Study Guide
To Accompany Brinkle

The Unfinished Nation

A Concise History
of the American People

STUDY GUIDE
TO ACCOMPANY BRINKLEY:

The Unfinished Nation

A CONCISE HISTORY
OF THE AMERICAN PEOPLE

Second Edition

Harvey H. Jackson

Jacksonville State University

Bradley R. Rice

Clayton State College

The McGraw-Hill Companies, Inc.

New York St. Louis San Francisco Auckland
Bogotá Caracas Lisbon London Madrid Mexico City Milan
Montreal New Delhi San Juan Singapore
Sydney Tokyo Toronto

McGraw-Hill
*A Division of the **McGraw-Hill** Companies*

STUDY GUIDE to accompany Brinkley:
THE UNFINISHED NATION: A Concise History of the American People
Second Edition

Copyright © 1997, 1993 by McGraw-Hill, Inc. All rights reserved. Printed in the United States of America. Except as permitted under the United States Copyright Act of 1976, no part of this publication may be reproduced or distributed in any form or by any means, or stored in a data base or retrieval system, without the prior written permission of the publisher.

This book is printed on acid-free paper.

1 2 3 4 5 6 7 8 9 0 DOCDOC 9 0 9 8 7 6

ISBN 0-07-015105-9

This book was set in Times New Roman by Naomi Z. Sofer.
Project supervision was done by Sylvia Warren.
The editors were Monica Freedman and LG;
the production supervisor was Elizabeth J. Strange.
R. R. Donnelley & Sons Company—Crawfordsville was printer and binder.

Cover photo: *Street Scene with Snow* (57th Street, N.Y.C.), 1902. By Robert Henri. Yale University Art Gallery, New Haven, The Mabel Brady Carvan Collection 1947.185.

ABOUT THE AUTHORS

Harvey H. Jackson received his Ph.D. from the University of Georgia. With Bradley R. Rice, he wrote *Georgia: Empire State of the South*. He authored or coauthored books on early America, including *Lachlan McIntosh and the Politics of Revolutionary Georgia* (1979), and is now focusing his studies on the cultural environment of the South. In 1995 he published *Rivers of History: Life on the Coosa, Tallapoosa, Cahaba, and Alabama* (1995), and he has recently finished a book on the building of early hydroelectric dams in Alabama. Jackson is currently working on a study of the northern coast of the Gulf of Mexico since World War II. His articles have appeared in several anthologies and journals including the *Journal of Southern History* and the *William and Mary Quarterly*. Harvey Jackson is Professor and Head of the Department of History at Jacksonville State University, Jacksonville, Alabama.

Bradley R. Rice received his Ph.D. from the University of Texas at Austin. He coauthored *Georgia: Empire State of the South* with Harvey H. Jackson and wrote *Progressive Cities: The Commission Government Movement in America, 1901–1920* (1977). Rice is coauthor and coeditor of *Sunbelt Cities: Politics and Growth Since World War II* (1983), and his work has appeared in several edited collections and journals including the *Journal of Urban History*. Since 1982, Rice has been editor of *Atlanta History: A Journal of Georgia and the South*, which is published quarterly by the Atlanta Historical Society. Rice is Professor of History and Assistant Vice President for Academic Affairs at Clayton State College, Morrow, Georgia.

TABLE OF CONTENTS

Introduction		ix
CHAPTER ONE	The Meeting of Cultures	1
CHAPTER TWO	The English "Transplantations"	11
CHAPTER THREE	Life in Provincial America	22
CHAPTER FOUR	The Empire Under Strain	32
CHAPTER FIVE	The American Revolution	43
CHAPTER SIX	The Constitution and the New Republic	54
CHAPTER SEVEN	The Jeffersonian Era	66
CHAPTER EIGHT	Varieties of American Nationalism	80
CHAPTER NINE	Jacksonian America	91
CHAPTER TEN	America's Economic Revolution	103
CHAPTER ELEVEN	Cotton, Slavery, and the Old South	117
CHAPTER TWELVE	An Age of Reforms	128
CHAPTER THIRTEEN	The Impending Crisis	137
CHAPTER FOURTEEN	The Civil War	150
CHAPTER FIFTEEN	Reconstruction and the New South	162
CHAPTER SIXTEEN	The Conquest of the Far West	177
CHAPTER SEVENTEEN	Industrial Supremacy	188
CHAPTER EIGHTEEN	The Age of the City	198
CHAPTER NINETEEN	From Stalemate to Crisis	208
CHAPTER TWENTY	The Imperial Republic	218
CHAPTER TWENTY-ONE	The Rise of Progressivism	228
CHAPTER TWENTY-TWO	The Battle for National Reform	239
CHAPTER TWENTY-THREE	America and the Great War	250
CHAPTER TWENTY-FOUR	The New Era	261
CHAPTER TWENTY-FIVE	The Great Depression	271

CHAPTER TWENTY-SIX	The New Deal	282
CHAPTER TWENTY-SEVEN	The Global Crisis, 1921–1945	294
CHAPTER TWENTY-EIGHT	America in a World at War	305
CHAPTER TWENTY-NINE	America and the Cold War	317
CHAPTER THIRTY	The Affluent Society	329
CHAPTER THIRTY-ONE	The Ordeal of Liberalism	340
CHAPTER THIRTY-TWO	The Crisis of Authority	353
CHAPTER THIRTY-THREE	The Age of Limits	365
CHAPTER THIRTY-FOUR	Beyond the Cold War	378

Writing a Historical Book Review	390
Preparing a Historical Research Paper	394
Answers to Self-Test Questions	397

Introduction

Every history professor has heard hundreds of students complain that history is nothing but dry, irrelevant facts, names, and dates to be memorized quickly and just as quickly forgotten. To be sure, for students to have a good framework of historical understanding, they must have a basic knowledge of factual information, but history is much more than that. Names and dates are really people and time. History is society's memory, and society cannot function without history any more than an individual could function without his or her memory. The names represent real flesh-and-blood people, both famous and common, and the dates mark the time when those people lived and worked. This study guide will try to lead you toward the developing a historical perspective. You will be encouraged to go beyond the bare facts to think critically about the causes and consequences of historical decisions. Careful study of this guide in consultation with your instructor will help you use the text to its best advantage. With the guide, you can constantly test yourself to make sure that you have learned from what you have read.

Each chapter of the guide is composed of several parts: objectives, pertinent questions, identification, document, map exercise, summary, and a self-test. Your instructor may assign specific items from the guide that best complement his or her approach to the course, or you may be expected to use the guide on your own. It will work well with either approach. The guide is not a workbook or a shortcut. It does not recapitulate, outline, or simplify the work of Professor Brinkley. Rather, it is designed to challenge you to seek a better comprehension of the text in particular and American history in general.

It is best to look over the appropriate chapter in the guide before you read your assignment so that you will be better attuned to what to look for as you read. The objectives that are listed at the beginning of each chapter of the study guide will give you a general idea of what the chapter is about. The identification items are important names and terms covered in the text but not usually directly mentioned in the pertinent-questions section of the Study Guide. Of course, your instructor may add to and/or delete from these lists to meet the needs of the course.

The pertinent questions and the self-test questions are the heart of the study guide. The goal of these exercises is to provide you with a thoughtful method for self-assessment after you have read each chapter. Some students will wish to write out their answers in full; some will jot down a few key ideas; and others will simply check themselves "in their heads." Experiment and use whichever method works best for you (assuming it is acceptable to your instructor). You should keep in mind that no general survey text could possibly cover all the pertinent questions in American history or fully explicate those it does discuss. Do not become too preoccupied with incidental supporting detail. Look for the essence of the answer, and then seek out those facts and examples that support your conclusions.

The document exercises in each chapter provide an opportunity for you to discover how important the analysis of documents can be to the historian's task. The questions on each document should be treated much like the pertinent questions. The map exercises let you see how geography can help you form a historical perspective.

At the end of the guide are sections that will help you write a critical book review or research paper if your instructor so requires. Such assignments will give you the opportunity to exercise critical thinking skills and apply the historical perspective that you have cultivated while reading the text and using this guide.

Naturally, this all seems like a drawn-out process, and at first it may well be. But as you work at it, you will find that each chapter will take less time, until finally you will have developed a system of study habits and analysis that will serve you well in this course and in many others as well.

Harvey H. Jackson

Bradley R. Rice

CHAPTER ONE

The Meeting of Cultures

OBJECTIVES

A thorough study of Chapter 1 should enable you to understand:

1. What the New World was like at the time of Christopher Columbus.
2. The ways in which the peoples of the New and Old Worlds affected each other when their societies came in contact in the late fifteenth century.
3. The colonial policies of the colonizing nations, and the effect each had on the future of the Americas.
4. Some important aspects of the culture from which Negro slaves were taken.
5. The early development of slavery.
6. The role of religion in European efforts to colonize the New World.
7. The first efforts of the English to establish a colony and the reasons for their failure.

PERTINENT QUESTIONS

America before Columbus (pp. 1–6)

1. Identify and describe the elaborate native civilizations that developed in South and Central America and in Mexico.
2. Describe the way of life in the North American Indians—where they lived and how they supported themselves.
3. Describe the changes taking place among North American Indians during the century before Europeans arrived.

Europe Looks Westward (pp. 6–19)

4. What changes stimulated Europeans to look toward new lands?
5. What did Columbus hope to achieve through his voyages, and what did he actually accomplish?

6. Why did the *conquistadores* seek to eliminate the underpinnings of existing American civilizations? How was this destruction accomplished?
7. Explain the relationship between the Spanish and the Pueblo Indians. How did this relationship shape the development of New Mexico?
8. Describe the demographic differences between the Spanish empire in America and the empires to the north. What impact did European diseases have on colonization efforts?
9. What did Europeans gain from the Indians that proved more important than gold?
10. What did the intermarriage of Spanish and North Americans reveal about the Spanish colonial system and suggest about the Europeans who administered it?
11. What role did the Catholic church play in Spanish colonization efforts?
12. Describe the cultures from which African slaves were taken and brought to America.
13. How did the African slave trade originate, and how did it evolve?

The Arrival of the English (pp. 19–25)

14. What commercial factors contributed to England's decision to seek colonies in the New World?
15. How did the English Reformation differ from that of Luther and Calvin? Why did it fail to satisfy the religious desires of many English people?
16. What did the Puritans wish to accomplish, and why did they clash with James I?
17. How did the English colonization of Ireland influence the way in which the English colonized America?
18. Where did the French and Dutch establish colonies in North America, and how did their efforts differ from those of the Spanish and the English?
19. What inspired the English to get into the race for colonies?
20. Describe the colonization efforts of Sir Humphrey Gilbert and Sir Walter Raleigh.
21. How did James I settle the rivalry between London and Plymouth merchants over the exploration of North America?

IDENTIFICATION

Identify each of the following, and explain why it is important within the context of the chapter.

1. Tenochtitlàn
2. Iroquois Confederation
3. Francisco Pizarro
4. *mestizos*
5. Mali
6. John Cabot
7. *encomiendas*
8. mercantilism
9. Separatists
10. *coureurs de bois*

DOCUMENT

John Smith is one of the most famous names associated with the English colonization of America, and his writings did much to introduce Europeans to America and to promote English colonization efforts. The document that follows is from his *General Historie of Virginia, New England, and the Summer Isles*...(1624), a chronicle of English exploration that drew heavily on the earlier work of Richard Hakluyt. This account of a meeting in 1584 between English explorers and Indians, although seen through the eyes of the English, tells us much about Indian life before the transformation of the tribes was complete. While reading it, consider the culture and possessions of the Indians and the English attitude toward what the Indians obviously valued. Also pay particular attention to what the English noticed about the Indians, and speculate on why these things were important to them.

> Till the third day we saw not any of the people, then in a little Boat three of them appeared, one of them went on shore, to whome wee rowed, and he attended vs without any signe of feare; after he had spoke much though we vnderstood not a word, of his owne accord he came boldly aboord vs, we gaue him a shirt, a hat, wine and meate, which he liked well, and after he had well viewed the barkes and vs, he went away in his owne Boat, and within a quarter of a myle of vs in halfe an houre, had loaden his Boat with fish, with which he came againe to the poynt of land, and there devided it in two parts, poynting one part to the Ship, the other part to the Pinnace, and so departed.
>
> The next day came diuers Boats, and in one of them the Kings Brother, with forty or fifty men, proper people, and in their behauiour very ciuill; his name was *Granganameo*, the King is called *Winginia*, the Country *Wingandacoa*. Leauing his Boats

a little from our Ships, he came with his trayne to the poynt: where spreading a Matte he sat downe. Though we came to him well armed, he made signes to vs to sit downe without any shew of feare, stroking his head and brest, and also ours, to expresse his loue. After he had made a long speech vnto vs, we presented him with diuers toyes, which he kindly accepted. He was greatly regarded by his people, for none of them did sit, nor speake a word, but foure, on whom we bestowed presents also, but he tooke all from them, making signes all things did belong to him.

The King himselfe in a conflict with a King his next neighbour and mortall enemy, was shot in two places through the body, and the thigh, yet recouered: whereby he lay at his chiefe towne six days journey from thence.

A day or two after shewing them what we had, *Granganaraeo* taking most liking to a Pewter dish, made a hole in it, hung it about his necke for a brestplate: for which he gaue vs twenty Deere skins, worth twenty Crownes; and for a Copper Kettell, fiftie skins, worth fiftie Crownes. Much other trucke we had, and after two dayes he came aboard, and did eate and drinke with vs very merrily. Not long after he brought his wife and children, they were but of meane stature, but well fauoured and very bashfull; she had a long coat of Leather, and about her priuities a peece of the same, about her forehead a band of white Corrall, and so had her husband, in her eares were bracelets of pearle, hanging downe to her middle, of the bignesse of great Pease; the rest of the women had Pendants of Copper, and the Noblemen fiue or sixe in an eare; his apparrell as his wiues, onely the women weare their haire long on both sides, and the men but on one; they are of colour yellow, but their hayre is blacke, yet we saw children that had very fayre Chestnut coloured hayre.

After that these women had beene here with vs, there came downe from all parts great stores of people, with Leather, Corrall, and diuers kinde of dyes, but when *Granganarneo* was present, none durst trade but himselfe, and them that wore red Copper on their heads, as he did. When euer he came, he would signifie by so many fires he came with so many boats, that we might know his strength. Their Boats are but one great tree, which is but burnt in the forme of a trough with gins and fire, till it be as they would haue it. For an armour he would haue ingaged vs a bagge of pearle, but we refused, as not regarding it, that wee might the better learn where it grew. He was very iust of his promise, for oft we trusted him, and he would come within his day to keepe his word. He sent vs commonly euery day a brace of Bucks, Conies, Hares, and fish, sometimes Mellons, Walnuts, Cucumbers, Pease, and diuers roots. This Author sayeth, their come groweth three times in fiue moneths; in May they sow, in Iuly reape; in Iune they sow, in August reape; in Iuly sow, in August reape. We put some of our Pease in the ground, which in ten dayes were 14 ynches high.

John Smith, *Works*, ed. Edward Arber (Birmingham, Eng.: J. Grant, 1884), pp. 306–308.

MAP EXERCISE

Fill in or identify the following on the blank map provided. Use the maps on pages 8 and 10 of the text as your source.

1. The routes of exploration, and the nations that sponsored these ventures.

2. The principal Indian civilizations in North and Central America and in the Caribbean.
3. The centers of European settlement in North and Central American and in the Caribbean.

Interpretative Questions

Based on what you have filled in, answer the following. For some of the questions you will need to consult the narrative in your text for information or explanation.

1. In light of the European rivalries of the period, and considering the various areas explored, settled, or claimed by the various European nations, what potentials for conflict among them existed?
2. Still considering the areas explored by European rivals, what opportunities for intercolonial trade existed? For trade with the Indians? What might have prevented this trade from taking place?

3. Note the location of the Spanish missions. How might they have served a purpose other than religious? Why were forts often found with missions?
4. Consider the location of Spanish missions and forts. How might these have been sources of potential conflict with other European powers?

SUMMARY

Before European explorers arrived in the Americas, Native Americans had developed many forms of social organizations that differed from one another in their levels of achievement. Europeans, concerned first with exploiting the New World and its peoples, regarded the natives as savages and set out to destroy the societies and replace them with a variation of European culture. Helped in this by the biological disaster brought on by smallpox and other diseases, the Europeans were able to conquer the tribes and civilizations and impose on the Indians a number of different colonial systems. To help make up for the Indians' labor lost through conquest and epidemic, Europeans brought in African slaves, who added to the cultural diversity of America. Conflicts in the old world spilled over into the New as different nations got into the race for colonies. By the end of the sixteenth century, the age of discovery was all but over, and the great era of colonization, especially English colonization, was about to begin.

CHAPTER SELF-TEST

After you have read the chapter in the text and done the exercises in the Study Guide, the following self-test can be taken to see if you understand the material you have covered. Answers appear at the end of the Study Guide.

Multiple Choice

Circle the letter of the response which best answers the question or completes the statement.

1. The Indian Empire that dominated modern Mexico at the time of the Spanish conquest was the:
   a. Mayas.
   b. Inca.
   c. Aztec.
   d. Chaco.

2. At the time of the Spanish conquest, the economies of most of the native Americans in South and Central America and Mexico were based on:
   a. hunting and gathering.
   b. herding.
   c. fishing and gathering.
   d. agriculture.

3. The eastern third of what is now the United States was inhabited by the:
   a. Woodland Indians.
   b. Plains Indians.
   c. Mountain Indians.
   d. Coastal Tribes.

4. At least partly as a result of Columbus's voyages, Spain:
   a. got involved in the Indian slave trade.
   b. soon went to war with France.
   c. replaced Portugal as the foremost seafaring nation.
   d. opened trade with the great khan in China.

5. Through a combination of daring, brutality, and greed, the *conquistadores*:
   a. made possible the creation of a Spanish empire in America.
   b. brought capitalism to Mexico.
   c. founded St. Augustine.
   d. introduced African slavery into America.

6. The first and perhaps most profound result of the meeting of native and European cultures was the:
   a. exchange of plants and animals.
   b. importation of European diseases.
   c. native adoption of European ways of waging war.
   d. intermarriage of Europeans and natives.

7. Ultimately more important to Europe than the gold and silver found in the new world was the:
   a. importation of new crops that could feed larger numbers of people.
   b. discovery of new forms of religious worship.
   c. Indian labor force.
   d. architectural knowledge gained from the Aztecs.

8. In matrilineal Indian and African societies:
   a. the father is the sole authority in the family.
   b. local gods were the basis of religious beliefs.

c. women played a major, often dominant, role.
   d. slavery did not exist.
9. The African slave trade began:
   a. in the fifteenth century, soon after the Spanish conquest.
   b. as early as the eighth century.
   c. with the English settlement of Virginia.
   d. when the sugar industry moved to the Caribbean.
10. Which of the following was *not* an English incentive for colonization:
    a. to escape religious strife at home.
    b. to bring the Christian religion to the Indians.
    c. to escape the economic transformation of the countryside.
    d. to find new markets for English products.
11. According to the theory of mercantilism, a nation could be made strong by:
    a. exporting more than it imported.
    b. building up a large standing army.
    c. defeating its neighbors in war.
    d. importing more than it exported.
12. Members of the Church of England who claimed that the church had not given up Rome's offensive beliefs and practices were the:
    a. Baptists.
    b. Presbyterians.
    c. Methodists.
    d. Puritans.
13. The country that produced the most successful fur traders and trappers was:
    a. Spain.
    b. Holland.
    c. France.
    d. Germany.
14. The first permanent English settlement was:
    a. Massachusetts Bay.
    b. Jamestown, Virginia.
    c. Plymouth, Massachusetts.
    d. St. Augustine.

15. The man to whom Queen Elizabeth granted the land on which the "lost colony" was planted was:
    a. John White.
    b. Walter Raleigh.
    c. Humphrey Gilbert.
    d. James Cobb.

True/False

Read each statement carefully. Mark true statements "T" and false statements "F."

1. The Aztec capital built on the site of present-day Mexico City was Cuzco.
2. The large Indian trading center in the Mississippi River Valley near present day St. Louis was Cahokia.
3. The Iroquois Confederation consisted of tribes in the southernmost region of the Eastern seaboard.
4. Cortes might not have been able to defeat the Aztecs had it not been for an epidemic of smallpox that decimated the native population.
5. The oldest permanent European settlement in the present-day United States was St. Augustine.
6. New Mexico became one of the most important provinces in Spanish America.
7. The riches of America ultimately hurt Spain because it caused that country to ignore domestic economic growth.
8. The most important native American crop brought back by the Europeans was squash.
9. Europeans felt justified in their treatment of the Indians because they considered the Indians uncivilized savages.
10. Spaniards seldom intermarried with the native Americans.
11. Mercantilism was a theory which discouraged nations from having colonies.
12. Joint-stock companies were means by which investors could share the risks and the profits of colonizing ventures.
13. The doctrine that God "elected" some people to be saved and condemned others to damnation was preached by Martin Luther.
14. The English Reformation began with a political dispute between king and pope—not with a religious dispute over matters of theology.
15. England's first experience with colonization was in Virginia.

16. The first Europeans to settle in the Hudson River Valley were the Dutch.
17. In 1606, James I gave the exclusive right to colonize along the southeast coast to a group of London merchants.

Review Questions

These questions are to be answered with essays. This will allow you to explore relationships among individuals, events, and attitudes of the period under review.

1. Describe the Indian societies and their geographic distribution before the coming of the European explorers. What did these cultures contribute to the Europeans, and why, despite these contributions, did the invaders still think of the American Indians as savages?
2. Compare and contrast the Spanish and the English motives for colonization. How were both sets of motives reflected in the organization of the colonies that each nation established?
3. How did earlier exploration and colonization experiences influence the way England, Spain, and other European nations attempted to colonize America?
4. Explain the relationship between Spanish colonists and the Indians. Why did the Indians come out the loser?
5. Describe the social and cultural backgrounds of the Africans brought to America. How was this background different from Indians? Europeans? How were the backgrounds of these people alike?

Chapter Two

The English "Transplantations"

OBJECTIVES

A thorough study of Chapter 2 should enable you to understand:

1. The differences between the Jamestown and Plymouth colonies in terms of objectives, type of settlers, early problems, and reasons for success.
2. The causes and significance of Bacon's Rebellion.
3. The settlement of England's Caribbean colonies and why these provinces were significant.
4. The background of the Massachusetts Bay colony and its founders, the Puritans.
5. The conditions in Puritan Massachusetts Bay that spawned such dissenters as Roger Williams and Anne Hutchinson.
6. The reasons for the founding of each of the original thirteen colonies.
7. The early economic, religious, and political factors in the colonies that tended to produce sectional differences.
8. The effect of the Glorious Revolution on the development of the American colonies.

PERTINENT QUESTIONS

The Early Chesapeake (pp. 26–36)

1. What four conditions shaped the character of English settlements in America?
2. What serious difficulties did the Virginia colonists face from the moment they landed?
3. How did the motives of the Virginia colonists differ from those of the separatists who settled in Plymouth?
4. Explain the importance of tobacco in the development of the Virginia colony.

5. What led to Virginia's becoming a royal colony?
6. What were the origins of the colony of Maryland? How did Maryland's early development differ from that of Virginia?
7. What were the origins of the political turmoil in Virginia during the 1670s?
8. How was Bacon's Rebellion related to the political unrest in Virginia, and what effect did the rebellion have on the development of that colony?

The Caribbean Colonies (pp. 36–39)

9. Why were the Caribbean colonies the "most important destinations" for English immigrants throughout the first half of the seventeenth century?
10. What circumstances led to English colonization in the Caribbean?
11. What conditions led English planters to begin importing labor to the Caribbean islands?
12. Why did Caribbean planters fear slave revolts? What steps did they take to prevent uprisings?
13. Why was it difficult to establish a stable society and culture in the Caribbean colonies?

The Growth of New England (pp. 39–47)

14. Describe the background of the Pilgrims and their motives for coming to America.
15. How did the Pilgrims' experience with the Indians differ markedly from that of the settlers in Virginia?
16. How did the turbulent events in England generate interest in colonization among certain English Puritans? What did these Puritans hope to accomplish?
17. How did the charter of the Massachusetts Bay Company influence the colony's first government?
18. What did the Puritans believe to be their purpose in coming to America (their "mission"), and how did church and state cooperate to achieve this goal?
19. How did the colony of Connecticut originate? Rhode Island? What does this expansion ("exodus") reveal about the colony of Massachusetts Bay?
20. What was the controversy surrounding Anne Hutchinson, and what does it reveal about Puritan religious and social beliefs?
21. What factors made relations between Indians and colonists in New England such a disaster for native Americans?

22. According to William Bradford's description of the arrival of the Pilgrims (see "American Voices," page 42), what obstacles did the colonists have to overcome if they were to be successful in America?

The Restoration Colonies (pp. 47–54)

23. How did the Stuart Restoration affect those English colonies already established in America? How did it affect attitudes about founding more settlements?
24. How did the political, economic, social, and religious institutions established in Carolina reflect the proprietors' motives for starting the colony?
25. What sort of social order took root in the colony of Carolina? Why did it differ from that proposed under Carolina's Fundamental Constitution?
26. How did the existing Dutch settlements and institutions influence the development of New York?
27. What beliefs and practices characterized the Quakers, and how did their influence make Pennsylvania a unique colony?
28. How did the purposes for which Georgia was founded differ from those of previous colonies? How were they similar?

The Development of Empire (pp. 54–57)

29. What attempts did England make to regulate its colonies between 1660 and 1700? What moved the mother country to consider regulation at this time, and how was it enforced?
30. What were the origins of the Dominion of New England, and what was the colonial reaction to it?
31. What impact did the Glorious Revolution have on England's North American colonies?

IDENTIFICATION

Identify each of the following, and explain why it is important within the context of the chapter.

1. "starving time"
2. John Rolfe
3. headright system
4. House of Burgesses
5. Opechancanough
6. Maryland's Act Concerning Religion

7. Sir William Berkeley
8. Barbados
9. Scrooby congregation
10. William Bradford
11. John Winthrop
12. Fundamental Orders of Connecticut
13. Thomas Hooker
14. Roger Williams
15. King Philip's War
16. Society of Friends
17. James Oglethorpe
18. Georgia Trustees
19. Edmund Andros
20. William and Mary
21. Jacob Leisler
22. John Coode

DOCUMENT

An expedition under Captain Christopher Newport began the Jamestown settlement in May 1607. In June, Captain Newport sailed for England, leaving behind 104 settlers. In September, only 46 of them were still living. One of the survivors, George Percy, wrote an account of the terrible time at Jamestown.

> There were never Englishmen left in a foreign country in such misery as we were in this new discovered Virginia. We watched every three nights, lying on the bare cold ground, what weather soever came; and warded all the next day; which brought our men to be most feeble wretches. Our food was but a small can of barley, sodden in water, to five men a day. Our drink, cold water taken out of the river; which was at flood very salt; at low tide full of slime and filth, which was the destruction of many of our men. Thus we lived for the space of five months [from August 1607 to January 1608] in this miserable distress, not having five able men to man our bulwarks upon any occasion. If it had not pleased God to put a terror in the savages' hearts we had all perished by those wild and cruel pagans, being in that weak estate as we were; our men night and day groaning in every corner of the fort most pitiful to hear.
> ... It pleased God after a while to send those people which were our mortal enemies; to relieve us with victuals, as breed, corn, fish, and flesh in great plenty, which was the setting up of our feeble men; otherwise we had all perished.

MAP EXERCISE

Fill in or identify the following on the blank map provided. Use the map on page 39 of the text as your source.

The English "Transplantations"

1. Colonial grants to Massachusetts Bay, Plymouth, New Haven, Hartford, Rhode Island, and the Duke of York.
2. Connecticut, New York, New Hampshire, and Maine.
3. Principal settlements in these colonies and the dates they were founded.
4. Connecticut River and the Merrimack River.
5. Lake Champlain, Massachusetts Bay, Cape Cod, Narragansett Bay, and the main islands along the coast.
6. The Mason and Gorges grants.

Interpretative Questions

Based on what you have filled in, answer the following. For some of the questions you will need to consult the narrative in your text for information or explanation.

1. Note the patterns of settlement in New England. What geographic features contributed to the placement of these early settlements? Why did these geographic features make a difference to early settlers?
2. Looking again at a physical map of the United States, determine which settlements were in the coastal plain, which were in the piedmont, and which were along the fall line. How did the location of these settlements influence their economic growth? How did location and subsequent economic growth shape the sort of societies that developed there?
3. Note the dates these settlements were established. What conclusions about the evolution of the settlements can you draw from these dates? (Consider political events as well as geographic conditions.)
4. Note the location of Boston, Providence, Hartford, and New Haven. What geographic features helped determine their locations? How did these features help shape the local economy of these settlements?
5. Massachusetts Bay was, or at least attempted to be, the dominant force in New England. How did that colony's land claims and expansion contribute to this? How did the location of new colonies serve to check the influence of Massachusetts Bay?

SUMMARY

During the seventeenth century, colonies were established in British North America, and the colonists began to perceive themselves as a hybrid breed. Before 1660, most colonies began as private ventures (with charters from the king), but the motives that brought them into being were as varied as the sociopolitical systems they developed. After 1660, proprietary colonies became the norm, and charters indicated a closer tie between the "owners" of a colony and the king, who granted the charter. As a result of this colonization effort, by the 1680s England had an unbroken string of provinces stretching from Canada to the Savannah River, as well as a number of island provinces in the Caribbean. As the colonies matured, their inhabitants began to exhibit an interest in exercising control over local affairs and an independence of interests that eventually led to trouble and confusion on both sides of the Atlantic. The problem was that at the very time that the American colonists were developing attitudes and institutions distinctly American, England, fully aware of the potential of its colonies, began to tighten control over its possessions.

CHAPTER SELF-TEST

After you have read the chapter in the text and done the exercises in the Study Guide, the following self-test can be taken to see if you understand the material you have covered. Answers appear at the end of the Study Guide.

Multiple Choice

Circle the letter of the response which best answers the question or completes the statement.

1. Which of the following did *not* shape the character of English settlements in America?
   a. The colonies were business enterprises.
   b. The colonies promoted freedom of religion.
   c. The colonies were designed to transplant society from the old world to the new.
   d. The colonies were able to develop their own political and social institutions.

2. The Englishman who first cultivated tobacco in Virginia was:
   a. John Smith
   b. Lord De La Warr.
   c. John Rolfe.
   d. Walter Raleigh.

3. The year 1619 was important in the history of Virginia because that year the colony:
   a. elected its first House of Burgesses.
   b. made its first profit.
   c. received its first royal governor.
   d. put down an Indian uprising.

4. In 1619, two new elements were introduced into the Virginia social order. They were:
   a. women and catholics.
   b. *mestizos* and blacks.
   c. blacks and women.
   d. women and *mestizos*.

5. Which of the following colonies allowed freedom of religion to all Christians?
   a. Massachusetts.
   b. Virginia.

c. Plymouth.
d. Maryland.

6. Bacon's Rebellion was significant because:
   a. it revealed the bitterness of competition among rival elites in Virginia.
   b. it was evidence of the continuing struggle to define the Indian and white spheres of influence in Virginia.
   c. it demonstrated the potential for instability in the colony's large population of landless men.
   d. a and c.
   e. all of the above.

7. Many Virginians turned to slaves rather than indentured servants for labor because Africans:
   a. already knew how to raise tobacco.
   b. did not have to be released, so there was no fear that they might become an unstable, landless class.
   c. were cheaper to purchase at the outset.
   d. were more naturally subservient and caused the master no trouble.

8. In the Caribbean planters turned to slave labor because:
   a. slaves already knew how to raise rice.
   b. slavery tended to make the society and culture more stable.
   c. sugar cultivation required a great deal of labor, which the native population could not supply.
   d. slaves could be kept for a long period of time and remain valuable.

9. The majority of colonists who first settled in Plymouth were:
   a. members of a Puritan Separatist congregation.
   b. not members of a Puritan Separatist congregation.
   c. upper-middle-class Puritans from the London area.
   d. moderate Puritans who wanted only minor reforms in church practices.

10. The first governor of the Massachusetts Bay colony was:
    a. John Winthrop.
    b. William Bradford.
    c. Roger Williams.
    d. Thomas Hooker.

11. Anne Hutchinson's teaching threatened to undermine the spiritual authority of the established clergy because she:
    a. claimed believers could communicate directly with God.
    b. preached that the clergy was corrupt.

c. denounced clergymen who were also politicians.
   d. stressed faith over good works.
12. The Restoration colonies had in common that they were all:
   a. located in the south.
   b. profitable for the crown.
   c. proprietary ventures.
   d. royal colonies.
13. Slavery in Carolina was greatly influenced by slavery in:
   a. Virginia.
   b. Barbados.
   c. St. Augustine.
   d. England.
14. The Navigation Acts were designed to:
   a. regulate commerce according to the theory of mercantilism.
   b. destroy the power of rising colonial merchants.
   c. keep the price of tobacco low.
   d. raise money to pay off England's war debts.
15. The overthrow of James II in the Glorious Revolution was:
   a. well received in New England.
   b. criticized by colonial merchants.
   c. the result of pressure on Edmund Andros.
   d. hardly felt by colonial politicians.
16. In America, the Glorious Revolution of 1688 led to changes which revealed:
   a. a colonial desire for self-government.
   b. that local issues were more important than questions over the nature of the empire.
   c. that the institution of monarchy was unpopular.
   d. that the established church was unpopular.

True/False

Read each statement carefully. Mark true statements "T" and false statements "F."

1. Virginia was a profitable colony from the start.
2. The "headright" system was used to attract colonists to Virginia.
3. Of the more than 8,500 settlers who came during Virginia's first seventeen years, more than 80 percent either abandoned the colony or died.

4. Bacon's Rebellion successfully overthrew the government of Sir William Berkeley.
5. The population of the English Caribbean colonies was equally divided between whites and blacks, freemen and slaves.
6. The first enduring European settlement in New England was at Scrooby.
7. Roger Williams insisted that the land on which Massachusetts was settled belonged to the Indians, not to the king.
8. After New Englanders defeated the local Indians, the French refused to aid the native Americans.
9. John Locke was the author of the Fundamental Constitution for Carolina.
10. When the English took New Amsterdam, they were able to quickly rid the colony of Dutch influences.
11. Soon after Pennsylvania was founded, the Quakers became its largest religious group.
12. The majority of colonists who came to Georgia were taken from debtors prison.
13. New Englanders liked the idea of centralized authority under the Domain of New England.
14. The Navigation Acts increased the authority of the crown and decreased that of local governments.
15. The colony that the crown could usually count on to support its policies was Massachusetts.
16. As a result of the Glorious Revolution, religious toleration in Maryland continued.

Review Questions

These questions are to be answered with essays. This will allow you to explore relationships among individuals, events, and attitudes of the period under review.

1. Compare and contrast Virginia and Plymouth—their origins, their goals, and their early social, political, and economic development.
2. Between 1660 and 1700, the American colonies were shaken by a series of "revolts" that, it has been contended, were the result of tensions in colonial society. Examine the protests that took place in Virginia, Maryland, Massachusetts, and New York, and then compare and contrast the internal divisions that helped spark the outbreaks.

3. Explain the way in which England applied the principles of mercantilism to its North American colonies.
4. Compare and contrast the institution of slavery in England's mainland colonies with the institution as it existed in the Caribbean.

Chapter Three
Life in Provincial America

OBJECTIVES

A thorough study of Chapter 3 should enable you to understand:

1. The disagreement among historians concerning the origins of slavery.
2. The sources of colonial labor, including indentured servants, women, and imported Africans.
3. Immigration patterns and their effect on colonial development.
4. The ways in which factors of soil and climate determined the commercial and agricultural development of the colonies, despite crown attempts to influence production.
5. The emergence of the plantation system, and its impact on Southern society.
6. The New England witchcraft episode as a reflection of Puritan society.
7. The reasons for the appearance of a variety of religious sects in the colonies, and the effect of the Great Awakening on the colonists.
8. The beginnings of colonial industry and commerce, and the early attempts at regulation by Parliament.
9. The ways in which colonial literature, education, science, law, and justice were diverging from their English antecedents.

PERTINENT QUESTIONS

The Colonial Population (pp. 58–69)

1. Explain the system of indentured servitude that developed in the American colonies.
2. What impact did freed indentures have on colonial sociopolitical development?

3. What factors contributed to the rapid increase in colonial population during the last half of the seventeenth century?
4. How did the importance of reproduction in the labor-scarce society of colonial America affect the status and life cycle of women?
5. How and why did the status of women in colonial America differ from region to region?
6. Describe the steps that led to the establishment of black slavery in the English American colonies.
7. Why is 1697 considered a "turning point in the history of the black population in America"? What had this change resulted in by 1760?
8. What were the major non-English groups to migrate to America, and why did they come?
9. What were the general characteristics of the colonial population in the first half of the eighteenth century—its rate of growth, cultural composition, and settlement patterns?
10. How was the experience of indentured servant Gottlieb Mittleberger (see "American Voices," page 60) similar to that of a slave brought from Africa?

The Colonial Economy (pp. 69–73)

11. Describe the economy of the Chesapeake region, and explain why it developed as it did.
12. How did the economy of South Carolina and Georgia differ from that of the Chesapeake? How was it similar?
13. Why did the Northern colonies turn to economic pursuits other than agriculture?
14. What factors gave rise to colonial commercial enterprises? What obstacles did these enterprises have to overcome and what effect did their success have on the colonial economy?
15. What was the "triangular trade," and what does it reveal about colonial economics?

Patterns of Society (pp. 74–79)

16. How did the plantation system in the American South illustrate both the differences between the colonial and English class systems and the way in which colonial communities evolved in response to local conditions?
17. What were the characteristics of plantation slavery?
18. What were the characteristics of communities that emerged in Puritan New England?

19. How was the family central to the Puritan community?
20. How did the experience of America affect the patriarchal family?
21. What caused the witchcraft hysteria of the 1680s and 1690s, and what did these incidents reveal about the nature of Massachusetts society?
22. What forces gave rise to colonial "cities"?
23. Describe urban life in colonial America.

The Colonial Mind (pp. 79–85)

24. What were the major religious groups in the colonies, what elements formed them, and where were they located?
25. What was the Great Awakening? Who brought it about, and what groups supported or opposed it?
26. What were the effects of the Great Awakening?
27. What colonial colleges were in operation by 1763? Why was each founded, and what subjects were studied in the mid-eighteenth century?
28. Explain the working of the law in colonial America—the concepts on which it was based and the way it functioned.
29. Was slavery the result of white racism or was racism the result of slavery? How has the debate over the origins of slavery revolved around this question?

IDENTIFICATION

Identify each of the following, and explain why it is important within the context of the chapter.

1. middle passage
2. Royal African Company
3. "slave codes"
4. Scotch-Irish
5. the Enlightenment
6. Peter Hasenclever
7. Stono Rebellion
8. town meeting
9. "visible saints"
10. "jeremiads"
11. George Whitefield
12. Jonathan Edwards
13. New Lights/Old Lights

14. "dame schools"
15. John Peter Zenger

DOCUMENT

Below is the report of the "confession" of Mary Osgood of Andover, Massachusetts, which was given on September 8, 1692, before a group of judges.

> She confesses that, about 11 years ago, when she was a melancholy state and condition, she used to walk abroad in her orchard; and upon a certain time she saw the appearance of a cat, at the end of the house, which yet she thought was a real cat. However, at that time, it diverted her from praying to God, and instead thereof she prayed to the devil; about which time she made a covenant with the devil, who, as a black man, came to her and presented her a book, upon which she laid her finger, and that left a red spot: and that upon her signing, the devil told her he was God, and that she should serve and worship him, and she believes she consented to it. She says, further, that about two years agone, she was carried through the air, in company with deacon Frye's wife, Ebenezer Baker's wife, and Goody Tyler, to five mile pond, where she was baptised by the devil, who dipped her face in the water and made her renounce her former baptism, and told her she must be his, soul and body, forever, and that she must serve him, which she promised to do.

Six weeks later, Mrs. Osgood visited the Puritan divine Increase Mather. He reported that she had recanted.

> Mrs. Osgood freely and relentingly said that the confession which she made upon her examination for witchcraft, and afterwards acknowledged before the honourable judges, was wholly false, and that she was brought to the said confession by the violent urging and unreasonable pressings that were used toward her; she asserted that she never signed the devil's book, was never baptised by the devil, never afflicted any of the accusers, or gave her consent for their being afflicted.

In the light of what you have read in your text, what do these documents tell you about religion in the Massachusetts Bay Colony, the relationship between church and state in that colony, and the impact of religion on the lives of the Puritans?

MAP EXERCISE

Fill in or identify the following on the blank map provided. Use the map on page 68 of the text as your source.
1. British North American colonies.
2. Colonial groups—Southern, Middle, and New England.
3. Principal settlements in each colony.
4. Principal rivers in each colony.
5. Using different colors, identify the dominant immigrant groups.

Interpretative Questions

Based on what you have filled in, answer the following. For some of the questions you will need to consult the narrative in your text for information or explanation.

1. What was the major non-English immigrant group in the Southern colonies? What circumstances led to their immigration to the New World? Why were they concentrated in the South rather than in other regions?
2. Who were the Scotch-Irish? Why did they leave their homeland, and why did they settle where they did? How would the conditions that led to their immigration and settlement have affected their attitude toward England and English colonial governments.
3. Note the location of German immigrant groups. Why did they leave their homeland, and why did they settle where they did? How would the conditions that led to their immigration and settlement have affected their attitude toward England and English colonial governments?
4. Note where the English are concentrated. Which are the most "English" colonies and regions? Why would the Southern colonies continue to have a strong English orientation despite the presence of a large immigrant group?

SUMMARY

After the turmoil of the late seventeenth century had subsided, it became evident that the English-American colonies and the colonists who populated them were beginning to develop characteristics that were distinctly "American." Although still essentially transplanted English subjects and still greatly influenced by European ideas and institutions, the colonists were also diverse, aggressive, and as concerned with their own success as with that of the empire of which they were part. New sources of wealth and new patterns of trade shaped the growth of the colonies, and new immigrants, not always from England, added a dimension unknown in the mother country. Although differences in geography, economy, and population gave each colony its own particular character and problems, there remained many common concerns—not the least of which was how to deal with, or avoid dealing with, British mercantile restrictions. In short, between 1700 and 1750, Britain's American colonies began to show signs of being both English and American; they were indeed "different," and it is this difference that Chapter 3 explores.

CHAPTER SELF-TEST

After you have read the chapter in the text and done the exercises in the Study Guide, the following self-test can be taken to see if you understand the material you have covered. Answers appear at the end of the Study Guide.

Multiple Choice

Circle the letter of the response which best answers the question or completes the statement.

1. During the seventeenth century, at least three-fourths of the immigrants who came to the Chesapeake colonies came as:
   a. slaves.
   b. artisans.
   c. indentured servants.
   d. convicts.

2. The high mortality rate in the colonies had the effect of:
   a. weakening the traditional patriarchal family structure.
   b. creating significant labor shortages in New England.
   c. making it difficult for women to find husbands.
   d. keeping the birth rate low.

3. In the Puritan colonies, the principal economic and religious unit in the community was the:
   a. family.
   b. meeting house.
   c. town meeting.
   d. small farm.

4. The year 1697 marked a turning point in the history of the black population in America because:
   a. planters from Barbados came to Carolina.
   b. slavery was introduced in Georgia.
   c. Massachusetts and Rhode Island abolished slavery.
   d. the Royal Africa Company lost its monopoly.

5. The one factor which determined whether a person was subject to the slave codes in the British American colonies was:
   a. their country of origin.
   b. the ancestry of their father.

c. the ancestry of their mother.
d. their African ancestry.

6. The most numerous of the non-English immigrants were the:
   a. Scotch-Irish.
   b. Pennsylvania Dutch.
   c. French Huguenots.
   d. Scottish Highlanders.

7. Which of the following was *not* one of the reasons why Africans were so valuable to planters along the Carolina and Georgia coasts.
   a. They could be forced to do work that white laborers refused to do.
   b. They often came from rice-producing regions of Africa.
   c. They were more accustomed to the hot and humid climate.
   d. They could be counted on to work the fields without protest.

8. A common problem in American commerce in the seventeenth century was:
   a. the lack of a commonly accepted currency.
   b. an insufficient number of ships to carry colonial goods.
   c. the large number of big companies in every colony.
   d. a small, unprofitable coastal trade.

9. The maze of highly diverse trade routes that involved the buying and selling of rum, slaves, and sugar was known as the:
   a. staple system.
   b. triangular trade.
   c. middle passage.
   d. Atlantic highway.

10. During the seventeenth century, colonial plantations were:
    a. rough and relatively small.
    b. English country estates on a smaller scale.
    c. seats of an entrenched, landholding aristocracy.
    d. insignificant in the colonial economy.

11. The characteristic social unit in New England was the:
    a. isolated farm.
    b. meeting house.
    c. town.
    d. plantation.

12. Which of the following was *not* a function of a colonial American city:
    a. They were trading centers.
    b. They were centers of industry.
    c. They were intellectual centers.
    d. They were areas of few social distinctions.

13. In matters of religion, Americans were:
    a. less tolerant than their English counterparts.
    b. more tolerant than their English counterparts.
    c. more inclined to be members of an Anglican congregation.
    d. unconcerned about piety, especially in New England.

14. The Great Awakening was:
    a. an effort to alert colonists to British efforts to control them politically.
    b. the way the Enlightenment influenced American education.
    c. the opening of new commercial opportunities in the West.
    d. the first great American revival.

15. During the first half of the eighteenth century colonial legislatures were generally:
    a. able to act independently of Parliament.
    b. controlled by the governor.
    c. free from class distinctions.
    d. a reflection of democracy in their respective colonies.

True/False

Read each statement carefully. Mark true statements "T" and false statements "F".

1. After the 1650s natural increase became the most important source of population growth in New England.
2. The survival rate for children was higher in the South than in any other section.
3. The "middle passage" was the route taken by settlers trying to get to the Ohio valley.
4. Africans were enslaved from the time of their arrival.
5. Between 1700 and 1775 the colonial population increased from under 300,000 to over 2 million.
6. Tobacco was the major cash crop in Georgia and South Carolina.
7. Industries which exploited the natural resources are known as extractive industries.

8. A great landowner in colonial America was powerful on his estate, but generally had no influence beyond the boundary of his property.
9. There were no significant slave rebellions during the colonial era.
10. The rigid patriarchal structure of the Puritan family limited opportunities for younger male members to strike out on their own.
11. What happened during the witch trials at Salem was not repeated in other parts of New England.
12. The outstanding preacher of the Great Awakening was Jonathan Edwards.
13. With access to "dame schools," American women were able to enjoy a higher degree of literacy than men.
14. Most of the early colleges in America were started for religious reasons.
15. In the John Peter Zenger case, the court held that criticism of the government was not libelous if factually true.

Review Questions

These questions are to be answered with essays. This will allow you to explore relationships among individuals, events, and attitudes of the period under review.

1. Compare and contrast the economy of the Northern colonies with that of the Southern colonies. What made the two regions develop as they did? How did these economic systems reflect social systems emerging at the same time?
2. Write an essay in which you describe the diverse population that settled the British colonies in the sixteenth and seventeenth centuries, and assess its growth during this period.
3. By violating the Navigation Acts and developing their own trading patterns, were the American colonies creating their own mercantile system? Discuss this question and its implications for future relations between the colonies and England.
4. What role did religion play in the advance of education in America? In what way did religion also hinder education? After assessing these two relationships, show the extent to which the fruits of education (reading, writing, science, and law) flourished in America; at the same time, show how these helped to form a character that was "American."

CHAPTER FOUR

The Empire Under Strain

OBJECTIVES

A thorough study of Chapter 4 should enable you to understand:

1. The primary reasons for the growth of the differences between colonial Americans and the British government that resulted in a clash of interests.
2. The colonial attitudes toward England and toward other colonies before the Great War for the Empire.
3. The causes of the Great War for the Empire, and the reasons for the French defeat.
4. The effects of the war on American colonists and on the status of the colonies within the British Empire.
5. The options for dealing with the colonies available to the British in 1763, and the reasons for adopting the policies that they chose to implement.
6. The importance of the series of crises from the Sugar Act through the Coercive Acts, and how each crisis changed colonial attitudes toward the mother country.
7. The change in American attitudes toward Parliament, the English constitution, and the king.
8. What slogans such as "No taxation without representation" really meant.
9. The significance of the convening of the First Continental Congress, and what it accomplished.

PERTINENT QUESTIONS

Origins of Resistance (pp. 88–90)

1. How did the relationship between king and Parliament change during the early eighteenth century? What role did the prime minister play in this change?

2. How were the American colonies administered by Britain, from Britain, during this period? What was the effect of this policy?
3. How was England's hold on the colonies weakened between 1700 and 1775? What role did colonial assemblies play in this weakening?
4. What factors helped promote colonial unity during this period?
5. What was the Albany Plan, and what did it reveal about colonial unity?

The Struggle for the Continent (pp. 90–96)

6. To what areas of North America had the French laid claim by 1750?
7. What were the causes and results of Anglo-French conflicts between 1686 and 1748? What role did the American colonies of each play in these conflicts?
8. What caused the Great War for the Empire, and why is it called by that name?
9. How did the Great War for the Empire become a "global war," and how did Britain carry out its part in the struggle?
10. What role did the French and British colonies play in this war?
11. What were the terms of the Treaty of Paris of 1763?

The New Imperialism (pp. 96–102)

12. What dilemma faced London policymakers at the end of the Great War for the Empire?
13. What initial policy changes occurred when George III ascended the throne, and what were the king's motives in making these changes?
14. How were the policy changes cited in question 13 reflected in the acts passed under the Grenville administration? Deal with the specific acts as well as general policy objectives.
15. What was it about post-1763 British policy that would cause colonists in every section to see the disadvantages rather than the advantages of being part of the British Empire?

Stirrings of Revolt (pp. 102–111)

16. Why did the Stamp Act so antagonize the American colonists?
17. Who sounded the "trumpet of sedition" in Virginia over the Stamp Act? What reasons, other than those stated in the resolutions proposed, contributed to this action? What was the effect of this, and what were the results?

18. What was England's response to the American protests over the Stamp Act? How did the action by Townshend attempt to anticipate American attacks on future acts?
19. How did the policies of Lord North differ from those of his predecessors? In what ways were they alike?
20. What role did Samuel Adams play in the American protests? How did his view of the need for American independence differ from those of most other colonial leaders at the time?
21. How did the colonial view of the nature of the British Empire differ from the view by George III and his supporters?
22. What were the theories of government advanced by John Locke, and how did the American colonists apply them to their struggle with England?
23. Why was the Tea Act seen by many Americans as a threat to themselves and their institutions?
24. What were the Coercive Acts? How did the Quebec Act help to unite the colonies, with Boston, in opposition to these acts?

Cooperation and War (pp. 111–114)

25. What role was played by committees of correspondence in the American protests?
26. What were the five major decisions made at the First Continental Congress, and what was their significance?
27. What were the circumstances that led to the fighting at Lexington and Concord?

IDENTIFICATION

Identify each of the following, and explain why it is important within the context of the chapter.

1. Treaty of Utrecht
2. King George's War
3. William Pitt
4. James Wolfe
5. Proclamation of 1763
6. Sugar Act of 1764
7. Paxton Boys
8. Regulators
9. Sons of Liberty
10. Declaratory Act

11. Massachusetts Circular Letter
12. Boston Massacre
13. "internal"/"external" taxes
14. "virtual" representation
15. Intolerable Acts
16. Continental Association

DOCUMENT

Below is an extract from the resolutions of the Stamp Act Congress, passed in 1765. Note the line of argument. How do the resolutions reflect attitudes toward local control of local affairs developed over the preceding century?

> I. That His Majesty's subjects in these colonies owe the same allegiance to the Crown of Great Britain that is owing from his subjects born within the realm, and all due subordination to that august body the Parliament of Great Britain.
>
> II. That His Majesty's liege subjects in these colonies are entitled to all the inherent rights and liberties of his natural born subjects within the kingdom of Great Britain.
>
> III. That it is inseparably essential to the freedom of a people, and the undoubted right of Englishmen, that no taxes be imposed on them but with their own consent, given personally or by their representatives.
>
> IV. That the people of these colonies are not, and from their local circumstances cannot be, represented in the House of Commons in Great Britain.
>
> V. That the only representatives of the people of these colonies are persons chosen therein by themselves, and that no taxes ever have been, or can be constitutionally imposed on them, but by their respective legislatures....

MAP EXERCISE

Fill in or identify the following on the blank map provided. Use the map on page 98 of the text as your source.

1. Britain's North American colonies.
2. Other territory claimed by Britain.
3. Spanish claims.
4. Provincial capitals (British and Spanish).
5. Other principal colonial towns.
6. Non-Indian settlement before 1700.
7. Non-Indian settlement between 1700 and 1763.
8. Frontier line in 1763.

9. Proclamation Line of 1763.
10. Principal rivers, the Great Lakes, and the Appalachian Mountains.

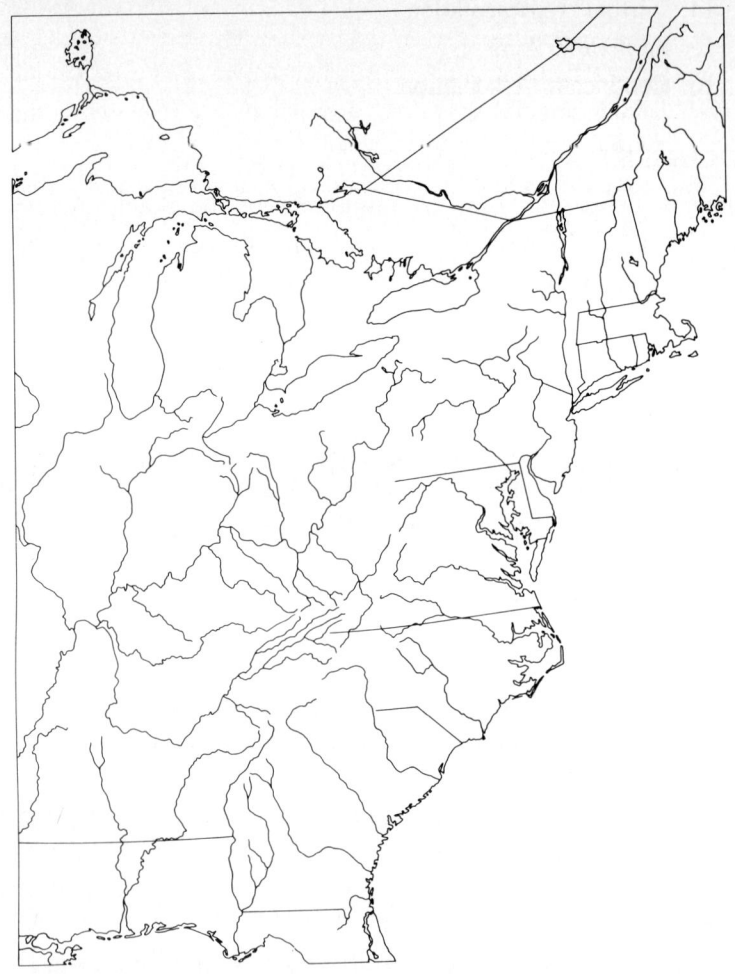

Interpretative Questions

Based on what you have filled in, answer the following. For some of the questions you will need to consult the narrative in your text for information or explanation.

1. Note the frontier line in 1763 and consider how much territory east of this line had been settled. How would this settlement pattern support Britain's post-1763 policy concerning western expansion?

2. How does the Proclamation Line of 1763 correspond to the frontier line? Which areas would have been immediately affected by the line?
3. If settlement west of the Appalachian Mountains was restricted, where would the expanding population go? Which colonies might have actually benefited from the Proclamation Line? Explain.
4. Which colonies would be most negatively affected by the Proclamation Line of 1763? Explain.
5. From the names and locations of the settlements west of the Proclamation Line of 1763, do you think they would hinder or help the British accomplish their policy objectives in that region? Explain.

SUMMARY

Despite a number of disagreements, by 1763, Anglo-American ties seemed stronger than ever. The colonies had prospered under British rule, had developed local institutions through which they seemed to govern themselves, and finally, with the defeat of France, appeared ready to expand into the heart of the continent. However, no sooner was the war ended than the British began to alter the pre-1763 system in an effort to make it more efficient and more responsive to control from London. The means chosen to do this (enforced regulations to end the illegal trade that had flourished under salutary neglect, plus taxation to pay for the colonial administration) were seen in the colonies as threats to the way of life they had come to accept as rightfully theirs. Rising in protest, the colonies faced a British government determined to assert its authority, and, with neither side willing to give in, the cycle of action and reaction continued. Finally, spurred on by a propaganda campaign that characterized the mother country as a tyrant determined to bring America to its knees, the colonies acted. The Intolerable Acts proved the final straw, and in September 1774, twelve British provinces met in a Continental Congress in hopes that a united front would cause London to reconsider and that conflict would be avoided. But it did not work, and in the spring, fighting occurred at Lexington and Concord. Although independence was not yet declared, the American Revolution had begun.

CHAPTER SELF-TEST

After you have read the chapter in the text and done the exercises in the Study Guide, the following self-test can be taken to see if you understand

the material you have covered. Answers appear at the end of the Study Guide.

Multiple Choice

Circle the letter of the response which best answers the question or completes the statement.

1. By the 1750s, colonial legislatures had come to see themselves as:
   a. little Parliaments.
   b. agents of the royal governor.
   c. powerless.
   d. agents for democratic reform.

2. The British victory in the Great War for the Empire:
   a. expelled France and Spain from North America.
   b. gave England control of the settled regions of North America, including Canada and Florida.
   c. resulted in the defeat of all North American Indian tribes.
   d. resulted in less contact between British authority and American colonists.

3. Prior to the Great War for the Empire, the Iroquois Confederacy:
   a. traded exclusively with the English.
   b. traded exclusively with the French.
   c. maintained their autonomy by avoiding a close relationship with both the French and the English.
   d. traded only with the five tribes that made up the Confederacy.

4. Which of the following did *not* occur during the Great War for the Empire:
   a. Americans were reimbursed for supplies requisitioned in their British colonies.
   b. Colonial assemblies were in charge of recruitment in their respective colonies.
   c. The French lost the city of Quebec.
   d. Most of the fighting was done by colonial militia.

5. For which of the following was the result of the Great War for the Empire a disaster:
   a. English frontiersmen and traders.
   b. Colonial merchants.

c. the Iroquois Confederacy.
d. the Royal Africa Company.

6. The English decision to reorganize the British Empire after 1763 was the result of:
   a. colonial demands for more efficient government.
   b. problems in the merchant community and their desire for regulation.
   c. colonial unrest, which the British government planned to put down before it became serious.
   d. a need to administer an empire that was now twice as large as it had been.

7. In an effort to keep peace between frontiersmen and Indians, and provide for a more orderly settlement of the West, the British government:
   a. forbade settlers from crossing the mountains that divided the Atlantic coast from the interior.
   b. gave Indian tribes and confederations colonial status.
   c. allowed interior settlement only if settlers bought land from the tribes.
   d. put forts in the Ohio Valley to protect settlers there.

8. Which of the following was a consequence of the policies of the Grenville ministry?
   a. British tax revenues in the colonies increased 10 times.
   b. Colonists effectively resisted and paid little tax.
   c. Many colonial merchants went out of business.
   d. Colonial assemblies assumed the responsibility for taxing their individual colonies.

9. British policies after 1763:
   a. destroyed the economy of the American colonies.
   b. stripped colonial assemblies of their authority.
   c. created a deep sense of economic unease, particularly in colonial cities.
   d. actually helped the colonial economy.

10. Colonists argued that the Stamp Act was not proper because:
    a. it affected only a few people, so the burden was not shared.
    b. the money raised would not be spent in the colonies.
    c. colonies could be taxed only by their provincial assemblies.
    d. the tax was too high.

11. Townshend believed his taxes on the colonists would not be protested because they were:
    a. "external" taxes—taxes on goods brought from overseas.
    b. not going to be strictly enforced.
    c. lower than the Stamp Act taxes.
    d. to be used to support colonial projects.

12. Colonial "committees of correspondence" were created to:
    a. keep colonial intellectuals in contact with each other.
    b. publicize grievances against England.
    c. improve the writing skills of young gentlemen.
    d. correspond with English radicals who supported the American cause.

13. Colonists felt that when the English constitution was allowed to function properly, it created the best political system because it:
    a. distributed power among the three elements of society—the monarchy, the aristocracy, and the common people.
    b. created a republican government.
    c. created a democracy.
    d. put power in the hands of those best suited to govern.

14. The Coercive Acts, or Intolerable Acts:
    a. isolated Massachusetts from the other colonies.
    b. made Massachusetts a martyr in the eyes of other colonists.
    c. created no concern among any group other than merchants.
    d. increased the power of colonial assemblies.

15. Which of the following was *not* a step taken by the First Continental Congress?
    a. It adopted a plan for a colonial union under British authority.
    b. It endorsed a statement of grievances.
    c. It called for military preparations.
    d. It called for a series of boycotts.

True/False

Read each statement carefully. Mark true statements "T" and false statements "F."

1. By the 1750s, most Americans felt little loyalty to the British crown.
2. The French were able to forge good relations with the Indian tribes because they were more tolerant of the Indian way of life than the British.

3. Before the Great War for the Empire, England, France, and Spain had been at peace with each other for nearly half a century.
4. The Seven Years War, the French and Indian War, and the Great War for the Empire are all the same war.
5. After the Peace of Paris of 1763, the English were inclined to let the colonies go their own way, with few restrictions.
6. England was fortunate that King George III was young, bright, and surprisingly mature for his age.
7. Because they needed protection, colonists in both the East and the West were glad to have regular British troops stationed permanently in America.
8. The formation of groups known as the "Paxton Boys" and the "Regulators" revealed that colonists in the West believed they were not being treated fairly by colonists in the East.
9. Colonists were concerned over the immediate impact of the Stamp Act, not its long-range implications.
10. Parliament repealed the Stamp Act, and in the Declaratory Act it declared that it would not tax the colonies in this way again.
11. Colonists responded to the Townshend Duties with agreements not to import the taxed goods.
12. Americans wanted their representatives to "actually" represent them, while the British claimed that Parliament represented all British citizens, no matter where they lived.
13. Women, especially southern women, took no part in the protests and boycotts rising from the Coercive Acts.
14. Those who attended the Continental Congress did not intend for it to be a continuing organization.
15. The fighting at Lexington and Concord caused many to rally to the rebel cause who previously had little enthusiasm for it.

Review Questions

These questions are to be answered with essays. This will allow you to explore relationships among individuals, events, and attitudes of the period under review.

1. Explain the role that colonial assemblies played in the American protests of British policies after 1763. Why did the assemblies take such a leading role, and what effect did the British attitude (and action) toward these legislatures have on the American decision to revolt?

2. It has been said that Americans revolted against tyranny anticipated, rather than against tyranny inflicted. Define tyranny as you believe an eighteenth-century American might have, and then assess this point of view.
3. From the outset, Massachusetts was the leader of the anti-British protest studied in this chapter. Why? What was it in the economic, political, and intellectual climate of that colony that made it such a hotbed of revolution? What part did Puritanism play in shaping this climate?

Chapter Five
The American Revolution

Objectives

A thorough study of Chapter 5 should enable you to understand:

1. American war aims, and the problems experienced by the Revolutionary governments in carrying on a protracted war.
2. The aim of the Declaration of Independence, the reasons for its issuance, and its influence throughout the world since 1776.
3. The indispensable contributions of George Washington to the successful outcome of the Revolution.
4. The diplomatic triumph for American negotiators embodied in the Treaty of Paris.
5. The features of the Articles of Confederation, and the reasons for its creation.
6. The problems faced by the government under the Articles of Confederation and how they were addressed.

Pertinent Questions

The States United (pp. 115–119)

1. List the divisions within the Second Continental Congress, and give the aim of each faction. How did they attempt to gain their ends?
2. How did the pamphlet *Common Sense* address the problem of the aim of the war, and what was its impact on American opinion?
3. What were the philosophical roots of the Declaration of Independence, and what effect did the Declaration have on the struggle?
4. What problems did the Americans face in providing the necessary supplies and equipment for the war in paying for them?

5. What were the American advantages in the struggle, and why was George Washington selected as the best person to make the most of these advantages?

The War for Independence (pp. 119–130)

6. What were the initial setbacks in the war during 1776, and what was the significance of the Battles of Trenton and Princeton in this regard?
7. What was the initial plan for the British campaign of 1777? How was this altered, and what effect did this alteration have on the outcome?
8. What were the American diplomatic goals at the start of the war? What problems did they face, and what efforts were made to overcome them?
9. How did the victory at Saratoga affect American diplomatic efforts? How did England and France respond to this news? What was the result?
10. Why did the British decide to launch a campaign against the Southern colonies in 1778? What advantages and disadvantages did each side have in this region?
11. How was the campaign in the South conducted, and why was the victory at Yorktown so significant for the Americans?
12. What were the provisions of the Treaty of Paris in 1783, and how did the Treaty affect relations among the United States, France, and Spain?
13. According to Joseph P. Martin's account of the Battle of Long Island ("American Voices," page 123), what aspects of warfare most concerned the common soldier?

War and Society (pp. 130–135)

14. Who were the Loyalists? What elements in America remained loyal to the king, and for what reasons?
15. What impact did the American Revolution have on Native Americans?
16. How did the Revolution affect the way American women thought about their status, and what changes resulted from this new awareness?
17. What changes did the Revolution produce in the structure of the American economy?

The Creation of State Governments (pp. 135–139)

18. What was it about the concept of a republican government that so appealed to Americans?
19. How did Americans propose to avoid what they considered to be the problems of the British system they were repudiating?
20. What were the characteristics of the state constitutions written during the early years of the struggle? How did they reflect the general spirit of the Enlightenment—the belief that freedom was the natural state of humanity?
21. What impact did the Revolution have on slavery in New England? in the middle states? in the South?

The Search for a National Government (pp. 139–147)

22. What type of government did the Articles of Confederation create? What were its major features?
23. How did the Treaty of Paris of 1783 fail to resolve, or in some cases help to create, strain among the United States, England, and Spain?
24. What commercial arrangements did American shippers and traders want above all others after the war had ended? Why did they feel this was needed, and how successful were they in accomplishing their aims?
25. What effect did the American westward movement have on diplomatic relations with Great Britain and Spain?
26. How did the Confederation Congress attempt to solve the problem of the status of western territory the states had ceded to it? Which interest groups favored which plans for the sale and distribution of land?
27. What were the sources of the Confederation's postwar economic problems, and how did the government attempt to solve them? What were the results?
28. How was paper money seen as a solution to the economic problems of one element in American society? Who opposed this and why?
29. How did the action of Daniel Shays and his followers relate to the economic problem of the Confederation period? What was the significance of the movement he led?
30. How did the debate over the origins of the American Revolution focus on whether the Revolution was (a) largely a political and intellectual event, a defense of ideals and principles, or (b) a so-

cial and economic phenomenon in which material interests were at the heart of the rebellion?

IDENTIFICATION

Identify each of the following, and explain why it is important within the context of the chapter.

1. Benedict Arnold
2. Sir William Howe
3. John Burgoyne
4. Count de Vergennes
5. Sir Henry Clinton
6. Lord Cornwallis
7. Nathanael Greene
8. count de Rochambeau
9. Dragging Canoe
10. Judith Sargent Murray
11. Virginia Statute of Religious Liberty
12. Little Turtle
13. Ordinance of 1784
14. township
15. Northwest Ordinance
16. Treaty of Greenville
17. Robert Morris

DOCUMENT 1

Read the Declaration of Independence, reproduced in the Appendices to your text. This is a statement of the causes for the colonists' rebelling against England. How do these causes set down by Jefferson compare with those you have identified earlier in your reading?

The Declaration of Independence also suggests the type of society that Americans hoped would result from this struggle. Identify the major characteristics of the independent nation that Jefferson hoped would be created.

DOCUMENT 2

The following is an excerpt from the Articles of Confederation, approved by all the states by 1781. How does it reflect the principles for which

Americans said they were fighting the Revolution? What goals and objectives of the Revolution still remained to be achieved?

1. [Article II] "Each state retains its sovereignty, freedom, and independence, and every Power, Jurisdiction and right, which is not by this confederation expressly delegated to the United States, in Congress assembled."

2. [Article IV] The free inhabitants of each state "shall be entitled to all privileges and immunities of free citizens in the several states" and "full faith and credit" shall be given by each state to the judicial and other official proceedings of other states.

3. [Article V] Each state shall be represented in Congress by no less than two and no more than seven members, shall pay its own delegates, and shall have one vote (regardless of the number of members).

4. [Article VI] No state, without the consent of Congress, shall enter into diplomatic relations or make treaties with other states or with foreign nations, or engage in war except in the case of actual invasion.

5. [Article VIII] A "common treasury" shall be supplied by the states in proportion to the value of their land and improvements; the states shall levy taxes to raise their quotas of revenue.

6. [Article IX] Congress shall have power to decide on peace and war, conduct foreign affairs, settle disputes between states, regulate the Indian trade, maintain post offices, make appropriations, borrow money, emit bills of credit, build a navy, requisition soldiers from the states, etc.—but nine states must agree before Congress can take any important action.

7. [Article X] A "Committee of the States," consisting of one delegate from each state, shall act in the place of Congress when Congress is not in session.

8. [Article XIII] No change shall be made in these articles unless agreed to by Congress and "afterwards confirmed by the legislatures of every state."

MAP EXERCISE

Fill in or identify the following on the blank map provided. Use the map on page 141 of the text as your source.

1. States with western land claims.
2. States without western land claims.
3. Western lands claimed by the respective states and the dates these lands were ceded.
4. Claims that were disputed.
5. British, French, and Spanish possessions.
6. Major rivers and lakes.

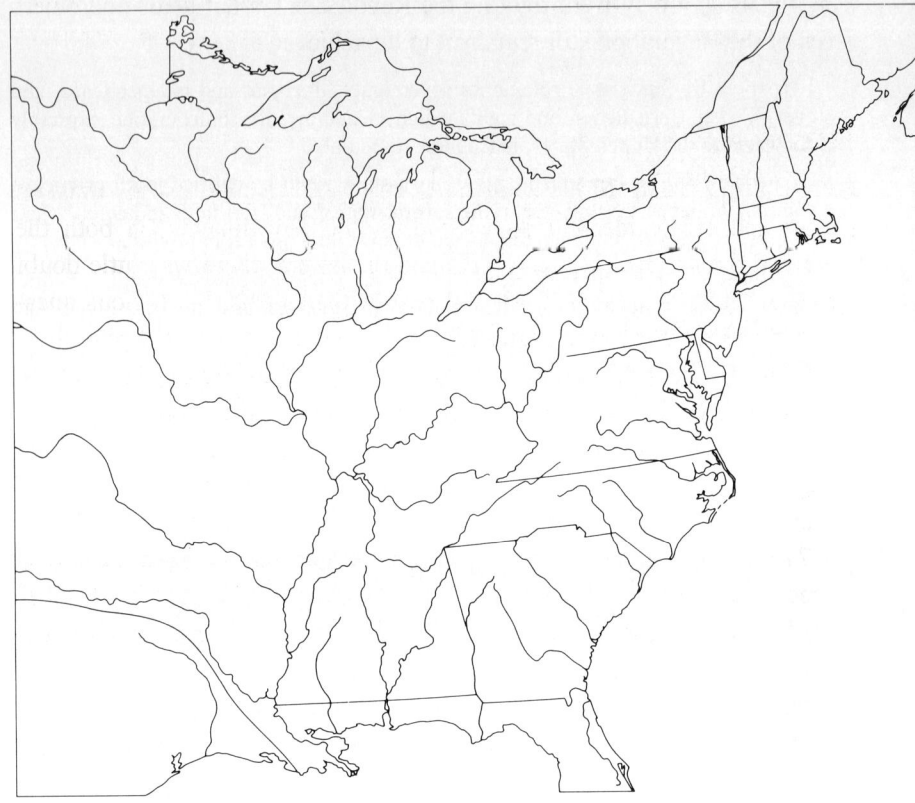

Interpretative Questions

Based on what you have filled in, answer the following. For some of the questions you will need to consult the narrative in your text for information or explanation.

1. Why was the question of western land claims so important in the ratification of the Articles of Confederation? What advantages were to be gained from western lands?
2. How did the Ordinance of 1784 propose to deal with the lands ceded to the national government? What is significant about this with regard to the political development of the West?
3. How did the Ordinance of 1787 (the Northwest Ordinance) differ from the Ordinance of 1784? What factors caused these differences?

4. Note the territory held by Spain. How did Spanish holdings (especially along the Gulf of Mexico) threaten the westward movement of Americans?

SUMMARY

Between 1775 and 1787, Americans struggled to win a war, make a peace, and create ideologically sound, stable governments on both the state and the national levels. By the end of the era, there was little doubt that they had accomplished the first two of their goals, but serious questions were being raised concerning the success of the last. Despite problems that would have stopped lesser men, George Washington and his army had been able to successfully keep the British at bay, winning when they could and losing as seldom as possible. Meanwhile, the Continental Congress, blessed with some remarkable diplomats, maintained a foreign policy the success of which can be seen in the Franco-American alliance of 1778 and the Treaty of Paris of 1783. But once the war ended, the government that the British threat had held together found that its member states' unwillingness to centralize power created more problems than it solved. Economic dislocation, exemplified by Daniel Shays and his followers, plagued the nation, as many thoughtful men searched for a way to transform Revolutionary rhetoric into reality and to restore order without sacrificing liberty.

CHAPTER SELF-TEST

After you have read the chapter in the text and done the exercises in the Study Guide, the following self-test can be taken to see if you understand the material you have covered. Answers appear at the end of the Study Guide.

Multiple Choice

Circle the letter of the response which best answers the question or completes the statement.

1. Thomas Paine's *Common Sense* is an important work because it:
   a. helped Americans reconcile their differences with England.
   b. persuaded Americans that no reconciliation with Britain was possible.
   c. supported the concept of the English constitution.
   d. argued that Parliament, not the King, was the enemy.

2. The Declaration of Independence stated that governments were formed to:
   a. give men an opportunity to exert power.
   b. reward loyal servants of the state.
   c. promote democracy.
   d. protect a person's life, freedom, and right to pursue happiness.

3. The Articles of Confederation actually:
   a. confirmed the weak, decentralized system of government already in operation.
   b. drew the states together into a strong government.
   c. put power in the hands of the military.
   d. put power in the hands of the executive and his appointees.

4. Congress financed the revolution by:
   a. selling bonds.
   b. minting gold and silver coins.
   c. borrowing from other nations.
   d. taxing the wealthy.

5. The choice of George Washington as commander in chief was a good one because of his:
   a. knowledge of military affairs.
   b. image among the people, who trusted and respected him.
   c. successful military experience in the Great War for the Empire.
   d. relaxed, informal way with his men.

6. At the end of 1776 the American army under Washington had:
   a. won no victories, major or minor.
   b. become badly divided and scattered.
   c. retreated into western Pennsylvania.
   d. won two minor victories and remained intact.

7. Which of the following was not part of the British strategy to cut the United States in two in 1777.
   a. To move forces up the Hudson from New York City.
   b. Prepare a two-pronged attack along the Mohawk and the upper Hudson.
   c. Capture Charleston.
   d. Bring an army down from Canada to meet the one coming up from New York.

8. John Burgoyne's surrender at Saratoga:
   a. convinced the French that they should help the Americans.
   b. caused the British to consider giving up the fight.

c. made George Washington a military hero.
   d. had little effect on the war in the long run.
9. After 1777 the British decided to focus their efforts in the South because:
   a. there was less population there.
   b. they believed there were more Loyalists there.
   c. they thought slaves would help them.
   d. they had more Indian allies there.
10. The British were forced to surrender at Yorktown because:
    a. French troops and a French fleet helped trap the British.
    b. Washington was able to defeat the British in the field.
    c. Americans were better trained than the British.
    d. the British commander underestimated the size of Washington's army.
11. Even though the British wanted to end the war, the French were reluctant to negotiate because:
    a. they feared the Americans might take Canada.
    b. British agents were at work among the common folk of Paris.
    c. they were committed to staying in the war until Spain got Gibraltar.
    d. Spain was insisting on getting the Virgin Islands.
12. Of all the Loyalists groups in America, the one which suffered most as a result of the Revolution was:
    a. western farmers.
    b. slaves.
    c. traders and trappers.
    d. Anglicans.
13. During the Revolution women took on new responsibilities. After the war:
    a. things generally went back to the way they were before and few concrete reforms in the status of women occurred.
    b. women were able to translate wartime gains into peacetime reforms.
    c. women were recognized and honored for their contributions with new careers.
    d. women got the right to vote in most Northern colonies.
14. If postwar Americans agreed on nothing else, they agreed that:
    a. there should be no property qualifications to vote.
    b. states should have democratic governments.

c. new governments should be republican.
d. some men were born to govern and some were born to follow.

15. Under the Articles of Confederation, the only institution of national authority was the:
    a. Supreme Court.
    b. Congress.
    c. President of the United States.
    d. Senate.

True/False

Read each statement carefully. Mark true statements "T" and false statements "F."

1. When the fighting began, most Americans wanted the colonies to be independent from Great Britain.
2. The rebelling colonies had access to sufficient local resources to fight a successful revolution.
3. The British lacked the resources to conduct a war on the American continent.
4. At the outset of the war, American leaders hoped that Canada would become the fourteenth state.
5. The surrender of Burgoyne at Saratoga had no effect on the Iroquois Confederacy, since most of the Indians supported the American cause.
6. There is no actual proof that Benedict Arnold committed treason.
7. As a result of the treaty of Paris of 1783, the new American nation's western boundary was the Blue Ridge Mountains.
8. At least one-fifth, and maybe as many as one-third, of the American colonists were loyal to Britain during the Revolution.
9. Native Americans were pleased with the outcome of the Revolution because it reduced the desire of colonists for western land.
10. The first state constitutions written during the American Revolution generally reduced the power of the executive.
11. In the newly created states, the privileges that churches enjoyed in the colonial era were largely stripped away.
12. After independence, the United States quickly and easily persuaded Great Britain to abide by the terms of the treaty of 1783.
13. The system for surveying and selling western lands set up under the Ordinance of 1785, favored small farmers.
14. The Northwest Ordinance laid out the requirements for western territories to become states.

15. During the period under consideration in this chapter, Congress did nothing to limit the expansion of slavery.

Review Questions

These questions are to be answered with essays. This will allow you to explore relationships among individuals, events, and attitudes of the period under review.

1. Explain how conflicts and rivalries among European nations both helped and hindered the American struggle for independence.
2. Compare and contrast the British and the American conduct of the war. How did each side propose to "win," how realistic was its assessment of the situation, and how did this prewar assessment influence the ultimate outcome of the war?
3. Examine the relative successes and failures of the Articles of Confederation. Do you think that this government was capable of providing the stability that the new nation needed? Why or why not?
4. How did Revolutionary ideology challenge the way minorities were treated in America? What changes in this treatment resulted from this challenge, and why did some minorities find their circumstances improved while others did not?
5. Explain how the political ideology that was the foundation of the American Revolution influenced the writing of state constitutions and the Articles of Confederation.

CHAPTER SIX

The Constitution and the New Republic

OBJECTIVES

A thorough study of Chapter 6 should enable you to understand:

1. The groups that advocated a stronger national government, and how they, probably a minority, were able to achieve their objective.
2. The origin of the Constitutional Convention, who the delegates were, how well they represented the people, and how well they were able to achieve a consensus.
3. Federalism and how the Constitution is designed to make it work.
4. The importance of *The Federalist Papers* in the ratification struggle, and their significance in years since.
5. The effectiveness of George Washington's solutions to the problems of the presidency, and how Washington, as its first occupant, affected the office and the nation.
6. The financial program of Alexander Hamilton, and its contribution to the success of the new government.
7. The ways in which the weak new nation coped with international problems, and the importance of such events as Washington's decision for neutrality and the "quasi war" with France.
8. The emergence of political parties, their political philosophies, and their influence through the election of 1800.

PERTINENT QUESTIONS

Toward a New Government (pp. 151–157)

1. Who were the advocates of centralization, and why did they want to alter or abolish the Articles of Confederation?

2. What did those who favored centralization see as the most serious problem of the Articles, and how would they have changed them? What had prevented these changes?
3. What were the characteristics of the men who met at the Constitutional Convention in Philadelphia? Whose presence was essential to the meeting's success? Why?
4. What were the two major points of view that divided the convention? What plans did each side propose to carry its view?
5. How were the differences between the "large state" and the "small state" plans resolved? What other issues divided the convention, and how were they resolved?
6. What was to be the role of various branches of government under the new Constitution?

Adoption and Adaptation (pp. 157–617)

7. Why did the supporters of the new Constitution call themselves "Federalists"? Were they actually Federalists, or did their philosophy of government reveal them to be something else? If so, what?
8. What method did the Federalists employ to get their views across to the people? What were their arguments, and how did the "Antifederalists" respond?
9. What was the process by which the Constitution was finally ratified? Which states supported it, by what margins, and which states did not? What objections were raised by the states?
10. What was the process by which the new government set up operations? What were the initial matters discussed, and how were they resolved?
11. In what way did Congress continue the work of the Constitutional Convention? What "gaps" in the Constitution did Congress fill?
12. Who were the men Washington selected for his cabinet, and on what basis did he choose them?

Federalists and Republicans (pp. 161–166)

13. How did the divisions of the 1790s reflect the differences in philosophy that were at the heart of debate over the Constitution?
14. What was the view of society and politics held by Hamilton? Who did he feel should govern, and why?
15. What was Hamilton's plan for paying the nation's debts and restoring credit on a sound basis? To which social-economic-political group would this have appealed?

16. How did Hamilton propose to enact his programs? Who opposed him, and to what degree was he successful?
17. How did political parties rise as a result of Hamilton's programs?
18. What was the political philosophy of Jefferson and Madison? How did it differ from that of Hamilton?
19. How did the French Revolution highlight the differences between the Federalists and the Republicans?.

Asserting National Sovereignty (pp. 166–169)

20. How did Washington's reaction to the Whiskey Rebellion underscore the difference between the Constitution and the Articles of Confederation?
21. How did the government under the Constitution guarantee that people on the frontier would be loyal to it? What was the impact on Native Americans?
22. What diplomatic problem did the French Revolution and the war that followed pose for the United States? How did Washington and Congress deal with this problem?
23. What were the circumstances that sent John Jay to England, and what were the results of his mission?
24. How did Jay's Treaty affect American relations with Spain?

The Downfall of the Federalists (pp. 169–174)

25. Why was John Adams selected as the Federalist candidate in 1796?
26. What circumstances led to an administration with a Federalist president and a Republican vice president?
27. What caused the "quasi war" with France during the Adams administration? What was the result of this struggle?
28. How did the Federalists attempt to silence those who opposed the undeclared war, and what groups did these attempts most affect?
29. What gave rise to the Virginia and Kentucky Resolutions, and what attitude toward the nature of the federal government did these resolutions reveal?
30. What were the issues in the election of 1800, and what strategy did each party employ to get elected?
31. What was the outcome of the election of 1800, and what were the reactions of the losers and the victors?

IDENTIFICATION

Identify each of the following, and explain why it is important within the context of the chapter.

1. Annapolis Conference
2. Virginia plan
3. New Jersey plan
4. "Great Compromise"
5. Antifederalists
6. *The Federalist Papers*
7. Bill of Rights
8. Judiciary Act of 1789
9. XYZ Affair
10. Hamilton's Bank Bill
11. Hamilton's Report on Manufactures
12. Jay's Treaty
13. Pickney's Treaty
14. Alien and Sedition Acts
15. Virginia and Kentucky Resolutions
16. Aaron Burr
17. Judiciary Act of 1801
18. "midnight appointments"

DOCUMENT

The document to be studied is the Constitution of the United States and its first twelve amendments. First, read the Constitution, in the Appendices to your text; then, consider the following.

1. How does the organization and election of the House and the Senate reflect attitudes that existed in 1787? Why is the impeachment held in the House and the trial in the Senate? What does this tell you about the Founding Fathers' attitude toward "popular" government?

2. Why are all revenue bills required to originate in the House of Representatives?

3. Examine the powers given Congress in Article I, Section 8. How does this section make the Constitution different from the Articles?

4. Outline how the president was elected before the ratification of the Twelfth Amendment. What role did the popular vote play in this process? Why was it designed this way?

5. List the specific powers given the president, and be prepared to follow the evolution of these powers.

6. Why are Supreme Court justices (and judges on inferior courts) appointed rather than elected, and why do they "hold their offices during good behavior"? Look at the terms of office for the other branches. What does this reveal about what the people can, and cannot, do regarding changes in their government? Why was it done this way?

7. How does the amendment process under the Constitution differ from that under the Articles? Why was this change made?

8. Reread the second paragraph of Article VI. According to this article, is the Constitution creating a national or a federal government?

Now read the first ten amendments to the Constitution—the Bill of Rights—and consider the following.

1. Look carefully at Amendments I and V, and consider the relations between Great Britain and its colonies from 1700 to 1776. It has been contended that these amendments were insisted on to make sure that the abuses experienced at the hands of the mother country would not be repeated. What evidence of this do you find?

2. Examine Amendments VI to VIII. What fears do these amendments reflect, and how were these fears resolved?

3. What seems to have been the purpose of Amendments IX and X? How do these amendments reflect concerns felt by opponents of the Constitution?

4. Compare and contrast the provisions in Amendment XII for electing the president with those in Article II, Section 1. What circumstances gave rise to this change?

MAP EXERCISE

Fill in or identify the following on the blank map provided. Use the maps in the text as your sources and consult maps in your library as needed.

1. Original thirteen states.
2. States admitted to the Union between the Revolution and 1800.
3. Ohio, Mississippi, Tennessee, and Missouri rivers.
4. Territory held or claimed by Spain.
5. New Orleans, Mobile, and Pittsburgh.
6. The Appalachian Mountains.

Interpretative Questions

Based on what you have filled in, answer the following. For some of the questions you will need to consult the narrative in your text for information or explanation.

1. Thomas Jefferson "believed that farmers were God's chosen people and that an ideal republic would consist of sturdy citizens, each tilling his own soil." Furthermore, he advocated policies designed to make this republican ideal a reality. Which groups would have been most likely to support Jefferson because of this? Where were they located?

2. Which groups were most likely to oppose Jefferson? Where were they located? Why were members of this opposition less inclined to support the admission of new states.
3. Why did farmers in western Pennsylvania challenge federal authority in 1794? What does their location, and the nature of their economy, have to do with this?
4. What Indian problems did the new nation experience? What role did the Spanish play in this? How were these problems solved?
5. Identify the settlements and area of the United States affected by Jay's Treaty. Why did some regions oppose this treaty?
6. Identify the areas of the United States affected by Pickney's Treaty. How did this treaty solve (for the time being) one of the major problems facing western expansion?

SUMMARY

The period between 1785 and 1800 was one of the most politically productive in American history. During these fifteen years, the nation, guided by some of the most talented men in history, reorganized itself under a new framework of government and then struggled to define (for itself as well a for others) just what had been created. It was a period marked by the rise of a party that called itself Federalist, although the philosophy it espoused was, as its opponents were quick to point out, more "nationalist" in emphasis. Arguing that to prosper, the United States had best follow the economic and political example of Great Britain, these Federalists, led by Hamilton, interjected foreign policy into domestic differences and set the stage for one of the earliest and most serious assaults by the government on individual civil liberties. Seeing their less elitist, pro-agriculture, Republican opponents as supporters of France in an undeclared conflict between that nation and the United States, the Federalists set out to suppress dissent and those who promoted it. This assault brought a swift response and so heightened tensions that many feared that the nation could not survive. It was against this background that a shift of power occurred, and by the end of the decade, the Federalists, who had been the moving force for so many years, were clearly losing ground to the Republicans. This meant that if wounds were to be healed and divisions mended, it would have to be done by the man many believed to be the personification of all that separated the two groups—Thomas Jefferson.

CHAPTER SELF-TEST

After you have read the chapter in the text and done the exercises in the Study Guide, the following self-test can be taken to see if you understand the material you have covered. Answers appear at the end of the Study Guide.

Multiple Choice

Circle the letter of the response which best answers the question or completes the statement.

1. By 1786, even defenders of the Articles of Confederation accepted the fact that it was necessary to strengthen:
   a. the power to tax.
   b. the executive.
   c. the court system.
   d. the army.

2. Which of the following was *not* a characteristic of the men who attended the Constitutional Convention in 1787?
   a. They represented the great property interests.
   b. They were relatively young.
   c. They believed in democracy.
   d. They were well educated.

3. The most significant division in the Constitutional Convention was between:
   a. slave and free states.
   b. large and small states.
   c. Eastern and Western interests.
   d. agricultural and manufacturing interests.

4. The most important issue left unaddressed when the Constitutional Convention adjourned was:
   a. the question of counting slaves for representation.
   b. whether to have an executive or not.
   c. the absence of a list of individual rights.
   d. the question of the power of the national government to tax.

5. The Constitution's most distinctive feature was its:
   a. "separation of powers" with "checks and balances."
   b. system for the direct election of the executive.

c. lack of a national judicial system.
d. single-house legislature.

6. Which of the following was *not* addressed by the first Congress under the new Constitution?
   a. a Bill of Rights.
   b. a federal court system.
   c. an executive department.
   d. the role of political parties in the election of a president.

7. Which of the following was *not* a belief of Alexander Hamilton?
   a. The best leaders are those democratically elected.
   b. A stable and effective government requires an elite ruling class.
   c. The new government needed the support of the wealthy and powerful.
   d. A permanent national debt was desirable.

8. Small farmers, who comprised the majority of the population, opposed Hamilton's plan on the grounds that it:
   a. taxed them excessively.
   b. favored a small, wealthy elite.
   c. created too many government offices.
   d. put power in the hands of slaveholders.
   e. a and b.
   f. c and d.

9. Jefferson and his followers believed the Federalists were creating a political party because they were:
   a. using their offices to reward supporters and win allies.
   b. forming local associations to strengthen their stand in local communities.
   c. working to establish a national network of influence.
   d. all of the above.

10. Which of the following was *not* a belief held by Jefferson and his followers?
    a. The ordinary farmer-citizen could, if properly educated, be trusted to govern through elected representatives.
    b. Urban people posed a danger to a republic, because they could easily become a lawless mob.
    c. The best citizen was one who tilled his own soil.
    d. Commercial activity was a danger to the republic.

11. Under the Constitution, the status of the western Indian tribes was:
    a. not clearly defined.
    b. that of independent nations.
    c. that of conquered nations.
    d. the same as states.

12. Although the treaty between England and the United States that John Jay negotiated in 1794 fell short of his instructions, it did:
    a. produce reasonably satisfactory commercial relations with England.
    b. give America undisputed sovereignty over the entire Northwest.
    c. end the impressment of American soldiers.
    d. indicate that the United States and France were not going to war with each other.

13. In the election of 1796:
    a. Thomas Jefferson was the choice of southern Federalists.
    b. the Federalist party united behind Adams.
    c. George Washington took an active role.
    d. the Federalist party divided, when southern Federalists refused to support Adams.

14. Republicans pinned their hopes for a reversal of the Alien and Sedition Acts on the:
    a. Supreme Court.
    b. state legislatures.
    c. House of Representatives.
    d. Army of the United States.

15. Which of the following is *not* true of the campaign and election of 1800?
    a. It was probably the ugliest in American history.
    b. Parties and party organization played an important role.
    c. It underscored problems in the method of electing a president.
    d. It resulted in a clear victory for the winning candidate.

True/False

Read each statement carefully. Mark true statements "T" and false statements "F."

1. The most resourceful advocate of a centralized government was Alexander Hamilton.
2. The intellectual leader of the Constitutional Convention was James Madison.

3. The "Great Compromise" was important because it solved the problem of representation.
4. The Constitution did not resolve the question of which law—state or national—would be the supreme law of the land.
5. Abiding by the rules set up under the Articles of Confederation, the Constitution could not go into effect until it was ratified by all the states in the union.
6. The essays known collectively as the *Federalist Papers* called for the ratification of the Constitution.
7. The Constitution had little chance of success unless it was ratified by Virginia and New York.
8. After the Constitution was ratified, Americans agreed that the government should strive to create a highly commercial, urban nation.
9. The Federalist vision for America included government by a wealthy, enlightened ruling class.
10. Virginia agreed to support Hamilton's "assumption" bill in return for locating the national capital in the South.
11. Most of the framers of the Constitution believed organized political parties were evil and should be avoided.
12. The national government's response to the Whiskey Rebellion was to win allegiance through intimidation.
13. In 1796, Thomas Jefferson ran for vice president on the Federalist ticket.
14. Aaron Burr's role in the election of 1800 was not very significant.
15. After the election of 1880, Federalists tried to hold on to power through the federal judiciary.

Review Questions

These questions are to be answered with essays. This will allow you to explore relationships among individuals, events, and attitudes of the period under review.

1. Explain Hamilton's motives for proposing his plans for taxation, assumption, and currency regulation. What was it in his motives that so upset Jefferson and Madison?
2. The Bill of Rights is generally recognized as protecting the citizens of the United States from their government, but what safeguards are contained in the Constitution to protect the states from violations of their rights? What additional safeguards were proposed by Jefferson and Madison in the Virginia and Kentucky

Resolutions, and what were the implications of these resolutions with regard to the growth of the central government?
3. Compare and contrast the political, economic, and social philosophies of Thomas Jefferson and Alexander Hamilton. Explain the sort of nation each wished created.
4. During the period we have just studied, two opposing political parties arose. Both had their roots in the era governed under the Articles, but unlike competing groups during that period, both factions claimed to support the Constitution. If both felt that the Constitution created the best form of government, what was the basis for their disagreement? Compare and contrast the two parties—their goals, methods, and philosophies.
5. During the "Federalist era," events in other countries did much to shape political party growth and domestic policy. Look at American relations with England, Spain, and France; analyze how these relations affected the two political parties that emerged during this period; and explain the way the government responded to this foreign influence on the parties.

Chapter Seven
The Jeffersonian Era

OBJECTIVES

A thorough study of Chapter 7 should enable you to understand:

1. Thomas Jefferson's views on education, and the role of education in the concept of a "virtuous and enlightened citizenry."
2. The indications of American cultural nationalism that were beginning to emerge during the first two decades of the nineteenth century.
3. The effects of the revolutionary era on religion, and the changing religious patterns that helped bring on the Second Great Awakening.
4. The evidence noticeable in the first two decades that the nation was not destined to remain the simple, agrarian republic envisioned by the Jeffersonians.
5. The political philosophy of Jefferson, and the extent to which he was able to adhere to his philosophy while president.
6. The Jeffersonian-Federalist struggle over the judiciary—its causes, the main points of conflict, and the importance of the outcome for the future of the nation.
7. President Jefferson's constitutional reservations concerning the Louisiana Purchase, the significance of the decision to accept the bargain, and the importance of the Lewis and Clark expedition.
8. What Thomas Jefferson and James Madison were attempting to accomplish by "peaceable coercion," and why their efforts were not successful.
9. The numerous explanations of the causes of the War of 1812, and why there is so much disagreement among historians.
10. The extent of the opposition to the American war effort, and the ways in which the peace settlement proved satisfactory for most citizens.

Pertinent Questions

The Rise of Cultural Nationalism (pp. 176–182)

1. What effect did Republican ideology have on education in the United States?
2. Explain the "cultural independence" that Jeffersonian Americans sought. What means of expression did this "independence" find?
3. What were the obstacles faced by Americans who aspired to create a more elevated national literary life? What efforts were made to overcome these obstacles?
4. How did the American Revolution affect traditional forms of religious practice? What challenges to religious traditionalism arose during this period?
5. What caused the Second Great Awakening?
6. Why were the Methodists, the Baptists, and the Presbyterians so successful on the frontier?
7. What were the "message" and the impact of the Second Great Awakening?

Stirrings of Industrialism (pp. 182–185)

8. What was the industrial revolution? Where and why did it begin?
9. Explain the role that Eli Whitney played in America's industrial revolution. What impact did his inventions have on the South? on the North?
10. What effect did America's transportation system have on industrialization?
11. What were the characteristics of American population growth and expansion in the years between 1790 and 1800?

Jefferson the President (pp. 185–190)

12. How did Jefferson's presidency represent a "fundamental change" in the direction of the federal government?
13. How was the relative "unimportance of the federal government" during the Jefferson administration symbolized by the character of the national capital?
14. What were the characteristics of the "spirit of democratic simplicity" that was the style set by Jefferson for his administration?
15. How did Jefferson combine his duties as president and as party leader in his efforts to govern the country?
16. Why did Jefferson, despite his views on government spending, go to "war" with the Pasha of Tripoli? What was the outcome?

17. What were the roots of Jefferson's conflict with the federal court system, and how did the case of *Marbury v. Madison* fit into the controversy? What is the significance of *Marbury v. Madison*?
18. What method did Jefferson employ to bring the judiciary under Republican control, and what were the results?

Doubling the National Domain (pp. 190–196)

19. Why was New Orleans "the one single spot" that made its possessor the "natural enemy" of the United States?
20. Which group in America was most concerned with the French possession of New Orleans, and how did this concern threaten Jefferson politically?
21. How were the negotiations for the Louisiana Purchase conducted, and what were the terms agreed on?
22. What were the reasons behind Jefferson's reservations over the purchase of Louisiana, and how was he able to reason these doubts away?
23. What was the purpose of the Lewis and Clark expedition, and what did the expedition accomplish?
24. What was the reaction of the New England Federalists to the Louisiana Purchase, and what was their plan to overcome its effects?
25. What were the circumstances that led to the duel between Hamilton and Burr?
26. What was the "Burr conspiracy," and what was its outcome?
27. How does the record kept by Lewis and Clark (see "American Voices," page 193) reflect the purpose of their expedition?

Expansion and War (pp. 196–203)

28. Why was America important to both sides in the conflict between England and France, and what role did the Americans hope to play in the struggle?
29. How did each belligerent nation attempt to prevent America from trading with the other, why was one more successful than the other, and what was the American response?
30. What was Jefferson's response to the *Chesapeake-Leopard* affair, and why did he take this action?
31. How did the Embargo affect the election of 1808, and what was the response of the new president to diplomatic problems that the Embargo had addressed?

32. How did conditions in the West heighten the tension between the United States and Britain?
33. What was Tecumseh's attitude toward the treaties previously negotiated between the United States and various Indian tribes? How did he plan to prevent the expansion of white settlements?
34. Why did Americans blame the British for Indian uprisings on the frontier, and what did frontier settlers see as the best solution to the problem?
35. Why did Americans want to wrest control of Florida from the Spanish? What attempts were made to do this before 1812? Which attempts were successful, and which failed?
36. Who were the "war hawks," and why were they able to exert such influence on America's drift toward war?

The War of 1812 (pp. 203–208)

39. What were the relative successes and failures of the American military during the first year of the war?
40. How did America's fortunes of war change during 1813 and early 1814, and what were the results of this change?
41. What were the plan and purpose of the British invasion of the United States in 1814? What was the result?
42. Why did New England oppose the War of 1812? Prior to 1814, what did the New England states do to hinder the war effort?
43. What caused the leaders of New England to regard the War of 1812 as a threat to their future as a meaningful force in the United States? What did they propose to remedy this situation?
44. What effect did the Hartford Convention have on the Federalist party?
45. What was the background to peace negotiations at Ghent? What did both sides initially demand, and why did they finally agree on the terms they did?

IDENTIFICATION

Identify each of the following, and explain why it is important within the context of the chapter.

1. "republican mother"
2. "noble savages"
3. deism
4. Unitarianism
5. Handsome Lake

6. Robert Fulton
7. Pierre L'Enfant
8. Barbary states
9. John Marshall
10. Lewis and Clark
11. "northern confederacy"
12. General James Wilkinson
13. "peaceable coercion"
14. Macon's Bill No. 2
15. Tecumseh
16. William Henry Harrison
17. Tenskwatawa
18. Battle of Tippecanoe
19. Henry Clay
20. Put-in Bay
21. Battle of Horseshoe Bend
22. Francis Scott Key
23. Battle of New Orleans
24. John Quincy Adams

DOCUMENT

Few inaugural addresses have had the lasting impact of Thomas Jefferson's first inaugural address, which he delivered in early 1801. Some historians have suggested that it was addressed not to his supporters, but to his political enemies. What evidence is there in the excerpt below to suggest that this is true? What evidence is there that this was in keeping with the principles that Jefferson had endorsed as long as he had been in public office? How do the principles espoused here relate to those in the Declaration of Independence? in the Virginia Statute of Religious Liberty?

> We are all Republicans, we are all Federalists. If there be any among us who would wish to dissolve this Union or to change its republican form, let them stand undisturbed as monuments of the safety with which error of opinion may be tolerated where reason is left free to combat it. I know, indeed, that some honest men fear that a republican government can not be strong, that this Government is not strong enough; but would the honest patriot, in the full tide of successful experiment, abandon a government which has so far kept us free and firm on the theoretic and visionary fear that this Government, the world's best hope, may by possibility want energy to preserve itself? I trust not. I believe this, on the contrary, the strongest Government on earth. I believe it the only one where every man, at the call of the law, would fly to the standard of the law, and would meet invasions of the public order as his own personal concern. Sometimes it is said that man can not be trusted

with the government of himself. Can he, then, be trusted with the government of others? Or have we found angels in the forms of kings to govern him? Let history answer this question.

MAP EXERCISE

Fill in or identify the following on the blank map provided. Use the map on page 204 of the text as your source.

1. United States and territories belonging to the United States.
2. British America and its principal towns.
3. Spanish Florida and its principal towns.
4. Principal ports on the Atlantic coast.
5. Routes of troop movements.
6. Battle sites and dates, indicating the victor.
7. Extent of the British blockade.

Interpretative Questions

Based on what you have filled in, answer the following. For some of the questions you will need to consult the narrative in your text for information or explanation.

1. Why did Northern and Southern frontiersmen want to expand into Canada and Florida? How did foreign occupation of these areas hinder western expansion in other regions?
2. Locate the major routes taken by the British when they invaded the United States. What geographic considerations played a part in the choice of where to attack? What made these sites important?
3. Locate the routes taken by American forces. What geographic considerations played a part in the choice of where to attack? What made these sites important?
4. Which region of the country gained the most from the War of 1812? Which felt that it lost as a result of the war? Explain.
5. Study America's expansion into Florida. What impact did the War of 1812 have on this?

SUMMARY

The period just covered was marked by definition and expansion. Having achieved political independence, Americans struggled to achieve cultural independence as well, and this search for self-identity touched almost every phase of the nation's life. "American" tastes in music, literature, and art developed, encouraged by a growing recognition that we were different from other countries and that the difference was worth calling attention to. Religious bodies with ties to the old, colonial ways declined as the Second Great Awakening swept America; technology, unrestrained by mercantile rules and regulations, expanded to solve problems that were particularly American; American politics began to take on characteristics and respond to needs that found little precedent in European systems. At the center of this activity, at times leading it and at times being led, was Thomas Jefferson, a president whose versatility seemed to mirror the diversity of the nation. An aristocrat with democratic sentiments, a strict constructionist who bought half a continent, Jefferson was as contradictory as the American people; but like those people, his ultimate goal was the freedom of individuals to pursue their interests, to expand their talents to the fullest. In that sense, Jefferson, although a pragmatic politician, was also a committed idealist—one who deserves to be the symbol of the age that bears his name.

Although Jefferson was out of office when the war between the United States and Britain began, events during his presidency did much to shape the course of the conflict. The War of 1812 did more than test the army and navy of the United States—it tested the nation's ability to survive deep internal divisions and threatened America's independence as surely as did the forces of Great Britain. Hoping to keep his nation out of war, Jefferson and Madison followed a policy that kept the peace but raised fears among their political enemies. Those opponents, their power and influence declining, saw the government's policies as much directed against themselves as the British; as war neared, many came to see it as part of the "plot" as well. In the meantime, the rest of the nation, feeling that Britain was insulting their sovereignty, rallied to President Madison, who brought the conflict to a successful (if somewhat ill-defined) conclusion.

CHAPTER SELF-TEST

After you have read the chapter in the text and done the exercises in the Study Guide, the following self-test can be taken to see if you understand the material you have covered. Answers appear at the end of the Study Guide.

Multiple Choice

Circle the letter of the response which best answers the question or completes the statement.

1. In the Republican vision of America, education was essential because:
   a. schools were the best place to teach children to be good party members.
   b. an ignorant electorate could not be trusted to preserve democracy.
   c. business leaders needed to be educated.
   d. schools were where religious values were taught.

2. Early in the eighteenth century, religious traditionalists were alarmed over:
   a. a decline in religious education.
   b. the popularity of immoral literature.
   c. demands to separate church and state.
   d. the rise of "rational" religious doctrines.

3. The Great Awakening:
   a. combined a more active piety with a belief in a God whose grace could be attained through faith and good works.
   b. turned back the doctrine of predestination.
   c. drew many converts to Unitarianism and Universalism.
   d. had no impact on women and slaves.

4. The work of Eli Whitney:
   a. improved transportation in the South.
   b. led to the expansion of the cotton culture and slavery.
   c. made the South a major textile-producing region.
   d. led to the decline of slavery, for fewer workers were needed to process the cotton.

5. During his administration, Thomas Jefferson:
   a. used the Alien and Sedition Acts against the Federalists.
   b. cut the national debt almost in half.
   c. showed little interest in westward expansion.
   d. made peace with Aaron Burr.

6. With Jefferson in the White House, the last Federalist stronghold was the:
   a. Senate.
   b. House of Representatives.
   c. Federal Judiciary.
   d. southern states.

7. In the case of *Marbury v. Madison,* the Supreme Court:
   a. affirmed its power to nullify an act of Congress.
   b. upheld Adam's right to make "midnight appointments."
   c. confirmed the power of Congress to expand judicial authority.
   d. ordered Madison to deliver Marbury's commission.

8. The greatest accomplishment of Chief Justice John Marshall was that he:
   a. stopped the growth of Republican power.
   b. prevented a Federalist revival in New England.
   c. refused to expand the power of the judiciary.
   d. made the judiciary a coequal branch of government.

9. What possibility concerned Jefferson when he said, "we must marry ourselves to the British fleet and nation"?
   a. An Indian uprising in the Ohio Valley.
   b. The French occupation of New Orleans.
   c. Increased Spanish strength in the Gulf of Mexico.
   d. A war between England, France, and Spain.

10. Jefferson had reservations about buying Louisiana because:
    a. he doubted his constitutional power to do so.
    b. he feared it would upset western Indian tribes.
    c. New Orleans had few Americans living there.
    d. the Spanish claimed the territory as theirs.

11. Americans learned what Louisiana actually was after:
    a. the French gave them detailed maps.
    b. the Lewis and Clark expedition returned.
    c. new states were carved from the territory.
    d. the Spanish allowed it to be explored.

12. Federalists were upset by the Louisiana purchase because they believed:
    a. it was unconstitutional.
    b. more slave states would come into the union.
    c. western states would be Republican states.
    d. the British were behind it.

13. The Essex Junto was:
    a. a Federalist organization created to support Jefferson.
    b. the anti-Burr coalition in New York.
    c. a literary club in New England.
    d. a group of radical Federalists who wanted to take New England out of the union.

14. The Burr-Hamilton duel took place because:
    a. Burr believed Hamilton was responsible for his defeat in the election for the governor of New York.
    b. Hamilton believed Burr was plotting treason.
    c. Burr refused to support Jefferson in 1801.
    d. Hamilton wanted to rid himself of a political rival.

15. The apparent goal of the "Burr conspiracy" was to:
    a. make Burr "king" of the American southwest.
    b. invade Mexico and take it from the Spanish.
    c. return Louisiana to France.
    d. force Jefferson to accept Burr back into the Republican party.

16. Early in the nineteenth century, the American merchant marine could be described as:
    a. weak and ineffective.
    b. one of the most important in the world.
    c. unable to compete with Britain in the West Indian trade.
    d. of little consequence in the American economy.

17. Jefferson refused to ask for war after the *Chesapeake-Leopard* incident because he:
    a. believed "peaceable coercion" would work.
    b. felt the British were within their rights.

c. did not want the Federalists to make it an issue.
d. was against war in general.

18. The Embargo Act hurt which of the following the most:
    a. England.
    b. France.
    c. New England.
    d. the South.

19. Jefferson told the Indians of the Northwest they could:
    a. convert themselves to farmers.
    b. move to the West.
    c. continue to live as they always had.
    d. a and b.
    e. none of the above.

20. The Prophet, Tenskwatawa, was significant because he:
    a. brought Indians to the Christian faith.
    b. inspired an Indian religious revival that helped unite the tribes.
    c. advocated a religious war with southern tribes.
    d. convinced the Indians to accept Jefferson's policies.

21. Tecumseh was important because he:
    a. advocated Indian unity to stop white expansion.
    b. allied the northwestern Indians with the British in Canada.
    c. was able to defeat the Americans at Tippecanoe.
    d. helped his brother, the Prophet, in his religious work.

22. The congressional election of 1810 was important because it:
    a. added a number of young, western, anti-British representatives to the House.
    b. greatly increased the strength of the Republican party.
    c. brought in a number of peace advocates.
    d. gave rise to a new political party.

23. The United States declaration of war was at first largely ignored by Great Britain because:
    a. England was preoccupied with Napoleon.
    b. the United States could not invade British territory.
    c. England's Indian allies would fight for them.
    d. England considered it only a bluff.

24. Apart from the British, the real losers in the War of 1812 were the:
    a. Spanish in Florida and Mexico.
    b. Canadians.

c. Indian tribes in the Southwest and Great Lakes region.
   d. Republicans in the West.
25. The Hartford Convention was held in an effort to:
   a. force Republicans to address the grievances New England Federalists had against the Madison administration.
   b. forge an alliance between the Northeast and the West.
   c. convince Republicans in New England that the region should secede from the union.
   d. reorganize the Federalist party and pick a candidate for the election of 1816.

True/False

Read each statement carefully. Mark true statements "T" and false statements "F."

1. In the Jeffersonian Era, schooling was primarily the responsibility of private institutions.
2. An argument for the education of women was that they could not be good "Republican mothers" unless they were educated themselves.
3. Once Americans won political independence from England, they had little interest in cultural independence.
4. Early in the nineteenth century most Americans abandoned traditional religious doctrines.
5. In the early nineteenth century, industrialization in the United States was hampered by an inadequate transportation system.
6. Thomas Jefferson refused to use political office to reward loyal supporters.
7. At Jefferson's urging, Justice Samuel Chase was impeached for political reasons, not because he had committed a crime.
8. Jefferson wanted to reduce internal taxes, but not abolish them.
9. Our strong navy made it unnecessary for us to pay tribute to the Barbary states, as weaker nations were doing.
10. Napoleon's plans for an American empire were blocked by a British invasion of Belgium.
11. The Louisiana Territory was organized on the same general pattern of the Northwest Territory.
12. Reports from explorer Zebulon Pike convinced Americans that land between the Missouri River and the Rockies was good for agriculture.

13. Federalists in New York tried to get Aaron Burr to join them in an anti-Jefferson coalition, but he refused.
14. The Burr Conspiracy was a plot by a desperate man, acting alone.
15. Both Jefferson and Marshall wanted Burr convicted for treason.
16. Americans agreed that the British should be free to search for deserters who might be serving in the American merchant marine.
17. Americans had little problem with French violations of our neutral rights.
18. After the *Chesapeake-Leopard* affair, Britain renounced its policy of impressment.
19. The Harrison Land Law of 1800 made it possible for white settlers to acquire farms from the public domain on easier terms than before.
20. Under Jefferson's Indian policy the tribes were granted their tribal lands forever.
21. The Indians in the West would not have risen against the United States if the British in Canada had not told them to do so.
22. White southerners wanted Florida because it blocked river access to the Gulf of Mexico.
23. American troops invaded Canada and held it for the entire War of 1812.
24. As a result of the Battle of New Orleans the United States was able to force Britain to sign the Treaty of Ghent.
25. In the Treaty of Ghent, England formally renounced impressment.

Review Questions

These questions are to be answered with essays. This will allow you to explore relationships among individuals, events, and attitudes of the period under review.

1. Considering the variety of movements covered in the section of your text entitled "The Rising Glory of America," how did American cultural life in the early nineteenth century reflect the Republican vision of the nation's future?
2. Jefferson and the Republicans championed the rights of the states and advocated a strict adherence to the Constitution, but once in office, they found new situations that demanded governmental actions that, in some cases, went beyond what the Federalists had done. What caused Jefferson and his party to change their approach to governing, what reservations did they have about what

they were doing, and how were they able to rationalize this apparent change in program and philosophy?
3. How did the Federalists respond to Republican programs? If the Federalists favored a loose interpretation of the Constitution, why did they protest when Jefferson used a loose interpretation as well? What was it in the Republican program that the Federalists saw as a threat, and how did they respond?
4. Many historians view the War of 1812 as the "second American war for independence," but is this an accurate characterization? In what way did British policies prior to 1812 threaten our independence? Had the United States not fought the war, what might the results have been? Assess these questions, and determine if we were indeed fighting for "independence."
5. What happened to the Federalists? For the first decade under the Constitution, the Federalist party held the nation together, started the government working on a day-to-day basis, and set precedents that are still valid. Twenty years later, they had all but ceased to exist as a party. Why? Examine the events and issues that accompanied the decline of the Federalists, and determine what caused this powerful party to fall.

CHAPTER EIGHT
Varieties of American Nationalism

OBJECTIVES

A thorough study of Chapter 8 should enable you to understand:

1. The effects of the War of 1812 on banking, shipping, farming, industry, and transportation.
2. Postwar governmental efforts to improve banking and transportation.
3. The westward expansion after the War of 1812 and its relation to the growing interest in internal improvements.
4. The settlement patterns that resulted from this postwar westward expansion.
5. The "era of good feelings" as a transitional period.
6. The causes of the Panic of 1819, and the effects of the subsequent depression on politics and the economy.
7. The arguments advanced by North and South during the debates over the admission of Missouri, and how they were to influence sectional attitudes.
8. The ways in which the status of the federal judiciary was changed by the Marshall Court, and how the Court's decision altered the relationships between the federal government and the states and the federal government and business.
9. The reasons why President James Monroe announced his "doctrine" in 1823, and its impact on international relations at the time.
10. Presidential politics in the "era of good feelings," and how they altered the political system.
11. The frustrations experienced by John Quincy Adams during his term as president.
12. The reasons why Andrew Jackson was elected in 1828, and the significance of his victory.

Pertinent Questions

Stabilizing Economic Growth (pp. 210–214)

1. How did America's wartime experience underline the need for another national bank?
2. How did Congress propose to promote manufacturing in the United States?
3. How was transportation improved during this period? What serious gaps remained in the nation's transportation system?
4. What were the arguments in favor of internal improvements financed by the government? What were the arguments against this idea?

Expanding Westward (pp. 214–218)

5. What were the reasons for the so called "great migration?"
6. What were the characteristics of life among white settlers in the Old Northwest?
7. How did life in the Old Southwest differ from that in other sections of the country?
8. Who were the "mountain men?" Why were they important in the settlement of the west?
9. Explain the perception that easterners had of the West.

The "Era of Good Feelings" (pp. 218–222)

10. Why were the leaders of New England disturbed at the nomination and election of James Monroe for president, and what did Monroe do to calm these fears?
11. Why was Florida such a problem for Americans in the South, and how did Andrew Jackson make the resolution of the problem an absolute necessity?
12. What were the critical points decided by the Adams-Onis negotiations?
13. What were the causes of the Panic of 1819?
14. What impact did the Panic of 1819 have on the American economy? What did the government do to try to ease the pain of this depression?

Sectionalism and Nationalism (pp. 223–229)

15. What were the major elements of disagreement in the debate over the admission of Missouri into the Union?

16. Which group opposed Missouri's entering the Union as a slave state? Why?
17. What was the Missouri Compromise? Why did nationalists regard it as a "happy resolution of a danger to the Union"? Why were others less optimistic?
18. What was the net effect of the opinions delivered by the Marshall Court? How did these opinions reflect John Marshall's philosophy of government?
19. Who led the opposition to the Marshall Court, and what was the position they took in denouncing it?
20. What was the long-range significance of the case of *Gibbons v. Ogden*? Of immediate importance, how did this case help to blunt criticism of the Court?
21. How was it that the United States's proclamation of neutrality in the wars between Spain and its colonies actually aided the colonies? Why did the United States do this?
22. Read the section in the text on the Monroe Doctrine, and answer these three questions:
a. Why did the president announce the "doctrine" when he did?
b. What specific dangers, if any, did he have in mind when he announced the "doctrine"?
c. Against what powers in particular was his warning directed?

The Revival of Opposition (pp. 230–233)

23. Why was the caucus system viewed with such disdain before the election of 1824?
24. Who were the candidates in the election of 1824? What was the "platform" of each?
25. What was the outcome of the election of 1824? How was that result arrived at, and what part did Henry Clay play in it?
26. What was the "corrupt bargain," and why did it take place?
27. What did John Quincy Adams plan to accomplish during his presidency? What role was the federal government to play in these plans? Was he successful? Why?
28. In the field of foreign affairs, what did Adams and Clay attempt to do? Were they successful? Why or why not?
29. What problems brought on the tariff debates of 1827 and 1828? In what way did the South respond to Northeastern demands for a higher tariff, and on what did the antitariff forces base their stand?

30. What was the outcome of these tariff debates, and why was it that few were pleased with these results?
31. How had Andrew Jackson's supporters prepared for the election of 1828? What were the issues in the campaign, and what was the outcome?
32. Who were the National Republicans? Who were their leaders? What programs did they support, and from what areas did they draw their strength?

IDENTIFICATION

Identify each of the following, and explain why it is important within the context of the chapter.

1. Second Bank of the United States
2. Francis C. Lowell
3. national road
4. Rocky Mountain Fur Company
5. "Presidential Jubilee"
6. Tallmadge Amendment
7. *Fletcher v. Peck*
8. *Dartmouth College v. Woodward*
9. *McCullough v. Maryland*
10. *Worcester v. Georgia*
11. "King Caucus"
12. William McIntosh

MAP EXERCISE

Fill in or identify the following on the blank map provided. Use the map on page 223 of the text as your source.

1. Free states and territories in 1820.
2. Slave states and territories in 1820.
3. Missouri Compromise line.
4. Dates states entered the Union.
5. Territory closed to slavery by the Missouri Compromise.

6. Territory open to slavery by the Missouri Compromise.
7. Mexico, British America, and Oregon.

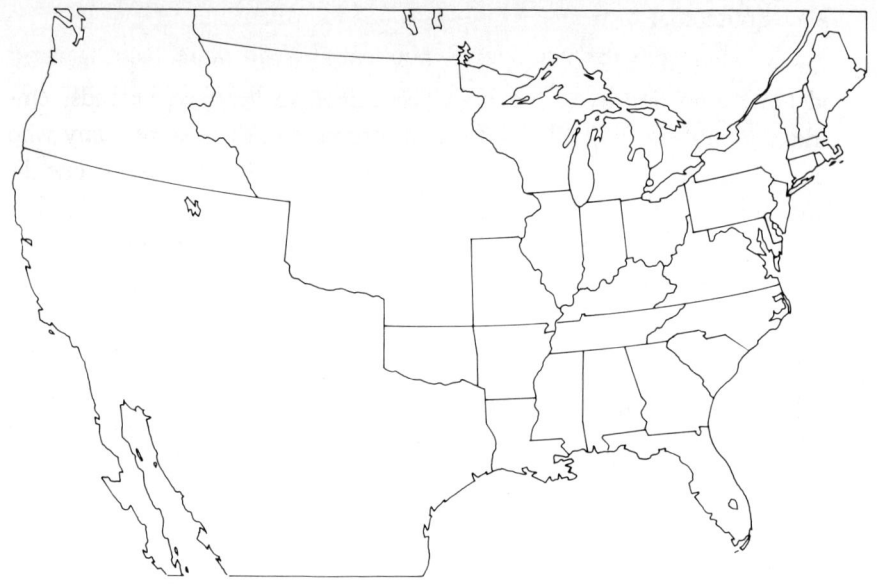

Interpretative Questions

Based on what you have filled in, answer the following. For some of the questions you will need to consult the narrative in your text for information or explanation.

1. What migration and settlement patterns helped determine that Missouri would want to enter the Union as a slave state?
2. What impact did the manner in which states were previously admitted to the Union have on the reaction to the admission of Missouri?
3. Why would the South accept the Missouri Compromise? What does this tell you about the nature of the plantation system and attitudes toward the institution of slavery and its ability to expand?
4. What potential existed (as a result of the Missouri Compromise) for an eventual upsetting of the balance between slave and free states? Which section seemed to gain the most from this?

5. How did the Missouri Compromise reflect the tensions between political parties at the time, especially tensions that were the result of the expansion of the nation?

SUMMARY

After the War of 1812 a new spirit of nationalism and expansion emerged, and the nation, led by a president determined to heal old wounds, embarked on an "era of good feelings." Unfortunately, there were many who did not feel very good for very long. During the 1820s two forces, one divisive and the other unifying, shaped American life and politics. The first appeared during the Missouri debates, which, despite overtones that resembled the earlier Federalist-Republican clashes, brought the issue of slavery and its expansion to the forefront. The immediate question—which section (North or South) would control the Senate—was dealt with through the Missouri Compromise, but the underlying problem was more difficult to resolve. What the debates revealed was that some in the nation saw the addition of slave states (not just western states, but slave states) as a threat. Southern politicians, it was apparent, had come to equate the expansion of slavery with the expansion of their own political philosophy (and power). How true these beliefs were is not the issue. What is important is that they were believed, and, as the years passed, more would come to share these convictions. Countering this divisive force was the spirit of nationalism and the emergence of two parties—both with a national following. These developments seemed to overshadow sectional concerns, and with the election of Andrew Jackson, one of the most popular political figures since George Washington, the nation seemed more concerned with unity than division. How long this was to last was another question.

CHAPTER SELF-TEST

After you have read the chapter in the text and done the exercises in the Study Guide, the following self-test can be taken to see if you understand the material you have covered. Answers appear at the end of the Study Guide.

Multiple Choice

Circle the letter of the response which best answers the question or completes the statement.

1. Which of the following did *not* occur after the War of 1812?
   a. Commerce revived and expanded.
   b. An economic boom was followed by a disastrous bust.
   c. All banking was left to the states.
   d. Westward expansion accelerated dramatically.

2. After peace was restored, American industries that prospered during the war:
   a. were strong enough to withstand British competition.
   b. expanded into foreign markets.
   c. were competitive with foreign imports.
   d. demanded that the government protect them from foreign competition.

3. After the war, the nation's most pressing economic need was:
   a. access to foreign markets that were not open to our commerce.
   b. a trained labor force to work in complex industries.
   c. a transportation system that would provide manufacturers access to raw materials and markets.
   d. a system by which worn out soil could be reclaimed.

4. Which of the following was *not* a reason behind the "great migration" after the War of 1812:
   a. population increase.
   b. free land.
   c. weakening Indian resistance.
   d. economic pressure.

5. Farmers seemed to prefer land in the Old Northwest rather than the Southwest because:
   a. the spread of the plantation system limited opportunity in the South.
   b. Indians were still active in the South.
   c. the Northwest had richer soil.
   d. land was cheaper in the Northwest.

6. As far as most Americans were concerned, the area west of the Mississippi was:
   a. a "Great American Desert."
   b. the next great agricultural frontier.
   c. too far from towns and cities to be attractive.
   d. fit only for a plantation style economy.

7. The administration of President James Monroe was called the Era of Good Feelings because:
   a. it was a time of few factional disputes and partisan divisions.
   b. there were no economic depressions.
   c. most Americans were content to remain where they were.
   d. the National Bank successfully managed the economy.

8. Because he favored American expansion, John Quincy Adams:
   a. called on the United States to occupy Oregon.
   b. felt a war with Mexico would help the nation's economy.
   c. supported Jackson's invasion of Florida.
   d. was unwilling to give up claims to Texas.

9. Although the Panic of 1819 had many causes, the West assigned the primary blame for the Panic on:
   a. state banks
   b. land speculators
   c. the National Bank
   d. Congress

10. John Marshall's influence on the Supreme Court was so great that he:
    a. was able to get whomever he wanted appointed to the bench.
    b. more than anyone other than the farmers themselves molded the development of the Constitution.
    c. was able to ignore the other justices.
    d. could single-handedly overturn acts of Congress.

11. The lasting significance of *Gibbons v. Ogden* was that it:
    a. opened the way for steamboat travel on the Mississippi.
    b. confirmed the state's right to regulate commerce.
    c. made peace between the court and the Adams administration.
    d. freed transportation systems from restraints by the states.

12. The decisions of the Marshall Court:
    a. established the primacy of the federal government in regulating the economy.
    b. gave strength to the doctrine of state rights.
    c. destroyed what was left of Hamiltonian Federalism.
    d. opened the way for an increased federal role in promoting economic growth.
    e. a and d.
    f. b and c.

13. In its rulings concerning the Indian tribes, the Marshall Court held that:
    a. the national government, not the states, had authority.
    b. Indians were citizens like everyone else.
    c. Indians had the same status as slaves.
    d. tribal lands belong to the states.

14. The charge of a "corrupt bargain" was raised when:
    a. Clay supported Adams for the presidency and was appointed secretary of state.
    b. Jackson promised to reward his supporters if he won.
    c. Adams won with the support of southern planters.
    d. the Republican caucus threw its support to Adams.

15. Adams's "nationalistic program," which was a lot like Clay's "American system," was not funded because:
    a. the nation could not afford it.
    b. business opposed it.
    c. western interests opposed it.
    d. Jackson's supporters in congress voted against it.

True/False

Read each statement carefully. Mark true statements "T" and false statements "F."

1. Difficulties in financing the War of 1812 underlined the need for a national bank.
2. Tariffs were generally favored by manufacturing interests but opposed by those who made their living from agriculture.
3. One reason for the growing interest in internal improvements was the sudden and dramatic surge in westward expansion in the years following the War of 1812.
4. The advance of the Southern frontier meant the spread not just of cotton but also of slavery.
5. During this period there was very little economic opportunity for Americans who wanted to trade with the far Southwest and Mexico.
6. Andrew Jackson took Florida and the Adams-Onis Treaty made it legal.
7. The Missouri Compromise upset the balance between slave and free states.

8. In *McCulloch v. Maryland* the Supreme Court declared the National Bank unconstitutional.
9. The decision in *Gibbon v. Ogden* was popular because it was a stand against monopoly power.
10. The Marshall Court's rulings concerning the Indian tribes were among its most popular decisions.
11. The Monroe Doctrine was passed by Congress and immediately became an important part of our foreign policy.
12. The political divisions that appeared in the late 1820s were in no way related to the divisions of the 1790s.
13. Henry Clay's "American System" included a national bank, a protective tariff, and federally funded internal improvements.
14. In 1828, Andrew Jackson lost the presidential election because he was too closely identified with an "economic aristocracy" that his enemies claimed controlled him.

Review Questions

These questions are to be answered with essays. This will allow you to explore relationships among individuals, events, and attitudes of the period under review.

1. After the War of 1812, there emerged a group of Republicans who urged the nation to consider "national" issues rather than "local" or "sectional" matters. So persistent were they that many of their party contended that they were abandoning the basic principles laid down by Jefferson. Were they? Could this new group be called "Jeffersonian," or did it represent something else? Examine the things the nationalists proposed for the nation, then go back to Chapter 6 and compare their plans with those of Jefferson and Hamilton. To which set of plans does the nationalists' program seem more closely allied? What does this tell you about the nature of political parties and political ideas at this time? Also, how does the emergence of the nationalists relate to the decline of the Federalists?
2. Nationalism was a unifying factor in the 1820s, but how did this nationalistic attitude, which was so evident in domestic affairs, influence foreign policy? What were the effects of nationalism on American foreign policy during this period, and what forces, if any, tended to negate its influence?
3. How did the career of John Marshall contribute to the rise of nationalism during this era? In what specific areas did he increase

the power of the national government? Of the two political parties, which was more likely to support Marshall? Why?

Chapter Nine
Jacksonian America

Objectives

A thorough study of Chapter 9 should enable you to understand:

1. Andrew Jackson's philosophy of government, and his impact on the office of the presidency.
2. The nullification theory of John C. Calhoun, and President Jackson's reaction to the attempt to put nullification into action.
3. The supplanting of John C. Calhoun by Martin Van Buren as successor to Jackson, and the significance of the change.
4. The reasons for the Jacksonian war on the Bank of the United States, and the effects of Jackson's veto on the powers of the president and on the American financial system.
5. The causes of the Panic of 1837, and the effect of the panic on the presidency of Van Buren.
6. The differences in party philosophy between the Democrats and the Whigs, the reasons for the Whig victory in 1840, and the effect of the election on political campaigning.
7. The negotiations that led to the Webster-Ashburton Treaty, and the importance of the treaty in Anglo-American relations.
8. The reasons why John C. Calhoun, Henry Clay, and Daniel Webster were never able to reach their goal—the White House.

Pertinent Questions

The Rise of Mass Politics (pp. 234–239)

1. What were the general characteristics of "Jacksonian Democracy," its philosophy, and its practice?
2. What role did the western states play in the growing democratization of American politics?
3. What was the reaction of the older states to these democratic trends? Cite some examples.

4. What groups were excluded from this widening of political opportunity? Why?
5. How did the spoils system fit into Jackson's "democratic" plans? What other means did he use to bring more people into the political process?
6. What was the effect of this growth of democracy? How did it change, or not change, the American political system? What is its significance?

"Our Federal Union" (pp. 239–244)

7. What was the dilemma faced by John C. Calhoun, and what factors gave rise to it?
8. How did Calhoun attempt to resolve this dilemma? What arguments did he use, and on which sources did he draw?
9. What did Calhoun really hope his theory of nullification would accomplish?
10. How did Martin Van Buren's and John C. Calhoun's backgrounds and rise to prominence differ?
11. What was the Kitchen Cabinet? Who were its members? Why did it come into existence?
12. What were the origins of the Calhoun-Jackson split? How did the Eaton administration contribute to the division? What effect did it have on the Jackson administration?
13. How did the Webster-Hayne debate fit into the controversy between Jackson and Calhoun? What brought about the debate, what was the major point of disagreement between the two, and what were the arguments advanced?
14. How did Calhoun and South Carolina propose to test the theory of nullification? What factors contributed to their decision?
15. What was Jackson's reaction to South Carolina's attempt at nullification? How did his action in this case correspond to his action in the case of the Cherokee removal? What accounts for this?
16. What was the outcome of the nullification crisis? What, if anything, did the antagonists learn from the confrontation?
17. Explain Jackson's position on states' rights. How did he apply this to the matter of internal improvements?

The Removal of the Indians (pp. 244–249)

18. What was the program (inherited by Jackson) designed to deal with the Indians who lived east of the Mississippi? What happened when this program was applied to the Cherokee in Georgia?

19. How did Jackson's action in the matter of the Cherokee removal correspond to his views on the role of the president and on the issue of states' rights?
20. Explain the different ways the Indians responded to Jackson's policies. What was the outcome for the different tribes?
21. How did white Americans justify their policies toward native Americans. What evidence is there to suggest that there were other alternatives available to expanding Americans?

Jackson and the Bank War (pp. 249–252)

22. What was Jackson's opinion on the Bank of the United States? On what did he base his views? What other factors contributed to his stand?
23. What was Nicholas Biddle's initial attitude toward the Bank's involvement in politics? What caused him to change his mind, what steps did he take, and who were his supporters?
24. How did Jackson respond to the efforts to recharter the Bank? What reasons did he give for his action, and what effect did the election of 1832 have on his Bank policy?
25. How did the supporters of the Bank respond to Jackson's action? What did Biddle do? What were the results?
26. How did the Supreme Court under Roger B. Taney differ from the Court under Marshall? What groups profited from Taney's decisions?

The Emergence of the Second Party System (pp. 252–256)

27. How did the "party philosophy" of the Whigs differ from that of the Democrats?
28. Who were the Whig leaders? How do they reflect the variety of political opinions found in the Whig party?
29. What was the Whig strategy in the election of 1836? Who was the Democratic candidate? Why was he selected? What was the result?

Politics After Jackson (pp. 256–261)

30. What was the general condition of the American economy in 1836? What factors contributed to this? What was the most pressing problem that Congress and the administration faced between 1835 and 1837, and how did they propose to solve it?
31. What caused the Panic of 1837? What effect did it have on the nation? on the Democratic party?

32. What programs did Martin Van Buren propose to ease the depression? Why did he act in this way?
33. Why did the Whigs select William Henry Harrison as their candidate in 1840? How did his campaign "set a new pattern for presidential contests"?
34. What did the selection of John Tyler as Harrison's vice-presidential candidate reveal about the composition of the Whig party?
35. What was the origin of the split between Tyler and Clay? What effect did it have on the administration? on the Whig party? What was the result?
36. Why did Daniel Webster not resign from the Tyler cabinet when the other Whigs did? What were the diplomatic problems on which he was working?
37. What were the accomplishments of Webster as secretary of state?
38. How has the debate over Jacksonian Democracy focused not only on Andrew Jackson but on American society in the Jacksonian era as well?

IDENTIFICATION

Identify each of the following, and explain why it is important within the context of the chapter.

1. "The reign of King `Mob'"
2. Dorr Rebellion
3. Albany Regency
4. William L. Marcy
5. Peggy Eaton
6. Webster's second reply to Hayne
7. Democrats' Jefferson banquet
8. force bill
9. Black Hawk War
10. Five Civilized Tribes
11. Trail of Tears
12. "soft money"/"hard money"
13. "pet banks"
14. Anti-Mason party
15. specie circular
16. independent treasury
17. "log cabin" campaign

18. *Caroline* affair
19. "Aroostook war"
20. *Creole*
21. Webster-Ashburton Treaty

DOCUMENT

Below is an excerpt from Daniel Webster's reply to Robert Y. Hayne's defense of the theory of nullification. What does Webster see as the danger inherent in Calhoun's doctrine? How is this speech in keeping with Webster's political views, especially his view of the nature of the Union and the role of the national government?

> I have not allowed myself, Sir, to look beyond the Union, to see what might lie hidden in the dark recess behind. I have not coolly weighed the chances of preserving liberty when the bonds that unite us together shall be broken asunder. I have not accustomed myself to hang over the precipice of disunion, to see whether, with my short sight, I can fathom the depth of the abyss below; nor could I regard her as a safe counsellor in the affairs of this government, whose thoughts should be mainly bent on considering, not how the Union may be best preserved, but how tolerable might be the condition of the people when it should be broken up and destroyed. While the Union lasts, we have high, exciting, gratifying prospects spread out before us, for us and our children. Beyond that I seek not to penetrate the veil. God grant that in my day, at least, that curtain may not rise! God grant that on my vision never may be opened what lies behind! When my eyes shall be turned to behold for the last time the sun in heaven, may I not see him shining on the broken and dishonored fragments of a once gorgeous Union; on States dissevered, discordant, and belligerent; on a land rent with civil feuds, or drenched, it may be, in fraternal blood! Let their last feeble and lingering glance rather behold the glorious ensign of the republic, now known and honored throughout the earth, still full high advanced, its arms and trophies steaming in their original lustre, not a stripe erased or polluted, not a single star obscured, bearing for its motto, no such miserable interrogatory as "What is all this worth?" nor those other words of delusion and folly, "Liberty first and Union afterwards"; but everywhere, spread all over in characters of living Light, blazing on its ample folds, as they float over the sea and over the land, and in every wind under the whole heavens, that other sentiment, dear to every true American heart,—Liberty *and* Union, now and for ever, one and inseparable!

Daniel Webster, *The Writings and Speeches of Daniel Webster*, National Edition (Boston, 1903), 6:75.

MAP EXERCISE

Fill in or identify the following on the blank map provided. Use the map on page 246 of the text as your source.

1. Tribal lands and the states and territories in which they were located.

2. Other states in the region.
3. Removal routes (including the towns and forts along the way).
4. Reservations and the forts within them.

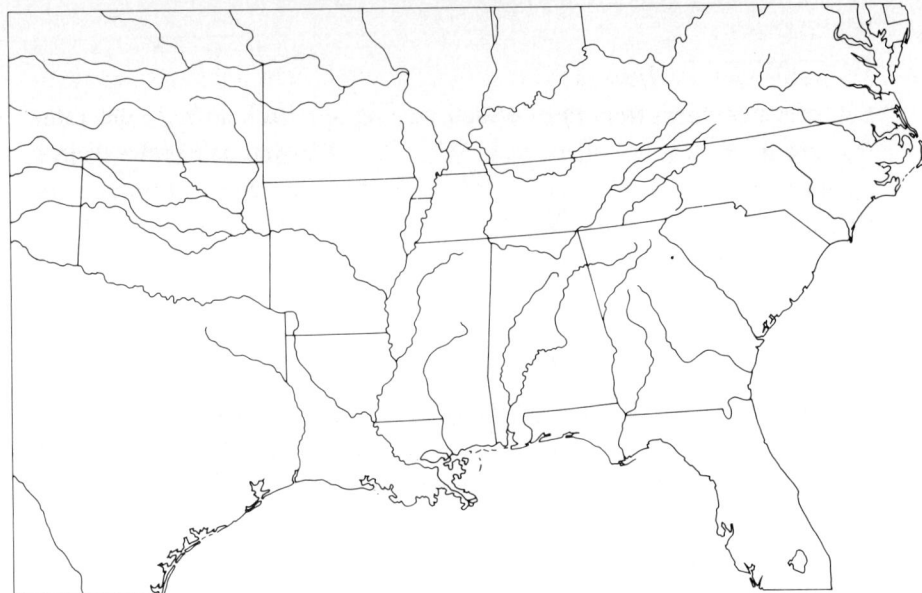

Interpretative Questions

Based on what you have filled in, answer the following. For some of the questions you will need to consult the narrative in your text for information or explanation.

1. Why did the states involved want the Indians removed? Look at the location of the tribal lands and explain why their continued occupation by the Indians represented not only the loss to the state of valuable territory but might also threaten the westward movement itself.
2. How did the land to which the Indians were removed differ from that on which they had lived? Were whites aware of the significance of the difference? What does this suggest about white attitudes toward the Indians?
3. Note the removal routes. What geographic features were considered in determining where the Indians would travel? Do you feel this made the trek easier or more difficult?
4. What geographic features made it possible for the Seminoles (and some Cherokees) to resist removal?

5. Note the location of the forts in or near the Indian Territory. Why were they placed as they were? What does this indicate about American Indian policy?

SUMMARY

At first glance, Andrew Jackson seems a study in contradictions: an advocate of states' rights who forced South Carolina to back down in the nullification controversy; a champion of the West who vetoed legislation that would have opened easy access to part of the area and who issued the specie circular, which brought the region's "flush times" to a disastrous halt; a nationalist who allowed Georgia to ignore the Supreme Court; and a defender of majority rule who vetoed the Bank after the majority's representatives, the Congress, had passed it. Perhaps he was, as his enemies argued, simply out for himself. But in the end, few would argue that Andrew Jackson was not a popular president, if not so much for what he did as for what he was. Jackson symbolized what American perceived (or wished) themselves to be—defiant, bold, independent. He was someone with whom they could identify. So what if the image was a bit contrived, it was still a meaningful image. Thus Jackson was reelected by an overwhelming majority and was able to transfer that loyalty to his successor, a man who hardly lived up to the image. But all this left a curious question unanswered. Was this new democracy voting for leaders whose programs they favored or, rather, for images that could be altered and manipulated almost at will? The answer was essential for the future of American politics, and the election of 1840 gave the nation a clue.

CHAPTER SELF-TEST

After you have read the chapter in the text and done the exercises in the Study Guide, the following self-test can be taken to see if you understand the material you have covered. Answers appear at the end of the Study Guide.

Multiple Choice

Circle the letter of the response which best answers the question or completes the statement.

1. The goal of the Jacksonians was to:
    a. redistribute the wealth of the nation.
    b. reduce the influence of southern planters.

c. ensure that people could rise to prominence on the basis of their own talents and energies.
   d. put as many of their own people in office as possible.

2. During the Jacksonian Era, the number of voters:
   a. increased at a more rapid pace than did the population as a whole.
   b. increased at a slower pace than in the previous decade.
   c. actually decreased as a percentage of the population.
   d. remained stable.

3. The most significant change regarding "party" to take place in the Jacksonian Era was the:
   a. recognition of the value of "third parties."
   b. view that institutionalized parties were a desirable part of the political process.
   c. view that party leaders should be presidential candidates.
   d. emergence of a hard core of party loyalists who picked all candidates for national office.

4. Which of the following did Jackson and the Jacksonians *not* attack:
   a. a "class" of permanent officeholders.
   b. the system by which presidential candidates were selected.
   c. the "spoils system."
   d. the party caucus.

5. John C. Calhoun advanced the theory of nullification as:
   a. a moderate alternative to secession.
   b. a means of making the national government secondary to the states.
   c. a concession to western interests.
   d. a way to force congress to pass a protective tariff.

6. The most significant result of the Eaton Affair was that:
   a. John C. Calhoun became the leader of the Kitchen Cabinet.
   b. it led to the Webster-Hayne debate.
   c. Martin Van Buren emerged as Jackson's choice to succeed him.
   d. John Eaton became Jackson's secretary of state.

7. Robert Y. Hayne supported the continued sale of western lands in an effort to:
   a. aid the expansion of slavery.
   b. help finance internal improvements.
   c. add to the deposits in the National Bank.
   d. get western support for efforts to reduce the tariff.

8. Daniel Webster's "second reply to Hayne" was made in an attempt to:
   a. refute Calhoun's theory of nullification.
   b. affirm the integrity of the Union.
   c. support the sale of western lands.
   d. a and b.
   e. b and c.

9. The "force bill" of 1832:
   a. authorized the president to use force to see that acts of Congress were obeyed.
   b. forced Jackson to stand up to Calhoun.
   c. forced the president to consult Congress if he planned to use troops against South Carolina.
   d. made it impossible for other southern states to nullify laws.

10. When the Indian removal was completed:
    a. every Indian west of the Mississippi River was gone.
    b. only elements of the Seminoles and Cherokees remained.
    c. the Indians were relocated in reservations much like the tribal lands they left.
    d. the Indians were far enough removed from whites where they would not face further encroachments.

11. Under Nicholas Biddle, the National Bank:
    a. withheld credit from new businesses.
    b. had a restraining effect on less well-managed state banks.
    c. did little general banking business.
    d. operated solely from its Philadelphia headquarters.

12. The National Bank was supported by:
    a. "hard-money" advocates.
    b. "soft-money" advocates.
    c. western farmers.
    d. eastern business interests.

13. Determined to reduce the Bank's power even before its charter expired, Jackson:
    a. fired most of its officials, including Biddle.
    b. removed government deposits from the Bank.
    c. removed government deposits from state banks.
    d. exposed the high officials who had been borrowing from the bank.

14. Roger B. Taney's tenure as chief justice:
    a. marked a sharp break with the Marshall court in constitutional interpretation.
    b. was little more than an extension of the Marshall court.
    c. helped modify Marshall's vigorous nationalism.
    d. was greatly influenced by the views of John C. Calhoun.
15. The Whig party:
    a. favored expanding the power of the federal government.
    b. encouraged industrial and commercial development.
    c. advocating knitting the country together into a consolidated economic system.
    d. all of the above.
    e. none of the above.

True/False

Read each statement carefully. Mark true statements "T" and false statements "F."

1. If the Jacksonians were consistent in nothing else, they were consistent Democrats.
2. During the Age of Jackson politics became open to virtually all the nation's white male citizens.
3. Jackson wanted to weaken the functions of the federal government and give the states more power.
4. Calhoun wanted his nullification theory to be put to the test as soon as possible.
5. Andrew Jackson's "Kitchen Cabinet" was a group of men the president wanted to have as little to do with as possible.
6. When South Carolina nullified the tariffs of 1828 and 1832, Jackson had no choice but to go along.
7. If Calhoun and his allies learned nothing else from the nullification crisis, they learned that no state could defy the federal government alone.
8. During the first decades of the nineteenth century the American view of Indians as "noble savages" changed to a view of them simply as "savages."
9. Indian removal was a purely Jacksonian idea.
10. Jackson believed the National Bank was a citadel of privilege and he was determined to destroy it.

11. Clay was able to use Jackson's veto of the bank to defeat him for the presidency.
12. When the Bank of the United States died in 1836, the country was left with a fragmented and chronically unstable banking system.
13. The Democratic party looked with suspicion on government efforts to stimulate commercial and industrial growth.
14. The Whig vision of America was one of a nation embracing the industrial future and rising to world greatness as a commercial and manufacturing power.
15. The Van Buren presidency was successful because he was able to quickly bring the nation out of the Panic of 1837.
16. The 1840 campaign illustrated how getting elected had become as important as governing.
17. Though Harrison died soon after he took office, John Tyler pushed ahead with Whig programs.

Review Questions

These questions are to be answered with essays. This will allow you to explore relationships among individuals, events, and attitudes of the period under review.

1. Andrew Jackson thought of himself as the "president of the people." Was he? What can you find in the career of Jackson that would support his assertion, and what can you find to deny it?
2. How did white American's attitudes toward native Americans evolve during the early nineteenth century? What factors led to the decision to remove the Indians from land east of the Mississippi. What other alternatives were available, and why were they rejected? How did the Indians respond to the government's policy toward them?
3. What was the ostensible reason for the split between Calhoun and Jackson? The Eaton affair is generally seen as a symptom, not a cause, which would indicate that the real division between the two men was much deeper. Assess the causes of the split, and speculate on its significance for the South and for the Democrats.
4. How did William Henry Harrison win in 1840? What were the issues that worked against him, and how did his party exploit them? Furthermore, how was this candidate presented to the people? What image were his managers trying to create, and what does this image tell you about the American electorate?

5. How did Calhoun (and South Carolina) justify and explain the theory of nullification? On what points did Webster (and Jackson) oppose this theory? Be sure to read your documents in the text.

CHAPTER TEN
America's Economic Revolution

OBJECTIVES

A thorough study of Chapter 10 should enable you to understand:

1. The changes that were taking place within the nation in terms of population growth, population movement, urbanization, and the impact of immigration.
2. The importance of the Erie Canal for the development of the West and of New York City.
3. The changes that were taking place in transportation, business, industry, labor, and commerce as the full impact of the industrial revolution was felt in the United States.
4. The reasons why the Northeast and Northwest tended to become more dependent on each other, while the South became isolated from the rest of the nation in the 1840s and 1850s.
5. The forces behind the rise of the factory and why this was the most profound economic development to take place in mid-nineteenth-century America.
6. The vast changes taking place in the Northeast as agriculture declined while urbanization and industrialization progressed at a rapid rate.
7. The characteristics of the greatly increased immigration of the 1840s and 1850s, and the immigrants' effects on the development of the free states.
8. The reasons for the appearance of the nativist movement in the 1850s.
9. The living and working conditions of both men and women in the Northern factory towns and on the Northwestern farms.

PERTINENT QUESTIONS

Foundations of Economic Development (pp. 265–269)

1. What were the reasons for and the effect of the rapid increase in population between 1820 and 1840?
2. Where did this increased population settle? What population shifts took place between 1820 and 1840, and how did they affect political division?
3. Why was the rise of New York City so phenomenal? What forces combined to make it America's leading city?
4. What major immigrant groups came to the United States during this period? What impact did they have on the character and distribution of the population in the North?
5. What impact did this immigration have on the political system? Which party was the most successful in attracting immigrant voters? Why?
6. What gave rise to the nativist movement? What were its political goals?

Transportation and Communications Revolutions (pp. 269–275)

7. Why were natural means of carrying commerce (lakes and river) unsatisfactory to most Americans?
8. How did Americans propose to overcome the geographical limitations on water travel?
9. Which area took the lead in canal development? What was the effect of these canals on that section of the country? How did other sections respond to this example?
10. What were the general characteristics of early railroad development in the United States? What innovations aided the progress of railroads, and what advantages did railroads have over other forms of transportation?
11. What innovations in transportation and/or communication, other than the growth of the railroads, took place during this period?

Commerce and Industry (pp. 275–279)

12. In the broadening of business described here, what shifts in manufacturing took place and what business innovations occurred, and what effect did this have on the general distribution of goods in America?

13. What influence did technology have on the growth of American industry?
14. What changes contributed to the rise of the factory? Why was this "the most profound economic development in mid-nineteenth-century America?"
15. How did technology and industrial ingenuity prepare the way for the expansion of industry and the growth of the American economy?
16. Who were the "merchant capitalists" and what contribution did merchant capitalism make to the American economy?

Men and Women at Work (pp. 279–285)

17. How did the textile mills recruit and use labor? What was the general response of workers to the Lowell method? Of observers? What caused the breakdown of this system?
18. What was the lot of working women in Lowell and other factory towns? How did this differ from conditions in Europe? What problems did these women have in adjusting to factory and factory-town life?
19. How did the circumstances of immigrant workers differ from those of native laborers?
20. What was the general condition of workers in Northeastern factories? What impact did factory work have on the artisan tradition in America?
21. What attempts were made to better conditions in Northeastern factories? What role did unions play in these attempts, and what was accomplished?

Patterns of Society (pp. 285–289)

22. Why was the increasing wealth of America not widely or equitably distributed? How was this unequal distribution manifested in daily life? Which groups were most likely to be found at the bottom of the economic scale?
23. Despite the gap between rich and poor, there was little overt class conflict in antebellum America. Why?
24. What "profound change in the nature and function of the family" took place during this era? What caused this change?
25. What conditions put women in a "separate sphere," and what were the characteristics of the "distinctive female culture" women developed?

26. What was the "cult of domesticity," and what costs and benefits did it bring to middle-class women? To working-class women?

The Agricultural North (pp. 289–293)

27. What caused the decline of farming in the Northeast? What did farmers in the Northeast do to overcome this decline, and what new patterns in agriculture resulted?
28. What was the basis of the economy in the Northwest? What goods were produced there?
29. Where were most of the goods produced in the Northwest marketed? What role did this play in the pre-1860 sectional alignment?
30. What factors contributed to the growth and expansion of the Northwest's economy? Who were the men responsible for this?

IDENTIFICATION

Identify each of the following, and explain why it is important within the context of the chapter.

1. Erie Canal
2. Supreme Order of the Star-Spangled Banner
3. Mohawk and Hudson Railroad
4. Samuel F. B. Morse
5. Eli Whitney and Simeon North
6. Charles Goodyear
7. the *Lowell Offering*
8. Factory Girls Association
9. National Trades' Union
10. *Commonwealth v. Hunt*
11. Central Park
12. Mary Lyon
13. "Domestic virtues"
14. John Deere
15. Cyrus H. McCormick

DOCUMENT 1

Few places better reflected the growth and diversity of the United States than the city of New York. With the opening of the Erie Canal, New York City became the gateway to the West, and its size grew with its importance. The following account of the city was written by James Silk Buckingham, an Englishman who visited America between 1837 and 1840. What impressed him most about the city? How did his English experience seem to shape these impressions? What evidence did Buckingham find of social customs and distinctions being different from those of Europe? What do you feel accounted for this?

What accounted for New York's growth and diversity? What forces combined to make it America's principal city? Considering the nationalistic spirit of the age, how would Americans have responded to Buckingham's description? Assuming that his assessment was accurate, would they have pointed with pride to the city? Why?

> The hotels are generally on a larger scale than in England. The great Astor House, which overlooks the Park from the west side of Broadway, is much larger in area than the largest hotels in London or Paris; it makes up 600 beds, and has a proportionate establishment to suit the scale of its general operations. It is built wholly of granite, is chaste in its style of architecture, and is called after the rich John Jacob Astor.
>
> Of places of public amusement there are a great number, including six theatres, which are well filled every night, though the majority of what would be called the more respectable classes of society, the most opulent, and the most religious members of the community do not generally patronize or approve of theatrical exhibitions under the present management.
>
> The private dwellings contain, as must be the case in all large cities, a great society of kinds and descriptions. The older houses are small, and most built of wood painted yellow or white. These are now confined to the residences of the poorer classes and are fast disappearing in every quarter, their places being occupied by substantial buildings of brick, though here and there are a few with granite fronts. The style of decoration, in the steps of ascent, the area of railings, and the doors, is more florid and ornamental than in the best parts of London, and the interior of the principal houses may be described as spacious, handsome, and luxurious, with lofty passages, good staircases, large rooms, and costly and gorgeous furniture. There are many individual houses of much greater splendour in London than any to be seen in New York, especially in the mansions of the English nobility; but, on the whole, the number of large, commodious, and elegantly furnished private dwellings in New York is much greater in proportion to the whole population than those in London, and approaches nearer to the ratio of Edinburgh or Paris.
>
> The streets are very unequal in their proportions and conditions. The great avenue of Broadway is striking from its continuous and unbroken length of three miles in a straight line; but its breadth, about eighty feet, is not sufficiently ample for the due proportion of its length. It is, moreover, wretchedly paved, both in the centre and on the sides. Large holes and deep pits are frequently seen in the former; and the latter, while before some houses the slabs of stone are large, uniform, and level, there is often an immediate transition from these to broken masses of loose stones, that require the greatest caution to pass over, especially in wet or frosty weather. The lighting and cleansing of the streets are not nearly so good as in the large towns of England, the gas being scanty in quantity, the lamps too far removed from each other, and the body of scavengers [garbage collectors] both weak in numbers and

deficient in organizations. Some of the smaller streets are almost impassible in times of rain and snow; and, when not incommoded by a profusion of mud or water, they are prolific in their supply of dust. Many of the streets have trees planted along the edge of the foot pavement on each side, which in summer affords an agreeable shade, but in autumn it has the disagreeable effect of strewing the path with falling leaves, and in winter it makes the aspect more dreary.

A custom prevails, in the principal streets for shops, of having wooden pillars planted along the outer edge of the pavement, with horizontal beams reaching from pillar to pillar, not unlike the stanchions and crosspieces of a ropewalk....

Broadway, which is greatly disfigured by these, is therefore much inferior to Regent Street in London in the general air of cleanliness, neatness, light, spaciousness, good pavement, and fine shops, by which the latter is characterized; and although the number of beautiful and gayly dressed ladies, who make Broadway their morning promenade, uniting shopping, visiting, and walking at the same time, gives it a very animated appearance of a fine day, between twelve and two o'clock, yet the absence of handsome equipages and fine horses, and the fewness of well-dressed gentlemen who have the leisure to devote to morning promenades of pleasure occasions Broadway to be inferior in the general effect of brilliance and elegance to the throng of Regent Street on a fine day in May, between three and four o'clock.

The population of New York is estimated at present to be little short of 300,000. Of these perhaps there are 20,000 foreigners, including English and persons from Canada and the British possessions, and 30,000 strangers from other states of the Union, making therefore the fixed resident population 250,000 and the floating population about 50,000 more. The greatest number of these are engaged in commerce or trade, with a due admixture of professional men, as clergy, physicians, and lawyers. But among them all there are fewer than perhaps in any other community in the world who live without any ostensible avocation. The richest capitalists still take a part in the business proceedings of the day; and men who have professedly retired and have no counting-house or mercantile establishment still retain so much of the relish for profitable occupation that they mingle freely with the merchants, and are constantly found to be the buyers and sellers of stock, in funds, or shares in companies, canals, railroads, banks, et cetera.

The result of all this is to produce the busiest community that any man could desire to live in. In the streets all is hurry and bustle; the very carts, instead of being drawn by horses at a walking pace, are often met at a gallop, and always in a brisk trot.

J. S. Buckingham, *America, Historical, Statistic, and Descriptive* (New York: Harper and Brothers, 1841). p. 4246.

DOCUMENT 2

The growth of American industry was one of the more remarkable aspects of the pre-Civil War era, and the town and factory of Lowell, Massachusetts, became known as the finest example of what American ingenuity could accomplish. One of those impressed by what he found at Lowell was the frontiersman and folk hero David Crockett, who left the following account.

What impressed Crockett most about the factory at Lowell? How did what he witnessed differ from the economy of the section from which he came? What did Crockett see as the general benefit of an operation such as the one at Lowell? With which political party did his views seem most closely associated?

What gave rise to the "prejudices against these manufactories" Crockett mentions as being held by the West and the South? What was taking place at the time this was written (1834) that would ease the prejudices in the former and heighten them in the latter?

> Next morning I rose early, and started for Lowell in a fine carriage, with three gentlemen who had agreed to accompany me. I had heard so much of this place that I longed to see it not because I had heard of the "miles of gals;" no, I left that for the gallantry of the president, who is admitted, on that score, to be abler than myself: but I wanted to see the power of the machinery, wielded by the keenest calculations of human skill; I wanted to see how it was that these northerners could buy our cotton, and carry it home, manufacture it, bring it back, and sell it for half nothing; and, in the mean time, be well to live, and make money besides....
>
> There are about fourteen thousand inhabitants [in Lowell]. It contains nine meeting houses; appropriates seven thousand five hundred dollars for free schools; provides instruction for twelve hundred scholars, daily; and about three thousand annually partake of its benefits. It communicates with Boston by the Middlesex canal (the first ever made in the United States); and in a short time the railroad to Boston will be completed, affording every facility the intercourse to the seaboard.
>
> This place has grown by, and must depend on its manufactures. Its location renders it important, not only to the owners, but to the nation. Its consumption not only employs the thousands of its own population, but many thousands far away from them. It is calculated not only to give individual happiness and prosperity, but to add to our national wealth and independence; and instead of depending on foreign countries, to have our own material worked up in our own country....
>
> I never witnessed such a combination of industry, and perhaps never will again. I saw the whole process, from the time they put in the raw material, until it came out completely finished. In fact, it almost came up to the old story of a fellow walking into a patent machine with a bundle of wool under his arm, and coming out at the other end with a new coat on.
>
> Nothing can be more agreeable than the attention that is paid by every one connected with these establishments. Nothing appears to be kept secret—every process is shown and with great cheerfulness. I regret that more of our southern and western men do not go there, as it would help much to do away with their prejudices against these manufactories.

David Crockett, *Life of David Crockett, The Original Humorist and Irrepressible Backwoodsman* (Philadelphia: Potter, 1865), pp. 213–317.

MAP EXERCISE

Fill in or identify the following on the blank maps provided. Use the maps on page 273 of the text as your source.

1. State boundaries.
2. Principal rivers.
3. Railroad routes in 1850.
4. Principal cities on the 1850 routes.
5. Railroad routes in 1860.
6. Principal cities on the 1860 routes.
7. Main East-West lines.

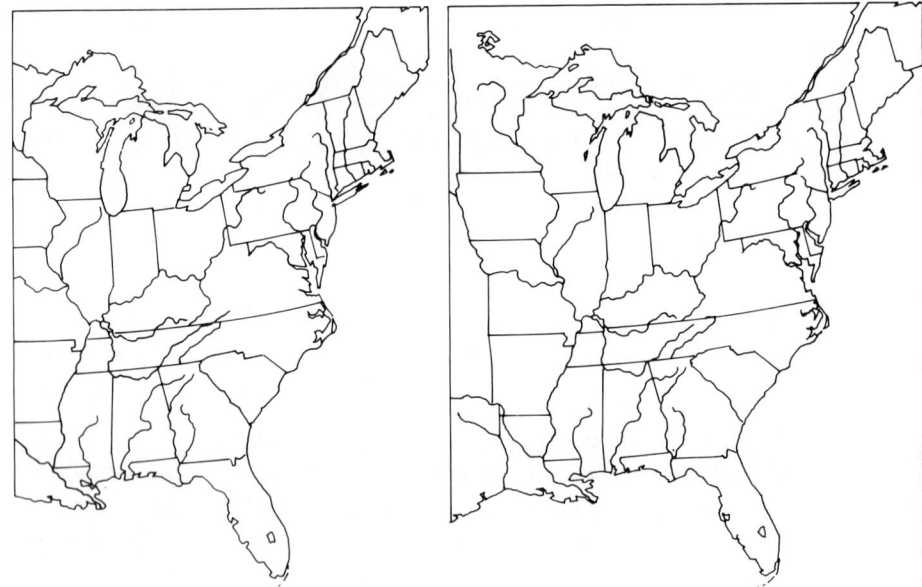

Interpretative Questions

Based on what you have filled in, answer the following. For some of the questions you will need to consult the narrative in your text for information or explanation.

1. Compare and contrast the 1850 and 1860 maps. Where did most of the railroad construction take place? How did this construction change earlier transportation patterns?

2. Where railroads went industry followed (and vice versa). What does the growth of railroads between 1850 and 1860 suggest about the industrial development of the nation?
3. Compare the principal cities in 1850 to those in 1860. Where were most of the rising urban centers located? What does this indicate about the economy and way of life in the North and the South?
4. Identify the railroad lines that linked North to South in 1850 and those that linked North to South in 1860. What does this suggest about how this transportation network united or divided the nation?

SUMMARY

In the 1830s and 1840s the United States underwent an economic revolution. This was especially evident in the North, where the economy was characterized by industrial expansion, by the growth of transportation systems (especially railroads), and by an increasingly diverse population. Cultural diversity produced uneasiness among some and a nativist movement appeared, while the gap between the rich and poor reflected an unequal distribution of wealth that disturbed some observers. But despite some labor unrest, there was little real class conflict, for where economic mobility might be lacking, geographic mobility often eased pressures. It was also in this era that the nature and the function of the family was changed by the forces of industrialization. Now many working-class women toiled in the mills, while their middle-class counterparts were assigned to the "female sphere" where their role in life was set out for them. In addition to the rapid expansion of business and industry in the region, the North also underwent agricultural changes that improved production and tied the Northeast economically to the Northwest.

CHAPTER SELF-TEST

After you have read the chapter in the text and done the exercises in the Study Guide, the following self-test can be taken to see if you understand the material you have covered. Answers appear at the end of the Study Guide.

Multiple Choice

Circle the letter of the response which best answers the question or completes the statement.

112 ~ Chapter Ten

1. At the time it was completed, the Erie Canal was:
   a. already obsolete.
   b. beginning to fill with silt from the Great Lakes.
   c. the greatest construction project Americans had ever undertaken.
   d. cited as an example of how not to construct a canal.

2. One of the immediate results of the new transportation routes constructed during the "canal age" was:
   a. an increased white settlement in the Northwest.
   b. an increased white settlement in the Southwest.
   c. the renewed cooperation between states and the national government on internal improvement projects.
   d. the conviction that the national government should be responsible for all internal improvements.

3. During the 1820s and 1830s, railroads:
   a. played only a secondary role in the nation's transportation system.
   b. replaced canals as the most important means of transportation.
   c. generated little interest among American businessmen.
   d. consisted of a few long lines, which were not connected to water routes.

4. In the period covered by this chapter, retail distribution of goods became:
   a. more dispersed and less efficient.
   b. increasingly systematic and efficient.
   c. more dependent on barter and trade.
   d. hostile to corporate ownership.

5. The most profound economic development in mid-nineteenth-century America was the:
   a. development of a national banking system.
   b. creation of corporations.
   c. decline of the small-town merchant and general store.
   d. rise of the factory.

6. The beginnings of an industrial labor supply can be traced to:
   a. overcrowding in American cities.
   b. a dramatic increase in food production.
   c. the use of slaves in manufacturing industries.
   d. an increase in European immigration.

7. The Lowell or Waltham system of recruiting labor was to:
   a. enlist young women from farm families.
   b. recruit whole families from rural areas.

c. recruit newly arrived immigrants.
d. enlist young men from farm families.

8. The paternalistic factory system of Lowell and Waltham did not last long because:
   a. workers resented being watched over so carefully.
   b. in the highly competitive textile market, manufacturers were eager to cut labor costs.
   c. unions undermined the owners' authority.
   d. men found jobs in the factories, and they disliked the paternalistic system.

9. Most of the industrial growth experienced in the United States between 1840 and 1860 took place in the:
   a. South and Southwest.
   b. Old Northwest.
   c. New England and the mid-Atlantic states.
   d. Ohio Valley.

10. Which of the following was *not* a technological advance that sped the growth of industry during this period?
    a. better machine tools.
    b. interchangeable parts.
    c. improved water power generators.
    d. new steam engines.

11. The railroad network that developed during this period linked the:
    a. Northeast to the Northwest.
    b. Northeast to the Gulf Coast.
    c. east coast to the west coast.
    d. New York to New Orleans.

12. Crucial to the operation of railroads was:
    a. a system of federal railroad regulations.
    b. the invention of the telegraph.
    c. slave labor to build the lines.
    d. a canal and river system that supported the lines.

13. Which of the following helped enlarge the urban population in this era?
    a. immigrants from Europe.
    b. Northeastern farmers.
    c. the growth of the population as a whole.
    d. all of the above.
    e. a and c.

14. The nativist movement wanted to:
    a. return all land to native Americans.
    b. enact more restrictive naturalization laws.
    c. increase aid to education so voters would be literate.
    d. make immigrants feel this was their home.

15. Which of the following did *not* inhibit the growth of effective labor resistance?
    a. ethnic divisions between natives and immigrants.
    b. the availability of cheap labor.
    c. slavery.
    d. the strength of the industrial capitalists.

16. Why did the unequal distribution of wealth not create more resentment?
    a. The actual living standard of the workers was improving.
    b. There was no social mobility, but people were content to stay where they were in the social system.
    c. Geographic mobility was limited, so there were few other opportunities.
    d. The political system offered few ways to express resentment.

17. In the middle-class family during this era, the role of women changed from:
    a. helpmate to workmate.
    b. "Republican Mother" to "Democratic Female."
    c. passive domestic to radical feminist.
    d. income producer to income consumer.

18. The growth of the agricultural economy of the Northwest effected the sectional alignment of the United States because:
    a. Northwestern goods were sold to residents of the Northeast.
    b. Northeastern industry sold its products to the Northwest.
    c. Northwestern grain was sold to the South, which allowed it to grow more cotton.
    d. the Northwest was able to feed itself so it did not align with any other section.
    e. a and b.
    f. a and d.

True/False

Read each statement carefully. Mark true statements "T" and false statements "F."

1. During the first half of the nineteenth century the United States grew more rapidly in population than Britain or Europe.
2. During the first half of the nineteenth century the African-American population increased as fast or faster than the white population.
3. The city which gained the most from the new transportation routes built in this era was New York.
4. Railroads had so many advantages over canals that, where free competition existed, they almost always prevailed.
5. Credit mechanisms in the early nineteenth century were well designed and efficient.
6. When compared to working conditions in European industries, the Lowell mills were a paradise for working women.
7. Artisans, displaced by the factory system, formed the first American labor unions.
8. The most conspicuous change in American life in the 1840s and 1850s was the rapid industrialization of the Northeast.
9. During this period international trade became increasingly important for the national economy.
10. The South was an important part of the national railroad network.
11. The majority of immigrants during this period came from Ireland and Russia.
12. Although conditions got worse in American factories, few workers tried to do anything about it.
13. Industrialization made no change in the nature and function of the American family.
14. Except for teaching and nursing, work by women outside the household gradually came to be seen as a lower-class preserve.
15. The typical white citizen of the Northwest was the owner of a reasonably prosperous family farm.

Review Questions

These questions are to be answered with essays. This will allow you to explore relationships among individuals, events, and attitudes of the period under review.

1. Examine the development of the system of roads and canals between 1815 and 1840. What geographical factors contributed to this? What sections did this transportation system link together, and what effect did did the linkages have on the economies of the sections thus connected? How might this transportation network

have influenced political alliances? In short, what effect did the system of canals and roads have on the nation as a whole?
2. According to the text, "the most conspicuous change in American life in the 1840s and 1850s was the rapid industrialization of the Northeast." What changes occurred in this region during the period under consideration, and how did these changes tend to draw the Northeast and the Northwest more closely together economically, socially, and politically?
3. What impact did the economic changes in the North have on society there? Explain how industrialization effected labor, family life, and the role of women in the North.

CHAPTER ELEVEN
Cotton, Slavery, and the Old South

OBJECTIVES

A thorough study of Chapter 11 should enable you to understand:

1. The nature of the cotton economy in the antebellum South and how it influenced the region's commerce and industrial development.
2. The economic differences between the South and the North.
3. The structure of Southern white society, and the role the various elements played in it.
4. The ways in which slavery could be both an economic and a social system.
5. What slavery was from the perspective of the slaveholder, the nonslaveholder, and the slave.
6. How and why some slaves resisted slavery, and how and why some seemed not to.
7. The "culture of slavery."

PERTINENT QUESTIONS

The Cotton Economy (pp. 294–301)

1. What was "the most important economic development in the South of the mid-nineteenth century"? What caused this, and what was its economic impact?
2. What role did the businessman of the South play in the region's economic development? What element was most important in this group? Why?
3. What elements were necessary for extensive industrial development? Did the South possess these? If not, why not?
4. What does the author mean by the statement that the antebellum South had a "colonial" economy?

Southern White Society (pp. 301–306)

5. What groups made up the planter aristocracy? Why did their influence far exceed their numbers?
6. What was the "cavalier" image, and how were Southern planters able to create it?
7. How was the role played by affluent Southern white women like that of their Northern counterparts? How was it different?
8. What accounted for the difference identified in question 7? Why did so few Southern white women rebel against their role?
9. If "the typical white Southerner was not a great planter," what was he? Describe and explain the way of life of the Southern "plain folk"—men and women.
10. Why did so few nonslaveholding whites oppose the slaveholding oligarchy? Where did these opponents live?

The "Peculiar Institution" (pp. 306–316)

11. What were slave codes? What function did they serve? How were they applied, and what resulted from their violation?
12. How was slave life shaped by the slave's relationship with his or her owner?
13. To a slave, what was life under slavery? Answer this question using your text and James L. Bradley's description of his bondage in "American Voices" (page 310).
14. Were there "classes" among the slaves? What evidence is there to support this?
15. How did slavery in cities differ from slavery on the plantation? What effect did urban slavery have on the "peculiar institution" and on the relationship between white and black?
16. What was life like for free blacks? How was freedom gained, and what were their opportunities once free?
17. How did slaves respond to slavery? What evidence exists to show that slaves did not accept their condition without protest and that, in some cases, they were strongly defiant?
18. What were the most widely recognized slave revolts? What effects did they have?

The Culture of Slavery (pp. 316–320)

19. What role did religion play in the life of slaves? How did slaves influence religion in America?
20. What role did the family play in the life of slaves?

21. Explain the legal restrictions that were placed on slave families and on the religious life of slaves.
22. How has the debate over the nature of plantation slavery evolved from the abolitionists' interpretation before the Civil War up to the present? How have the various interpretations in this debate reflected the times in which they appeared?

IDENTIFICATION

Identify each of the following, and explain why it is important within the context of the chapter.

1. "upper South"
2. Tredegar Iron Works
3. *De Bow's Review*
4. George Fitzhugh
5. "planters"
6. "hill people"
7. "crackers"
8. "cavalier myth"
9. gang system
10. task system
10. "head driver"
12. Elizabeth Keckley
13. "Sambo" image
14. Gabriel Prosser
15. Nat Turner
16. "slave patrols"

DOCUMENT 1

In the South, the plantation dominated the economy, much as industry did in the Northeast. Following is a description of and some observations on the plantation system and slave labor taken from the travel account of Frederick Law Olmsted. What similarities do you find between the regimentation of the factory workers at Lowell and the status of the slaves? What differences exist? How did the objectives of the plantation owner differ from the objectives of those who owned the mills at Lowell? Might the plantation owner have argued that he offered his charges many of the same things as the factory? What analogy was the South fond of drawing between the factory and the plantation? What does this excerpt tell you about that analogy?

> It is difficult to handle simply as property, a creature possessing human passions and human feelings, however debased and torpid the condition of that creature may be; while, on the other hand, the absolute necessity of dealing with property as a thing, greatly embarrassed a man in any attempt to treat it as a person. And it is the natural result of this complicated state of things, that the system of slave-management is irregular, ambiguous, and contradictory; that it is never either consistently humane or consistently economical.
>
> As a general rule, the larger the body of negroes on a plantation or estate, the more completely they are treated as mere property, and in accordance with a policy calculated to insure the largest pecuniary returns. Hence, in part, the greater proportionate profit of such plantations, and the tendency which everywhere prevails in the planting districts to the absorption of small, and the augmentation of large estates. It may be true, that among the wealthier slave-owners there is oftener a humane disposition, a better judgement, and a greater ability to deal with their dependents indulgently and bountifully, but the effects of this disposition are chiefly felt, even on those plantations where the proprietor resides permanently, among the slaves employed about the house and stables, and perhaps a few old favourites in the quarters. It is more than balanced by the difficulty of acquiring a personal interest in the units of a large body of slaves, and an acquaintance with the individual characteristics of each. The treatment of the mass must be reduced to a system, the ruling idea of which will be, to enable one man to force into the same channel of labour the muscles of a large number of men in various and often conflicting wills.

Frederick Law Olmsted, *The Cotton Kingdom* (London: Sampson Low, Son, 1862), p. 192.

DOCUMENT 2

As the section "Debating the Past" indicates, slavery has been debated for some time. Following is an excerpt from Joseph B. Cobb's *Mississippi Scenes,* published in 1851, that sheds some light on the question of the slave's response to slavery. Read it, and consider how it relates to the information and points of view presented in the text. From it determine, at least in this case, how slavery apparently changed blacks, and what elements of the system brought these changes about. In studying this question, reexamine Document 1. Would you call slavery a brutal system or, as many southerners (including Joseph B. Cobb) contended, a "positive good"?

> The late Hon. William H. Crawford, so affectionately and proudly remembered by all Georgians, owned four native Africans, brought to this country among the last importations of those unfortunate wretches who could be sold within the time prescribed by the Federal Constitution....In the same neighborhood, there happened to be residing another native African, rather more Americanized than the first, and these five old fellows...were treated with marked respect by all the other negroes for

miles and miles around.... Their illustrious owner himself always treated them with rather more kindness of manner and respect than his other slaves, and would never allow them to be subjected to the lash except in case of downright resistance to the authority of his overseer.... Their habits and dispositions were as unlike those of our native negroes as it is possible to conceive, when it is considered that they are of the same race. They had none of the merry-heartedness and vivacity...of our Southern negroes, and though not decidedly morose, or fractious, they were yet exclusive, and somewhat unapproachable. They require far less whipping to coerce attention to their tasks....On the other hand, our Southern negroes rarely ever resist..., but they are generally indolent and careless if they are allowed to think that whipping will not be resorted to. I never knew a native African to run away from his master's plantation. They stand their ground doggedly, like the Roman or British soldier, regardless of consequences; and to carry out the simile, they often fight with the same determined courage, unhappily for them!

Joseph B. Cobb, *Mississippi Scenes* (Philadelphia: Hart, 1851), pp. 173–174.

MAP EXERCISE

Fill in or identify the following on the blank maps provided. Use the maps on page 296 of the text as your source.

1. The slave states in 1820 and 1860
2. The distribution of slavery and cotton production in 1820 and 1860

Interpretative Questions

Based on what you have filled in, answer the following. For some of the questions you will need to consult the narrative in your text for information or explanation.

1. How did slavery relate to the growing of cotton? In what ways did slave labor serve the cotton economy, and how does this explain the relationship between the two.
2. In what non-cotton-growing areas did slavery exist? What economic role did slavery play in these areas?
3. Note the places where slavery did not exist. What was the economy of these areas? In what way did society in these areas differ from those areas where there was slavery?

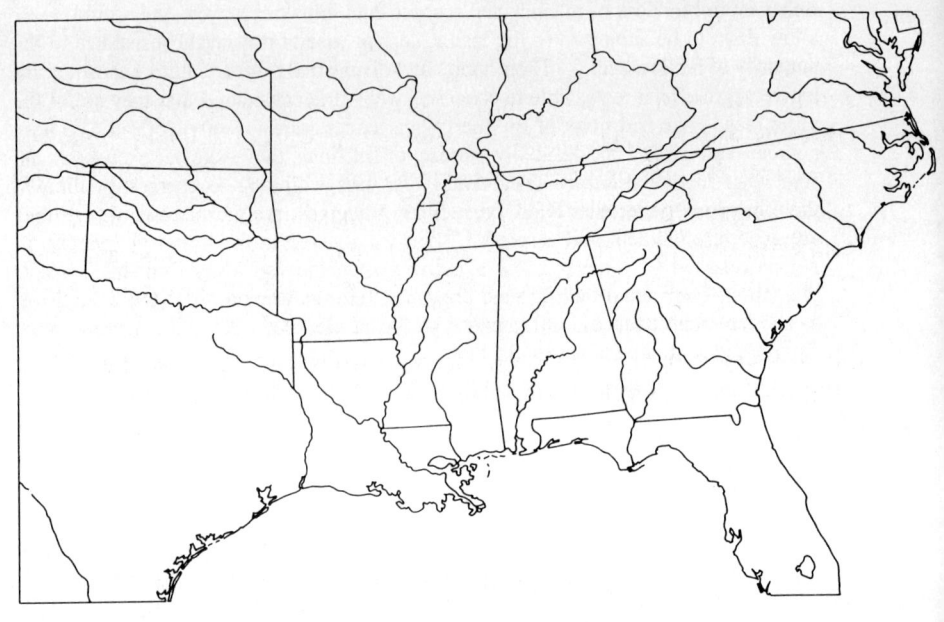

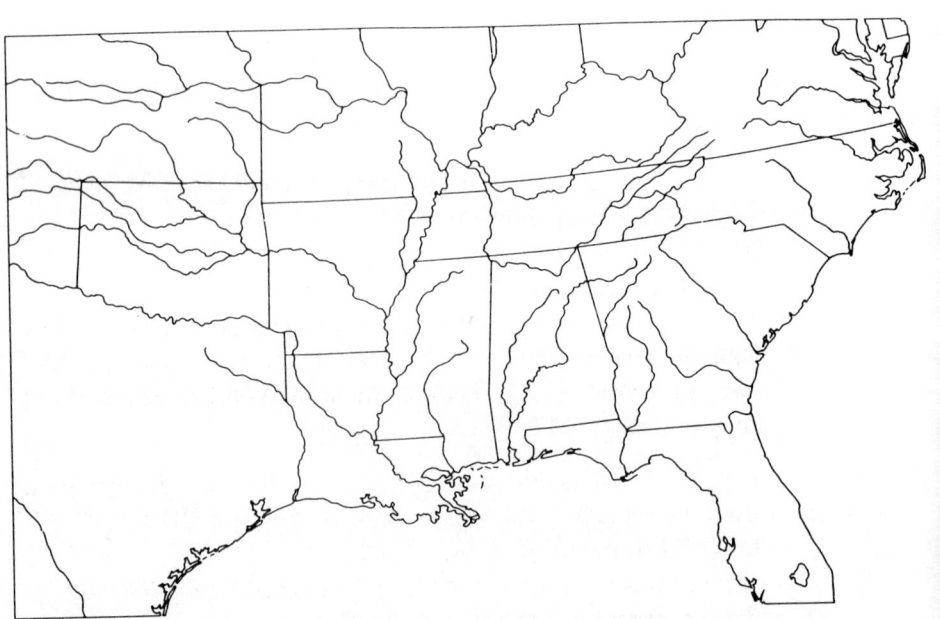

SUMMARY

During the 1830s and 1840s economic power shifted from the "upper South" to the "lower South," and with this shift came a shift in political power as well. During this period antebellum Southern society began to take on the features of what is popularly known as the "Old South." In the cotton kingdom planters and "plain folks," masters and slaves, plantation mistresses and farmers' wives coexisted, and together created a unique social order. Central to this was the region's "peculiar institution." More than just an economic system, slavery was a critical, creative force in the whole social order. Slaves contributed to white culture while creating a culture all their own. In the process they added to the complexity of a region that stood apart from the rest of the nation and seemed to pride itself in the differences.

CHAPTER SELF-TEST

After you have read the chapter in the text and done the exercises in the Study Guide, the following self-test can be taken to see if you understand the material you have covered. Answers appear at the end of the Study Guide.

Multiple Choice

Circle the letter of the response which best answers the question or completes the statement.

1. The Southern failure to create a flourishing commercial or industrial economy was in part the result of:
    a. a lack of business talent in the south.
    b. an unwillingness on the part of southerners to take risks.
    c. a set of values distinctive to the South that discouraged the growth of cities and industry.
    d. a slave labor force that could not work successfully in industry.

2. A minority of Southern whites owned slaves:
    a. and nonslaveholders dominated the political system in the region.
    b. but the slaveholding planters exercised power and influence far in excess of their numbers.
    c. so slavery was not very important in the lives of most whites.
    d. and most whites were happy with it that way.

3. In its efforts to develop industrially the South was hampered by:
   a. a rudimentary financial system.
   b. an inadequate transportation system.
   c. a "colonial dependency" on outside goods.
   d. all of the above

4. According to the "cavalier" myth, southern planters:
   a. were racially superior to common farmers.
   b. were chosen by God to dominate the South.
   c. were more concerned with a refined and gracious way of life than with industrial development.
   d. kept slaves even though it was unprofitable.

5. Most southern white "ladies" were:
   a. less subordinate to men than in the North.
   b. relatively isolated from people outside their own families.
   c. better educated than their Northern counterparts.
   d. more likely to engage in public activities or income-producing employment than their Northern counterparts.

6. The typical white southerner was:
   a. a planter with many slaves and a lot of land.
   b. a small-town merchant or professional man.
   c. extremely poor.
   d. a modest yeoman farmer.

7. Which of the following was *not* a condition of slave life in the South:
   a. an adequate if rough diet.
   b. hard work, even for women and children.
   c. the freedom to use the time after work as they wished to.
   d. isolation and control.

8. Slave women were:
   a. generally better treated than the men.
   b. not required to do household chores if they did field work.
   c. frequently required to do field work as well as take care of families.
   d. assigned mostly to household duties.

9. Free blacks were:
   a. seldom found in towns or cities.
   b. mostly found in Virginia and Maryland.
   c. financially as well off as most poor whites.
   d. better off in the South than in the North.

10. The most important method of slave resistance was:
    a. everyday behavior by which blacks defied their masters.
    b. open rebellion.
    c. running away.
    d. arson.

11. Slave religion:
    a. differed little from the Christianity practiced by masters.
    b. rejected all African religious forms.
    c. offered a means for natural leaders to emerge.
    d. accepted the master's interpretation of the Bible.

12. Slave religious services:
    a. were restrained and unemotional.
    b. stressed a hope for freedom in this world, not the next.
    c. often spoke of resistance and rebellion.
    d. focused on salvation and not on worldly things.

13. Family life under slavery was:
    a. limited by legal restrictions.
    b. encouraged to keep the slaves happy.
    c. encouraged as a means of producing more slaves for the master.
    d. of little or no concern to masters.

14. Among slaves, family ties were:
    a. weak because marriages were not legal.
    b. easily maintained because masters tried to keep families together.
    c. very different from what we call the "nuclear family" today.
    d. generally no less strong than those of whites.

15. Religion influenced the resistance efforts of:
    a. Gabriel Prosser
    b. Denmark Vesey
    c. Nat Turner
    d. all of the above

True/False

Read each statement carefully. Mark true statements "T" and false statements "F."

1. The South, like the North, changed from an agricultural to an industrial economy during this period.
2. The new product that made cotton "king" in the South was short-staple cotton.

3. According to *De Bow's Review,* the South had a "colonial" relationship with the North.
4. Planters in the South were just as much competitive capitalists as the industrialists in the North.
5. Most whites who did not own slaves lived far from the planters and their plantations.
6. Most southern planters did not think of themselves as aristocrats.
7. There is little evidence that southern planters had sexual relations with their slaves.
8. Most whites who did not own slaves opposed slavery and resented the planter class.
9. Nonslaveholders had little contact with slaveholders.
10. Because of slavery, the South was very undemocratic.
11. About the same percentage of slaves could read and write as poor whites.
12. There is no evidence that any sort of paternal relationship ever existed between master and slave.
13. Masters encouraged slaves to accept Christianity because they believed it would make them accept their lot in life.
14. Slaves were generally more healthy than whites in the South.
15. The dominant response of African Americans to slavery was a combination of adaptation and resistance.
16. One of the most frequent causes of flight from the plantation was a slave's desire to find family members.

Review Questions

These questions are to be answered with essays. This will allow you to explore relationships among individuals, events, and attitudes of the period under review.

1. What was "the Southern way of life" for the white Southerner? Be sure to look at more than the life of the planter.
2. If nothing else, slavery set the South apart, made it unique. But how did the institution function, and what was its impact on the slave? Analyze the plantation system, its social and its economic functions. How did it control its labor? And what was the response of these workers?
3. Compare and contrast the way of life of Southern white women and black women during the 1840s and 1850s. How did the institution of slavery affect them both?

4. What was slavery like for the slave? Examine the daily life of a slave—work, family life, diet, restrictions, and resistance.
5. What was the "culture of slavery"? How did slaves try to make their world a better place for themselves and their families?

CHAPTER TWELVE
An Age of Reforms

OBJECTIVES

A thorough study of Chapter 12 should enable you to understand:

1. The two basic impulses that were reflected in the reform movements, and examples of groups illustrating each impulse.
2. The transcendentalists and their place in American society.
3. The sources of American religious reform movements, why they originated where they did, their ultimate objectives, and what their leadership had in common.
4. The sources from which the philosophy of reform arose.
5. American educational reform in the antebellum period, and the contribution of education to the growth of nationalism.
6. The role of women in American society, and the attempts to alter their relationships with men.
7. The origins of the antislavery movement, and the sources of its leadership.
8. The role of abolitionism in the antislavery movement, and the strengths and weaknesses of that part of the movement.

PERTINENT QUESTIONS

The Romantic Impulse (pp. 322–328)

1. How was the work of James Fenimore Cooper the culmination of an effort to produce a truly American literature? What did his work suggest about the nation and its people?
2. Why was Whitman called the "poet of American democracy"?
3. Who were the transcendentalists? What was their philosophy, and how did they express it in literature?
4. How did the transcendentalists attempt to apply their beliefs to the problems of everyday life at Brook Farm? What was the result?

5. How did the utopian communities attempt to redefine the sex roles? Which communities were most active in this effort, and what did they accomplish?
6. Who were the Mormons? What were their origins, what did they believe, and why did they end up in Utah?

Remaking Society (pp. 328–334)

7. The "philosophy of reform" that shaped this era rose from what two distinct sources?
8. What gave rise to the crusade against drunkenness? What successes and failures resulted from the movement's efforts?
9. How did efforts to produce a system of universal public education reflect the spirit of the age?
10. What were the problems facing public education, and what types of institutions were created to deal with them?
11. How did the rise of feminism reflect not only the participation of women in social crusades, but also a basic change in the nature of the family?
12. How did feminists benefit from their association with other reform movements, most notably abolitionists, and at the same time suffer as a result?

The Crusade Against Slavery (pp. 335–341)

13. What was the antislavery philosophy of William Lloyd Garrison? How did he transform abolitionism into "a new and dramatically different phenomenon"?
14. What role did black abolitionists play in the movement? How did their philosophy compare with that of Garrison?
15. Why did many Northern whites oppose the abolitionist movement? How did they show this opposition?
16. What efforts did abolitionists make to find political solutions to the question of slavery? How successful were they initially?
17. How did abolitionists attempt to arouse widespread public anger over slavery through the use of propaganda? What was the most significant work to emerge from this effort? Why did it have such an impact?

IDENTIFICATION

Identify each of the following, and explain why it is important within the context of the chapter.

1. *Moby Dick*
2. "Resistance to Civil Government"
3. Nathaniel Hawthorne
4. *The Blithedale Romance*
5. "Owenites"
6. Shakers
7. *Book of Mormon*
8. Charles Grandison Finney
9. Horace Mann
10. asylums
11. Seneca Falls convention
12. Sarah and Angela Grimke
13. Catherine Beecher and Harriet Beecher Stowe
14. Elizabeth Cady Stanton
15. American Colonization Society
16. Monrovia
17. American Antislavery Society
18. Frederick Douglass
19. Elijah Lovejoy
20. *Prigg v. Pennsylvania*
21. personal liberty laws

DOCUMENT

At the women's rights convention held at Seneca Falls, New York in 1848, the delegates declared that "all men and women are created equal" and listed the "injuries and usurpations on the part of man toward woman." Then the convention adopted a series of resolutions for constructive action, among which were the following. What do these tell you about the goals of the early women's rights movement? What do they also tell you about the prejudices that women would have to overcome to gain the equality they sought?

> *Resolved,* That the same amount of virtue, delicacy, and refinement of behavior that is required of woman in the social state, should also be required of man, and the same transgressions should be visited with equal severity on both man and woman.
>
> *Resolved,* That the objection of indelicacy and impropriety, which is so often brought against women when she addresses a public audience, comes with a very ill grace from those who encourage, by their attendance, her appearance on the stage, in the concert, or in feats of the circus.
>
> *Resolved,* That it is the duty of the women of this country to secure to themselves their sacred right to the elective franchise.

Resolved, That the equality of human rights results necessarily from the fact of the identity of the race in capabilities and responsibilities.

Resolved, That the speedy success of our cause depends upon the zealous and untiring efforts of both men and women, for the overthrow of the monopoly of the pulpit, and for the securing to women an equal participation in the various trades, professions, and commerce.

SUMMARY

By the 1820s, America was caught up in the spirit of a new age, and Americans, who had never been shy in proclaiming their nation's promise and potential, concluded that the time for action had come. Excited by the nation's technological advances and territorial expansions, many set as their goal the creation of a society worthy to be part of it all. What resulted was an outpouring of reform movements the like of which had not been seen before and have not been seen since. Unrestrained by entrenched conservative institutions and attitudes, these reformers attacked society's ills wherever they found them, producing in the process a list of evils so long that many were convinced that a complete reorganization of society was necessary. Most, however, were content to concentrate on their own particular cause, and thus, at least at first, the movements were many and varied. But in time, most reformers seemed to focus on one evil that stood out above the rest. The "peculiar institution," slavery, denied all they stood for—equality, opportunity, and, above all, freedom. Slavery became the supreme cause.

CHAPTER SELF-TEST

After you have read the chapter in the text and done the exercises in the Study Guide, the following self-test can be taken to see if you understand the material you have covered. Answers appear at the end of the Study Guide.

Multiple Choice

Circle the letter of the response which best answers the question or completes the statement.

1. The reform movements of the first half of the nineteenth century reflected which of the following impulses:
   a. an optimistic faith in human nature.
   b. a rational view of man and his ability.

c. a desire for control and order.
d. a and c.

2. The first great American novelist was:
   a. Walt Whitman.
   b. James Fenimore Cooper.
   c. Herman Melville.
   d. Ralph Waldo Emerson.

3. Transcendentalists believed that:
   a. "understanding" was more important than "reason."
   b. man should repress instinct and strive for externally imposed learning.
   c. each individual should strive to "transcend" the limits of intellect and allow emotions to create an "original relation to the universe."
   d. individuals should avoid anything that would bring one too close to the natural world.

4. The Oneida Community:
   a. advocated "free love" to redefine gender roles.
   b. called for celibacy and attracted members for conversion.
   c. believed it liberated women from the demands of male "lust" and from traditional bonds of family.
   d. was widely accepted and had almost no critics.

5. Like other experiments in social organization of this era, Mormonism reflected:
   a. a strong antislavery bias.
   b. a celebration of individual liberty.
   c. a desire to improve the status of women.
   d. a belief in human perfectibility.

6. Evangelical Protestantism added major strength to which of the following reforms:
   a. temperance.
   b. education and rehabilitation.
   c. women's rights.
   d. peace.

7. The emphasis on educational reform was consistent with the spirit of the age because it:
   a. focused on the unleashing of individual talents.
   b. stressed educational equality.
   c. focused on external learning.
   d. stressed the importance of community.

8. As women in various reform movements confronted the problems they faced in a male-dominated society, they responded by:
   a. withdrawing from the movements.
   b. accepting the notion that men and women were assigned separate "spheres" in society.
   c. focusing their attention on religious matters.
   d. setting in motion the first important feminist movement.

9. Which of the following groups was most involved in the feminist movement?
   a. Baptist.
   b. Quakers.
   c. Mormons.
   d. Shakers.

10. After 1830, which of the following reform movements began to overshadow the others:
    a. antislavery.
    b. women's rights.
    c. temperance.
    d. education.

11. The most noted black abolitionist of the day was:
    a. Ralph Waldo Emerson.
    b. William Lloyd Garrison.
    c. Frederick Douglass.
    d. Joseph Smith.

12. Opponents of abolitionism in the North believed:
    a. abolitionists were dangerous radicals.
    b. the movement would lead to a war between North and South.
    c. the movement would lead to a great influx of free blacks into the North.
    d. all the above.

13. "Immediate abolition gradually accomplished" was the slogan of:
    a. moderate antislavery forces.
    b. Garrison and his followers.
    c. antislavery Southern planters.
    d. black abolitionists.

14. Personal Liberty laws:
    a. allowed masters to claim slaves who ran away to the North.
    b. freed slaves who escaped to states in the Old Northwest.

c. forbade state officials to assist in the capture and return of runaways.
   d. outlawed the interstate slave trade.
15. The movement that advocated keeping slavery out of the territories was known as the:
   a. "personal liberty" movement.
   b. "free soil" movement.
   c. John Brown Brigade.
   d. Garrison solution.

True/False

Read each statement carefully. Mark true statements "T" and false statements "F"

1. American intellectuals were pleased with the high regard in which their culture was held by Europeans.
2. Thoreau believed that a government which required an individual to violate his or her own morality had no legitimate authority.
3. Because transcendentalism was at heart an individualistic philosophy, its followers did not take part in communal living experiments.
4. The philosophy of reform in America drew heavily from Protestant revivalism.
5. At the beginning of the Civil War, the United States had one of the highest literacy rates in the world.
6. The idea of asylums for social deviants was not simply an effort to curb the abuses of the old system, but also an attempt to reform and rehabilitate the inmates.
7. Early feminists made their point by drawing a parallel between the plight of women and the plight of slaves.
8. The American Colonization Society failed because it challenged both property rights and Southern sensibilities.
9. The man who transformed the antislavery movement was Ralph Waldo Emerson.
10. Although there was opposition to abolitionism in the North, it was generally peaceful.
11. Radical abolitionists attacked slavery and the Constitution that seemed to sanction it.
12. Abolitionists were also pacifists, and therefore did not advocate violence to free the slaves.
13. Antislavery and abolition were different words for the same thing.

14. Although it sold well, the novel *Uncle Tom's Cabin* had little impact on American antislavery attitudes.
15. Only a relatively small number of people before the Civil War ever accepted the abolitionist position that slavery must be entirely eliminated in a single stroke.

Review Questions

These questions are to be answered with essays. This will allow you to explore relationships among individuals, events, and attitudes of the period under review.

1. During this period, how did American intellectuals create a national culture committed to the liberation of the human spirit? How do their efforts relate the efforts of social reformers?
2. What role did religion and religious leaders play in the reform movement described in this chapter?
3. Who were the major critics of slavery? On what grounds did they attack the institution, and what means to end it did they propose?
4. How did the reform movement affect the status of women? What role did women play in these efforts to change society, and what were they able to accomplish?

Chapter Thirteen
The Impending Crisis

OBJECTIVES

A thorough study of Chapter 13 should enable you to understand:

1. Manifest Destiny, and America's westward migration into Texas, California, and Oregon.
2. The origin of the Republic of Texas, and the controversy concerning its annexation by the United States.
3. The reasons why the United States declared war on Mexico, and how the Mexican War was fought to a successful conclusion.
4. The impact of the Wilmot Proviso on the sectional controversy.
5. The methods used to enact the Compromise of 1850, and its reception by the American people.
6. The role of the major political parties in the widening sectional split.
7. The enactment of the Kansas-Nebraska Act, and the effect of this act on the attitudes of the people in all sections.
8. The impact of the *Dred Scott* decision on sectional attitudes and on the prestige of the Supreme Court.
9. The reasons for Abraham Lincoln's victory in 1860, and the effect of his election on this sectional crisis.

PERTINENT QUESTIONS

Looking Westward (pp. 342–350)

1. What was Manifest Destiny? What forces created this concept?
2. What was the "empire of liberty"? How was it to be achieved, and what doubts were raised about its desirability?
3. How did Texas become available for annexation? What prevented its immediate annexation?
4. What was the history of American interest in Oregon?

5. What were the characteristics of western migrants? What problem did they face? How were these overcome?

Expansion and War (pp. 350–357)

6. How did Polk's campaign catch the spirit of the time? What effect did Clay's position on Texas have on his campaign in the presidential election?
7. What were the goals of President Polk? How did he resolve the Oregon question?
8. What tensions emerged in the Southwest that threatened to lead the United States into war with Mexico?
9. How did American interest in California develop?
10. On what grounds did Polk ask Congress to declare war on Mexico?
11. On what grounds was Polk's call for war criticized?
12. What was Polk's plan for the conduct of the war?
13. What were the objectives of the American offensives in the war? What did they accomplish? What were the terms of the Treaty of Guadalupe Hidalgo?

The Sectional Debate (pp. 357–364)

14. What was the Wilmot Proviso? What brought about its introduction, and what arguments were advanced in its favor?
15. What were the South's arguments against the Wilmot Proviso? On what points did they differ from the arguments of the North?
16. How did the gold rush change the cultural composition of California?
17. What problems faced President Zachary Taylor when he took office? How did he propose to solve them, and what action did Congress initially take?
18. What was the Compromise of 1850? How was it passed?
19. Who were the "younger" politicians who emerged after 1850? How did they differ from the leaders they replaced?
20. How did the Compromise of 1850 differ from the Missouri Compromise?

The Crisis of the 1850s (pp. 364–379)

21. How did the political parties react to the Compromise of 1850?
22. How did the sections of the country react to the Compromise of 1850?

23. What was the "Young America" movement? What national sentiment did it reflect? Who were its spokespersons? What did it accomplish?
24. How did the issue of a transcontinental railroad help to reopen the sectional controversy? Explain.
25. How did the North react to the Kansas-Nebraska Act? the South? What effect did it have on the Whigs? the Democrats?
26. Who were the Republicans? What caused their formation? Which groups composed this party, and what was the party's platform?
27. What problems were faced in the attempt to organize a legitimate government in Kansas? Why did these problems arise? How was it that Kansas became a battleground for the sectional controversy?
28. Explain the maneuvering by pro-slavery and antislavery forces to gain control of the Kansas government. What did both sides come to believe that Kansas symbolized for the nation?
29. What type of society did Northerners wish to create? How did "free soil" and "free labor" fit into their plans? Why did they feel that the South was holding them back?
30. How did the "free soil" ideology manifest itself in the Republican party? What diverse views did it unite?
31. What were the elements of the South's pro-slavery response? Who were its major spokespersons?
32. How did Southerners attempt to silence their opponents?
33. What effect did the depression of 1857 have on political divisions in America? How did it increase the tension between the North and the South? What did both sides see as the significance of this economic decline?
34. What were the origins of the *Dred Scott* case? What issues were involved, and what decision was handed down by the Court? How did the reaction to this case add to sectional tensions?
35. How did President James Buchanan respond to the Kansas question? What were his reasons, and what was the outcome? What does this tell you about the possibility of compromise on the issue of slavery in the territories?
36. Why did the Lincoln-Douglas debates take place, and why did they draw so much attention? How did Lincoln and Douglas differ on their solution to the question of slavery in the territories?
37. What were the goals of John Brown's raid, and why did it have such an impact on the South?

38. What caused the split between Northern and Southern Democrats in 1860, and what was the result of this division?
39. What was the Republican platform in 1860? To what specific political groups were the Republicans trying to appeal, and how did this platform propose to appeal to them?

IDENTIFICATION

Identify each of the following, and explain why it is important within the context of the chapter.

1. "penny press"
2. San Jacinto
3. John Jacob Astor
4. "Fifty-four forty or fight"
5. The Nueces River
6. General Winfield Scott
7. Nicholas Trist
8. "All Mexico"
9. Free Soil party
10. "Forty-niners"
11. Millard Fillmore
12. Jefferson Davis
13. Franklin Pierce
14. "Conscience" Whigs
15. Stephen A. Douglas
16. Ostend Manifesto
17. Gadsden Purchase
18. Pottawatomie Massacre
19. Preston Brooks
20. Free-soil ideology
21. "slaver-power conspiracy"
22. *Uncle Tom's Cabin*
23. John C. Breckenridge
24. John Bell

DOCUMENT 1

Below is an excerpt from a statement made in 1837 by John C. Calhoun that outlines his views on slavery. Note his comparison of the lot of slaves with that of European (and Northern?) workers. How might William Lloyd Garrison have responded to this?

> I hold that in the present state of civilization, where two races of different origin, and distinguished by color, and other physical differences, as well as intellectual, are brought together, the relation now existing in the slaveholding States between the two is, instead of an evil, a good—a positive good. I feel myself called upon to speak freely upon the subject where the honor and interests of those I represent are involved. I hold then, that there never has yet existed a wealthy and civilized society in which one portion of the community did not, in point of fact, live on the labor of the other.... I may say with truth that in few countries so much is left to the share of the laborer, and so little exacted from him, or where there is more kind attention paid to him in sickness or infirmities of age. Compare his condition with the tenants of the poor houses in the more civilized portions of Europe—look at the sick and the old and infirm slave, on one hand, in the midst of his family and friends, under the kind superintending care of his master and mistress, and compare it with the forlorn and wretched condition of the pauper in the poor house.

DOCUMENT 2

One of the most outspoken critics of the Mexican War was the Massachusetts poet James Russell Lowell. Like so many of his fellow New Englanders, he believed that the conflict was part of an effort to advance the interests of the South, a view he set forth in The *Bigelow Papers,* a collection of observations that Lowell attributed to one Hosea Bigelow. In the following poem, Bigelow confronts a recruiting sergeant and explains, in Yankee vernacular, his opposition to the war.

What does Bigelow see as the main purpose of the war with Mexico? Whom does he blame, and why? What role does he see the North playing in the war, and what does he feel the results will be? Look at the final verse. What solution does he propose? Remember this when we get to 1860. With such sentiments being expressed in the North, why will the Northern states be willing to fight to preserve the Union?

> 'T would n't suit them Southern fellers,
>   They're a dreffle graspin' set,
> We must ollers blow the bellers
>   Wen they want their irons het;
>
> May be its all right ez preachin'
>   By *my* narves it kind o' grates,
> Wen I see the overreachin'
>   O' them nigger-drivin' States.
>
> They may talk o' Freedom's airy
>   Tell they're pupple in the face,

It's a grand gret cemetary
  Fer the barthrights of our race;
They jest want this Californy
  So's to lug new slave-states in
To abuse ye, an' to scorn ye,
  An' to plunder ye like sin.

Aint it cute to see a Yankee
  Take sech everlastin' pains
All to git the Devil's thankee,
  Helpin' on 'em weld their chains?
Wy, it's jest ez clear ez figgers,
  Clear ez one an' one make two,
Chaps thet make black slaves o' niggers
  Want to make wite slaves o' you.

Ef I'd *my* way I hed ruther
  We should go to work an' part—
They take one way, we take t'other,—
  Guess it would n't break my heart;
Men hed ough' to put asunder
  Them thet God has noways jined;
An' I should n't gretly wonder
  Ef there's thousands o' my mind.

James Russell Lowell, *The Bigelow Papers* (London: Trubner, 1859), pp. 4–9.

MAP EXERCISE

Fill in or identify the following on the blank map provided. Use the map on page 361 of the text as your source.

1. Free states and territories.
2. Slave states and territories (with slave percentages of total population).
3. Areas where the decision on slavery was left to the territories.
4. Missouri Compromise line.
5. District of Columbia.

Interpretative Questions

Based on what you have filled in, answer the following. For some of the questions you will need to consult the narrative in your text for information or explanation.

1. Study the areas that remained open to slavery. As far as the expansion of the institution is concerned, did the South gain or lose from the Compromise of 1850?

2. After studying the map, what evidence do you find to support John C. Calhoun's fear that the South would be relegated to permanent minority status?
3. How had the knowledge of land west of the Mississippi River changed since the early 1800s, and what impact did this have on settlement patterns? In the light of these changes, how would the population be expected to expand in the next few decades and what impact would this have on the balance between slave and free states in the Senate?
4. What changes did the Kansas-Nebraska Act make in the agreements reached in the Missouri Compromise and the Compromise of 1850?

SUMMARY

Between 1845 and 1860, critical events and issues seemed to come in a rush, giving Americans little time to analyze what was happening and reflect on long-range solutions. Emotion seemed to replace reason as the debate grew increasingly repetitious and loud. The question, or so it seemed, was the expansion of slavery into the territories gained during the Polk administration. But something far more fundamental was at stake—the future of the nation. Northerners had become convinced that the expansion of slavery threatened the democratic foundations of the United States and that expansion would give the South control of the government that would lead to economic stagnation, unemployment, and financial ruin—all the effect of the depression of 1837, but magnified. From this point of view, the South, and its "peculiar institution," threatened the nation's growth and progress and had to be overcome. The South, however, convinced of the legality of its position and the validity of its institutions, fought back, and with remarkable success. By combining the power in the Democratic party (which gave it extraordinary influence in Congress and with the president) with its supporters on the Supreme Court, the slave states seemed secure. But still they were fearful. Convinced that they had given up all they could in earlier compromises, they feared future gains by those they considered to be enemies; and those they feared most were the Republicans.

CHAPTER SELF-TEST

After you have read the chapter in the text and done the exercises in the Study Guide, the following self-test can be taken to see if you understand the material you have covered. Answers appear at the end of the Study Guide.

Multiple Choice

Circle the letter of the response which best answers the question or completes the statement.

1. The idea that God and history had selected America to expand its boundaries over the continent of North America was known as:
   a. Manifest Destiny.
   b. divine right.
   c. white supremacy.
   d. nativism.

2. When the new republic of Texas requested annexation by the United States:
   a. the American government quickly agreed.
   b. Americans in the North opposed acquiring a large new slave territory.
   c. Southerners, led by President Jackson, pushed for annexation.
   d. Mexico gave up all claims to Texas.

3. Which of the following was *not* part of President Polk's policy regarding New Mexico and California?
   a. Sending troops to the Nueces River in Texas.
   b. Informing Americans in California that the United States would respond sympathetically to a revolt against Mexico.
   c. Instructing the Pacific naval commander to seize California ports if Mexico declared war.
   d. Ceasing all diplomatic contact with Mexico.

4. By combining the Oregon and the Texas issue in 1844, Democrats hoped to:
   a. start a war with Mexico and Great Britain.
   b. attract John Tyler to the Democratic party.
   c. divert attention from the slavery issue.
   d. appeal to both Northern and Southern expansionists.

5. The war with Mexico was criticized:
   a. by Southerners who believed Polk deliberately maneuvered the country into the conflict on behalf of Northern interests.
   b. by Northerners who believed it was part of a slaveholders' plot to bring in more slave states.
   c. by businessmen who believed it would hurt commerce with England and Mexico.
   d. none of the above.

6. The Wilmot Proviso:
   a. went into law without the president's signature.
   b. passed the House but not the Senate.
   c. was a compromise acceptable to the South and the North but not the West.
   d. drew very little attention outside of Congress.

7. The Compromise of 1850 included all of the following except the proviso that:
   a. California would come in as a free state.
   b. in the rest of the lands acquired from Mexico, territorial governments would be formed without restrictions on slavery.
   c. the national government would not pay the Texas debt.
   d. the slave trade, but not slavery, would be abolished in the District of Columbia.

8. The new leaders emerging in Congress after the Compromise of 1850 were:
   a. less able politicians.
   b. more concerned with narrow interest of self-promotion.
   c. as skilled at compromise as the older leaders.
   d. interested in broad national issues.

9. The question of statehood for Kansas and Nebraska became a critical issue because:
   a. of the question of whether they would be slave or free states.
   b. of Southern fear that a transcontinental railroad would be built through them.
   c. of Northern concern over new wheat states and depressed grain prices.
   d. many believed that they could never support a population sufficient to justify statehood.

10. Northerners who accepted the concepts of "free soil" and "free labor" believed:
    a. slavery was dangerous not because of what it did to blacks but because of what it did to whites.
    b. slavery opened the door to economic opportunity for whites.
    c. slavery was what made the South a glorious civilization and one that should be admired.
    d. slave labor would work in Northern factories and should be allowed to expand.

11. Southerners who believed in the "positive good" theory argued:
    a. slavery was good for blacks.
    b. slavery was maintained, even though it was not profitable for whites.
    c. northern factory workers were better off than slaves, but they deserved to be better off because they were white.
    d. blacks were not biologically inferior, they just needed time to catch up culturally.

12. The Dred Scott decision:
    a. affirmed the South's argument that the Constitution guaranteed the existence of slavery.
    b. was a victory for the antislavery movement.
    c. declared Scott a free man.
    d. outlawed the interstate slave trade.

13. Abraham Lincoln:
    a. believed slavery was morally wrong but was not a abolitionist.
    b. had been a Democrat before he became Republican.
    c. believed the expansion of slavery would hurt the spread of free labor.
    d. tried to avoid the slavery issue in his debates with Douglas.
    e. a and c.
    f. a and d.

14. The single event that did the most to convince white Southerners they could not live safely in the Union was:
    a. the election of Lincoln.
    b. the Pottawatomie Massacre.
    c. John Brown's raid.
    d. the Dred Scott decision.

True/False

Read each statement carefully. Mark true statements "T" and false statements "F"

1. The "penny press" was important because it exposed a significant proportion of the population to the rhetoric of nationalistic politicians.
2. Indian attack was the greatest danger westward migrants faced.
3. Texas was not able to get any European nation to recognize it as an independent nation.
4. Though a "dark horse" candidate, James K. Polk was not an obscure politician.
5. The Oregon question was finally settled by Britain surrendering claims below the 54th parallel.
6. The United States did not take all of Mexico because its invasion of that country was not successful.
7. The Wilmot Proviso prohibited slavery in the territory taken from Mexico.
8. The South supported Taylor because he was a Southerner and a slaveholder.
9. The Compromise of 1850 passed, despite the opposition of Webster and Calhoun.
10. After 1850 the Whig party emerged as the one party without sectional divisions.

11. The Kansas-Nebraska Act repealed the antislavery provision of the Missouri Compromise.
12. Northerners saw Preston Brook's attack on Charles Sumner as an example of the barbarism of the South, while Southerners believed Sumner had insulted Brook's uncle and got what he deserved.
13. Northerners saw the "gag rule" as evidence of the "slave power conspiracy" against their liberties.
14. President Buchanan proved a firm and decisive president at the very time the nation needed one.
15. The Republican party became the party of the "free soil-free labor" ideology.
16. With Lincoln's election, the Republicans controlled both the legislative and the executive branches of the government.

Review Questions

These questions are to be answered with essays. This will allow you to explore relationships among individuals, events, and attitudes of the period under review.

1. What was the concept of Manifest Destiny and how did it influence American expansion west of the Mississippi River? What impact did this concept have on American foreign policy during this period?
2. Why did the South perceive the Wilmot Proviso as such a threat? What did the proviso indicate about the North's attitude toward slavery? Was the abolition of slavery the issue, or was it something else? Examine the proviso, its implications, and the Southern response.
3. Eventually the majority of Northerners came to believe that the existence of slavery was dangerous not because of what it did to blacks but because of what it threatened to do to whites. How did this feeling shape the Northern attack on slavery, and how did Southerners attempt to defend their institution?
4. Kansas became a symbol for both the North and the South—but a symbol of what? What did both sides find in the controversy over Kansas to support their charges against their adversaries? What did Kansas come to mean to the nation? Assess Kansas as a symbol of the positions and problems that characterized the divisions in the United States?

5. One historian has claimed that a lack of leadership contributed to the inability of the nation to overcome its divisions. This argument contends that a "blundering generation" of politicians who failed to understand the nature of the divisions offered solutions that resolved issues but did not deal with the real problems. Look at the concerns expressed by both the North and the South, and look at the proposals advanced to ease these concerns. From this assessment, do you feel that the "blundering generation" theory has merit, or were these deeper, fundamental questions that even the most capable leaders could not have resolved? In short, had the conflict between North and South become "irrepressible"?

CHAPTER FOURTEEN
The Civil War

OBJECTIVES

A thorough study of Chapter 14 should enable you to understand:

1. The reasons why all attempts to reach a compromise in the time-honored way failed in 1860 and 1861.
2. The unique problems faced by the newly inaugurated President Lincoln, and his use of executive powers to solve them up to July 4, 1961.
3. The ways in which the Confederate States of America compared with the United States in manpower, natural resources, finances, industrial potential, and public support.
4. The significant legislation enacted by Congress once Southern members were no longer a factor.
5. The considerations involved in President Lincoln's decision to issue the Emancipation Proclamation, and its reception in the North, in the South, and in Europe.
6. The basic structure of the government of the Confederate States of America, how it differed from that of the United States, and how it dealt with the vital question of states' rights.
7. The efforts of presidents Lincoln and Jefferson Davis to act as commander in chief under their respective constitutions.
8. How other nations, particularly England and France, viewed the struggle, and how their courses of action affected the outcome.

PERTINENT QUESTIONS

The Secession Crisis (pp. 380–384)

1. Which states were the first to secede, and what was the reaction of the United States government to this?
2. What compromises were proposed to bring these states back into the Union, and why did they fail?

3. What was Abraham Lincoln's opinion on the legality of secession, and how was that opinion reflected in his action concerning Fort Sumter?
4. What advantages did the Union have in the Civil War? What were the advantages of the Confederacy?

The Mobilization of the North (pp. 384–391)

5. How did the Republican party act to expand the American economy during the war? To which prewar party was their program similar? Why were they able to enact it, whereas the previous party had not been?
6. How did the Union propose to finance the war? How successful was this? What was the effect of the economy?
7. How did the Union propose to raise troops? To what extent was it forced to use conscription? What was the reaction to this, and why was it so varied?
8. What were the characteristics of Lincoln as a leader? How were these characteristics reflected in his selection of his cabinet?
9. What was Lincoln's view of the extent of presidential war powers? Who were the opponents of the war, and how did Lincoln use these powers against them?
10. For what reason was the "Union party" created? Who were its candidates?
11. What were the two factions trying to control the Republican party and what were the goals of each? Which faction did Lincoln support?
12. How was this split in the Republican party revealed in the debate over what to do about slavery? What action did each faction propose? What did Lincoln do, and why?
13. What factors, other than political pressure, brought about the Emancipation Proclamation? What did the proclamation really accomplish? When did full emancipation really come?
14. What impact did the Civil War have on the Northern industrial economy?
15. What impact did the Civil War have on women in the North? What part did women play in the war effort?

The Mobilization of the South (pp. 391–395)

16. Explain the origins of the Confederate government. How did its constitution differ from that of the United States? Who were chosen as its leaders, and what problems did they face?

17. How did the Confederacy attempt to finance the war? What problems did it face, and what were the results?
18. How did the Confederacy propose to raise troops for the war? How did these plans compare with those of the Union, and how successful were they? Why?
19. Why was states' rights the greatest source of division in the Confederacy's war effort? What caused this division, and what was the effect?
20. How did the Civil War "transform" Southern society? How was this transformation like that which took place in the North? How was it different?
21. What was the "principal social effect of the war on the South," and what impact did this have?

Strategy and Diplomacy (pp. 395–399)

22. Compare and contrast Abraham Lincoln and Jefferson Davis—their backgrounds, abilities, and objectives. Why was Lincoln more successful at organizing a command system than Davis?
23. What role did Lincoln propose for the United States Navy? How did the Confederacy attempt to overcome this naval advantage, and what was the result?
24. What were the foreign-policy objectives of the Union and the Confederacy? How did each attempt to achieve these objectives, which was most successful, and why?

Campaigns and Battles (pp. 399–416)

25. What major engagements were fought in 1861? What did they reveal about the possibility of an early end to the struggle and about the readiness of the two sides for a major conflict?
26. What was the Union plan for the conquest of the West? How did the Confederates propose to defend this area? How did the campaign advance, what battles took place, and which of the two armies more nearly achieved its objectives?
27. What was the Union plan on the Virginia front in 1862? Who was the general selected to carry this out? Who was the Confederate general he faced, and what was the relative strength of the two armies?
28. Outline the battles fought in the East in 1862. How did Lincoln's action toward his commanders affect the war effort? What were the relative positions of the two armies at the end of 1862? Which side had been more successful in achieving its objectives?

29. Why was 1863 the "Year of Decision"? What took place in 1863 to swing the advantage to the side of the Union? Where did these battles occur? Who were the generals involved? What did the battles accomplish? Why were they so important?
30. What was Grant's grand strategy for 1864? Who was to be in charge of the armies involved, and what were their objectives?
31. How was the Confederacy finally defeated? In what way did the Union forces destroy the South's will to carry on the fight?
32. Read J. J. Hill's description of Lincoln's visit to Richmond after that city's fall (see "American Voices," page 415). What do his words reveal about his view of the reason for which the war had been fought?
33. How has the scholarly debate over the causes of the Civil War resolved around the question of whether it was a "repressible" or an "irrepressible" conflict?

IDENTIFICATION

Identify each of the following, and explain why it is important within the context of the chapter.

1. Maj. Robert Anderson
2. Crittenden Compromise
3. Homestead Act
4. Morrill Land Grant Act
5. greenbacks
6. Copperheads
7. Joseph Brown and Zebulon M. Vance
8. *Monitor* and *Merrimack* (Virginia)
9. *Trent* affair
10. King Cotton Diplomacy

Where did each of the following battles occur? Who was the victor, and what was the significance of the outcome?

1. First Bull Run
2. Shiloh
3. Murfreesboro
4. Seven Days
5. Second Bull Run
6. Antietam
7. Chancellorsville

8. Gettysburg
9. Chickamauga
10. Chattanooga
11. Wilderness Campaign
12. Atlanta

DOCUMENT

Daniel O'Leary, a captain in the Union army, took part in the bloody fighting of the Chattanooga and Atlanta campaigns and by the fall of 1864, had seen all of the war that he wanted to see. Having lost a brother fighting for the Union in Virginia and a brother-in-law, who fell in Dallas, Georgia, fighting for the Confederacy, he had every reason to feel tired and perhaps a bit disillusioned. The following is from a letter that he wrote to his wife just after his regiment had withdrawn from Atlanta and returned to Chattanooga, where they were to be discharged. What does his letter tell you about the status of the struggle at this time?

What of O'Leary's attitude toward black soldiers? The fall of Athens, Alabama, was not exactly what he had heard. About 400 black troops were captured, but some contended that the surrender had been the fault of their white commander. Nevertheless, what does O'Leary's reaction to the rumor tell you about the difficulties that blacks faced in being accepted? Also, what does this indicate about what men like O'Leary considered themselves to be fighting for?

What other evidence of disillusionment can you find in this letter? Who was the "Little Mac" whom O'Leary mentioned? How might this reference have been an indication of O'Leary's feelings about the way the war was being run? In general, what does the letter tell you about one group of Union soldiers?

Chattanooga, Tenn.
October 8th, 1864

MY DEAR WIFE

I shall endeavor to write you a few lines under difficulties. My frail canvass house is not proof against the stiff north wind that is blowing, shaking my desk so that it is almost impossible to write even if I had anything to write about....

There has been some trouble along our lines of communications of late. Forrest with a large force of cavalry was between here and Nashville and deprived us of a mail for more than a week, but he had to seek other quarters in which to operate after having captured about 1,500 Negro Soldiers at Athens, Alabama. Another strong force of the enemy has been threatening the railroad between here and Atlanta, but they came to grief. They made an attack on our forces near Allatoona Mountains and were repulsed leaving 500 dead on the field. White soldiers are not so easily captured as their *colored brethren,* although Republican papers are loud in their praise of the bravery and soldierly qualities of the "down trodden African." Three railroad bridges on the Atlanta road were washed away by the high water occasioned by the late heavy rains and had given us a good rest, there being no trains going from here to Atlanta, and will not be for the next week....

From all accounts the draft is causing a great many to tremble in the North, who were anxious to sacrifice the last man and the last dollar to prosecute the war, but when they are called in it is quite a different thing. I will be glad to hear of some being forced to come out and enjoy the pleasure of being shot at, and see how they like it. I think their love for "Sambo" would grow small and beautifully less in a short time.

I noticed today while in town that the approaching election was the only topic of conversation among the soldiers. They seemed to be pretty equally divided but the Lincoln men made the most noise. They called their brother soldiers who were for "Little Mac" traitors to their country and anything else in that line that they could think of.

Give my love to all the family....Hoping you are well and to hear from you soon I remain

your loving husband
D. O'LEARY

Courtesy of the Kentucky Historical Society, Frankfort, Kentucky.

MAP EXERCISE

Fill in or identify the following on the blank map provided. Use the maps in the text as your source.

1. States that seceded before the fall of Fort Sumter (with dates of secession)
2. States that seceded after the fall of Fort Sumter (with dates of secession)
3. Border states (slave states that did not secede)
4. Western counties of Virginia that remained loyal to the Union
5. States involved in the campaigns
6. Towns, cities, rivers, and streams that were principal landmarks in the campaigns
7. Troop movements of the Union and Confederate forces, with commanders indicated
8. Battle sites, including (a) names of the battles, (b) dates fought, and (c) the victors.

Interpretative Questions

1. Note the order in which the first seven states seceded. Now refer to the previous map on the Compromise of 1850 (see page 361) and note the percentage of the population in these states that were slaves. What does this suggest about the way the institution of slavery might have shaped Southern political attitudes?
2. Of the first seven Southern states to secede, Texas had the lowest percentages of slaves in its population (a percentage lower than some of the states that remained in the Union). What geographic factors might have worked in favor of secession in Texas? Did geographic factors influence the order of secession in the other states?
3. Why did four states that eventually seceded hesitate?
4. Why did the western counties of Virginia remain in the Union? What does this indicate about how geography shapes sociopolitical attitudes?
5. What effect did the secession of Virginia have on Union war strategy? Why was it necessary for the Union to focus so much of its attention on the Virginia theater?

6. What effect did the choice of Richmond as the capital of the Confederacy have on the South's war strategy? Why was it necessary for the South to focus so much of its attention on the Virginia theater?
7. Why did Lee invade the North in September of 1862? What engagements made this possible? What did he hope to accomplish? What was the outcome?
8. Why did Lee invade the North in the summer of 1863? What engagements made this possible? What did he hope to accomplish? What was the outcome?
9. Why were Chattanooga and Atlanta so important to the Union strategy and to Confederate hopes for winning (or at least continuing) the war?
10. What was the significance of Sherman's March to the Sea?
11. What was Lee trying to accomplish when he was cut off and forced to surrender at Appomattox? From the information on the map in the text, how realistic was his goal?

SUMMARY

Before 1860, references to the nation generally began "these United States are," but after 1865, it became more frequently "the United States is." In that change, one might well see the most important outcome of the American Civil War. The question of the nature of the Union, which had been debated since its inception, was settled—the nation was one and indivisible. The cost had been great, in both human and financial terms, but the war had done more than defeat a secessionist rebellion. It had set the nation on a new course. States' rights, as an alternative to nationalism, had been dealt a fatal blow. The tariff and internal improvements were law and would remain so. Slavery was abolished, free labor was triumphant, and industrial growth and material progress seemed to lie ahead. The war, therefore, was more than a victory for the armies of the Union—the real victor had been the Union itself. Never again would the supremacy of national laws be seriously questioned. The Civil War gave birth to the modern United States. Indeed, it did end an era and begin another.

CHAPTER SELF-TEST

After you have read the chapter in the text and done the exercises in the Study Guide, the following self-test can be taken to see if you understand

the material you have covered. Answers appear at the end of the Study Guide.

Multiple Choice

Circle the letter of the response which best answers the question or completes the statement.

1. By the end of the 1850s the two-party system in the United States:
   a. was the only thing holding the nation together.
   b. still focused on the issues that had created the "second party system."
   c. had reduced slavery to a minor issue.
   d. accentuated rather than muted regional controversy.

2. Which of the following stands did President Buchanan take after the first states seceded?
   a. No state has the right to secede from the Union.
   b. The federal government has no authority to stop a state from seceding from the nation.
   c. Federal troops should be called out to stop secession.
   d. Secession was a legal act.
   e. a and b.
   f. a and c.

3. Which of the following was true when the Civil War began:
   a. All the important material advantages lay with the North.
   b. The South had the active support of England.
   c. Southern industry was sufficient to conduct a war.
   d. The Union was prepared for a long war.

4. Which of the following was not an advantage enjoyed by the South at the outset of the war?
   a. It would be fighting, for the most part, a defensive war.
   b. Most of the white population of the South supported the war.
   c. Northern opinion on the war was divided.
   d. all of the above.

5. Which of the following was *not* enacted by the Republican party during the Civil War.
   a. A new National Bank Act.
   b. Increased taxes on almost all goods and services.
   c. Higher tariffs.
   d. Hard money policies requiring all payments in gold or silver.

6. In which of the following acts did Lincoln "ignore" the constitution?
   a. Sending troops into battle without asking for a declaration of war.
   b. Increasing the size of the regular army.
   c. Putting diplomatic pressure on England not to recognize the Confederacy.
   d. Unilaterally proclaiming a naval blockade of the south.

7. The Emancipation Proclamation freed slaves:
   a. in the North as well as the South.
   b. in areas of the Confederacy except those already under Union control.
   c. and offered compensation to the masters in slave states that remained loyal to the Union.
   d. in the South but offered to return them to masters who declared their loyalty to the Union.

8. The Civil War caused difficulties for American workers because it:
   a. cut off immigration and they had to work harder.
   b. drove prices up and cut purchasing power.
   c. prevented mechanization, so they had to work longer hours.
   d. removed almost all women from the workplace.

9. The Confederacy ultimately financed its war effort through:
   a. an income tax.
   b. requisitions from the states.
   c. paper money.
   d. tariffs on imported goods.

10. The greatest source of division in the South was:
    a. the doctrine of states' rights.
    b. the difference of opinion over the war.
    c. the question of whether to use slaves in combat.
    d. over King Cotton diplomacy.

11. In England, the South was supported by the:
    a. unenfranchised classes.
    b. ruling classes.
    c. Liberals.
    d. English manufacturers.

12. The United States was upset when England declared neutrality because:
    a. it meant that England might aid the South.
    b. the two sides in the conflict were of equal stature.

c. the South could easily get English loans.
   d. such a declaration usually led to diplomatic recognition.
13. The first battle of the Civil War was:
    a. Shiloh.
    b. the Seven Days.
    c. First Bull Run.
    d. Wilson's Creek.
14. The bloodiest engagement of the Civil War was fought at:
    a. Antietam.
    b. Gettysburg.
    c. Atlanta.
    d. Chickamauga.
15. Sherman's march through Georgia was designed to:
    a. find supplies for the Union armies in Virginia.
    b. free the slaves in central Georgia.
    c. get Lincoln re-elected.
    d. break the will of the Southern people.

True/False

Read each statement carefully. Mark true statements "T" and false statements "F"

1. The Crittenden Compromise failed because Republicans refused to give in on the question of the expansion of slavery.
2. Many Southerners believed that the dependence of English and French textile industries on American cotton would force them to intervene on the side of the Confederacy.
3. The Republican party did little to promote economic development during the war.
4. The Union's largest source of financing for the war was taxes and tariffs.
5. In both the North and the South, the draft was accepted with little protest.
6. Had the Union not taken Atlanta in September of 1864, Lincoln might have lost the presidency to McClellan.
7. The Civil War transformed the North from an agrarian to an industrial society.
8. The Confederate government was composed of the most radical Southern secessionists.

9. Despite many shortages, the South was at least able to grow enough food to meet its needs.
10. Lincoln's handling of the war effort faced constant scrutiny from the congressional Committee on the Conduct of the War, which seriously interfered with his work.
11. Despite the need for cotton, England's foreign policy was decidedly pro-Union.
12. No European nation offered diplomatic recognition to the Confederacy.
13. Though outmanned on the land, the Confederacy held the advantage at sea.
14. After General McClellan allowed Lee to retreat into Virginia following Antietam Creek, Lincoln removed McClellan from command.
15. After the battle of Chattanooga, the Confederacy's only hope was to hold on and exhaust the Northern will to fight.

Review Questions

These questions are to be answered with essays. This will allow you to explore relationships among individuals, events, and attitudes of the period under review.

1. Why did the South secede? What pushed the Southern states over the brink? Examine the events of late 1859 and 1860 in the light of Southern social and economic concerns and from the standpoint of Southern political philosophy. From this, determine why the South resorted to secession.
2. Some Northerners also regarded secession as an answer to the problem of slavery. Why were the majority willing to fight to hold the Union together?
3. Why did the North win? In an essay some years ago, Richard Current suggested that "God was on the side of the heaviest battalions," but is that a complete explanation? What other factors contributed to the outcome? Bring together these factors, and, after careful analysis, determine why the North did win.

CHAPTER FIFTEEN
Reconstruction and the New South

OBJECTIVES

A thorough study of Chapter 15 should enable you to understand:

1. The conditions in the former Confederacy after Appomattox that would have made any attempt at genuine reconstruction most difficult.
2. The differences between the Conservative and Radical views on the reconstruction process, and the reasons for the eventual Radical domination.
3. The functioning of the impeachment process in the case of President Andrew Johnson, and the significance of his acquittal for the future of Reconstruction.
4. Radical Reconstruction in practice, and Southern (black and white) reaction to it.
5. The debate among historians concerning the nature of Reconstruction, its accomplishments, and its harmful effects on the South.
6. The national problems faced by President Ulysses S. Grant, and the reasons for his lack of success as chief executive.
7. The diplomatic successes of the Johnson and Grant administration, and the role of the presidents in achieving them.
8. The greenback question, and how it reflected the postwar financial problems of the nation.
9. The alternatives that were available during the election of 1876, and the effects of the so-called Compromise of 1877 on the South and on the nation.
10. The methods used by white Southerners to regain control of the region's politics.
12. The reasons for the failure of the South to develop a strong industrial economy after Reconstruction.

13. The ways in which Southerners decided to handle the race question, and the origin of the system identified with "Jim Crow."
14. The response of blacks to conditions in the South following Reconstruction.

PERTINENT QUESTIONS

The Problems of Peacemaking (pp. 420–426)

1. What effects did the Civil War have on the economy and social system of the South?
2. What special problems did the freedmen face immediately after the war? What efforts were made the help them?
3. What political implications did the readmission of the Southern states pose for the political parties, especially the Republicans?
4. What were the differences among the Conservative, Radical, and Modern factions of the Republican party during Reconstruction?
5. What were the objectives and provisions of Lincoln's plan for Reconstruction? How did the Radical Republicans respond to it?
6. Describe Andrew Johnson's approach to Reconstruction. How was it shaped by his political background and his personality?

Radical Reconstruction (pp. 426–431)

7. Describe the Black Codes and the Congressional reaction to them. How did President Johnson respond to Congress?
8. What were the key provisions of the Fourteenth Amendment? What happened to it in 1866?
9. Explain the basic provisions of the congressional plan of Reconstruction of 1867 and tell how it was implemented. What were the implications of waiting so long after the war to get a comprehensive plan in place?
10. What measures did the Radical Republicans take to keep President Johnson and the Supreme Court from interfering with their plans? What ultimately happened to Johnson's influence?

The South in Reconstruction (pp. 431–436)

11. What three groups constituted the Republican party in the South during Reconstruction?
12. How do the facts of political life in the Reconstruction states compare to the oft-stated white charges of corruption, black domination, and misrule?

13. What changes in Southern education began to emerge during Reconstruction? Who pushed for these changes?
14. What changes in land ownership occurred in the South after the Civil War? What pattern of land occupancy characterized most blacks in the postwar South?
15. How did the typical agricultural credit system in the postwar South affect farmers—especially poor ones?
16. What economic advances did the freedmen make? How did the economic status of blacks compare with that of the average white Southerner?
17. How did freedom affect black family life?

The Grant Administration (pp. 436–440)

18. How did Ulysses S. Grant's political accomplishments compare with his military ability?
19. What episodes led to the Liberal Republican break over "Grantism" and later to the second-term scandals?
20. People in what financial condition were most likely to favor expansion of the currency supply with greenbacks? What sparked interest in greenbacks?

The Abandonment of Reconstruction (pp. 440–444)

21. What tactics did *white* Southern Democrats use to restrict or control black suffrage?
22. Why did Northern Republicans begin to take less interest in Reconstruction and the cause of the freedmen after about 1870?
23. Why was the presidential election of 1876 disputed? How was the controversy resolved by the "Compromise of 1877"?
24. What was President Rutherford B. Hayes's objective in the South? Did he succeed?
25. Compare white and black expectations for Reconstruction with the actual results. Why were most black hopes dashed? What black gains were made?

The New South (pp. 444–453)

26. What were the typical socioeconomic and political characteristics of the "Redeemers" (Bourbons)?
27. How did the policies of the "Redeemer" governments compare with those of the Reconstruction-era administrations?

28. In what particular products was industrialization in the South most advanced? What factors attracted industrial capital to the region after the war?
29. Describe the composition of the industrial work force in the South. What was life in a mill town like?
30. Describe the typical pattern of southern agriculture in the late nineteenth and early twentieth centuries. What problems confronted most farmers? What groups were most notably affected?
31. Describe the rise of the black middle class.
32. What was Booker T. Washington's prescription for black advancement as expressed in the "Atlanta compromise" and elsewhere?
33. How did the civil-rights cases of 1883 and *Plessy v. Ferguson* (1896) substantially negate the effect of the equal-protection clause of the Fourteenth Amendment?
34. What strategies and legal devices did the Southern states use to evade the spirit of the Fifteenth Amendment? What motivated the late nineteenth-early twentieth century crackdown on black voting?
35. Describe the pervasive nature of "Jim Crow" laws. How was the system enforced, formally and informally?

IDENTIFICATION

Identify each of the following, and explain why it is important within the context of the chapter.

1. Thirteenth Amendment
2. O. O. Howard
3. Thaddeus Stevens
4. Charles Sumner
5. Wade-Davis Bill
6. John Wilkes Booth
7. Alexander H. Stephens
8. Joint Committee on Reconstruction
9. Edwin M. Stanton
10. scalawag
11. carpetbagger
12. sharecropping
13. spoils system/civil service
14. Crédit Mobilier

15. "whiskey ring"
16. Hamilton Fish
17. "Seward's Folly"
18. "*Alabama*" claims
19. "redeemed"
20. Ku Klux Klan
21. Samuel J. Tilden
22. "solid" Democratic South
23. Henry W. Grady
24. lynching

DOCUMENT

Read the portions of the chapter that discuss the Black Codes. Also read the section "Debating the Past" (p. 452). The following selection is taken from the writings of William A. Dunning. Consider the following questions: How does Dunning's account reveal his racist assumptions? How would accounts such as Dunning's lead white Southerners in the twentieth century to conclude that they had been gravely wronged by Reconstruction? Which of the following statements is more convincing? The Black Codes were a necessary and realistic response to the situation. The Black Codes were a thinly disguised attempt to resubjugate the freedmen.

> To a distrustful northern mind such legislation could very easily take the form of a systematic attempt to relegate the freedmen to a subjection only less complete than that from which the war had set them free. The radicals sounded a shrill note of alarm. "We tell the white men of Mississippi," said the Chicago *Tribune,* "that the men of the North will convert the state of Mississippi into a frog-pond before they will allow any such laws to disgrace one foot of soil over which the flag of freedom waves." In Congress, Wilson, Sumner, and other extremists took up the cry, and with superfluous ingenuity distorted the spirit and purpose of both the laws and the law-makers of the South. The "black codes" were represented to be the expression of a deliberate purpose by the southerners to nullify the result of the war and reestablish slavery, and this impression gained wide prevalence in the North.
>
> Yet, as a matter of fact, this legislation, far from embodying any spirit of defiance towards the North or any purpose to evade the conditions which the victors had imposed, was in the main a conscientious and straightforward attempt to bring some sort of order out of the social and economic chaos which a full acceptance of the results of war and emancipation involved. In its general principle it corresponded very closely to the actual facts of the situation. The freedmen were not, and in the nature of the case could not for generations be, on the same social, moral, and intellectual plane with the whites; and this fact was recognized by constituting them a separate class in the civil order. As in general principles, so in details, the legislation was faithful on the whole to the actual conditions with which it had to deal. The restrictions in respect to bearing arms, testifying in court, and keeping labor contracts were

justified by well-established traits and habits of the negroes; and the vagrancy laws dealt with problems of destitution, idleness, and vice of which no one not in the midst of them could appreciate the appalling magnitude and complexity.

William A. Dunning, *Reconstruction: Political and Economic, 1865–1877* (1907; reprint, New York: Harper & Row [Harper Torchbooks], 1962), pp. 57–58).

MAP EXERCISE

Fill in or identify the following on the blank map provided.

1. Former Confederate states.
2. First state to be readmitted, including the year.
3. Last three states to be readmitted, including the years. (Note that the other seven were readmitted in 1868.)
4. First three states to reestablish Conservative government, including the years.
5. States in which Conservative government was not reestablished until 1876.

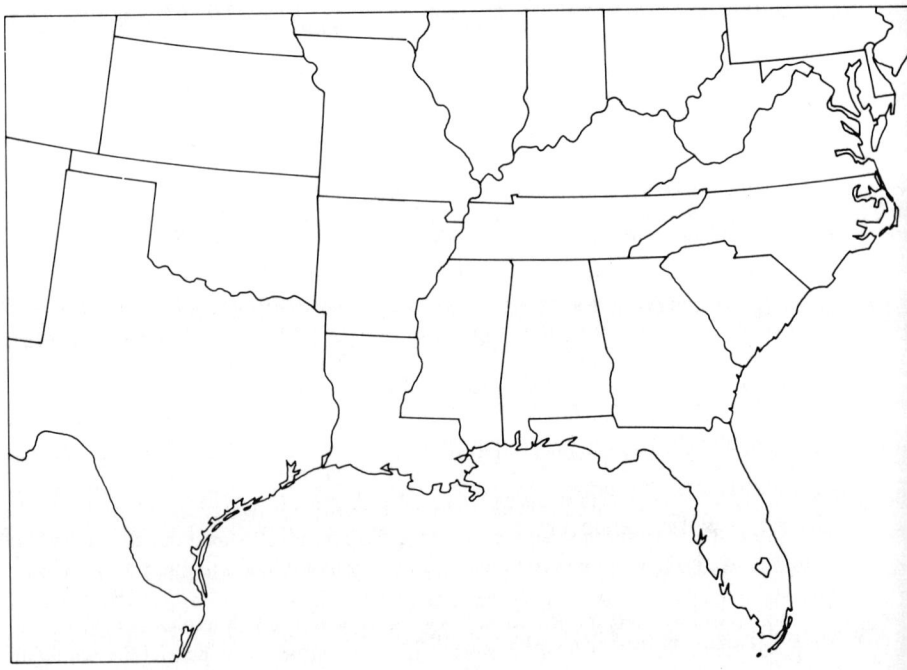

Interpretative Questions

Based on what you have filled in, answer the following. For some of the questions you will need to consult the narrative in your text for information or explanation.

1. Note the location of the first state to be readmitted by Congress, and explain why it was restored to the Union so quickly.
2. What did the other ten states have to do to gain their readmissions in 1868–1870?
3. Note the first three states to experience the reestablishment of Conservative government and explain why the restoration of Democratic party rule came so quickly there.
4. What forces delayed the reestablishment of the Conservative government in the other states? What episode symbolically marks the end of the Reconstruction era?

SUMMARY

The military aspect of the American Civil War lasted less than five years and ended in April 1865, but it would take another dozen years of Reconstruction to determine what the results of the war would be. The only questions clearly settled by the time of Appomattox were that the nation was indivisible and that slavery must end. The nation faced other issues with far-reaching implications. What would be the place of the freedmen in Southern society? How would the rebellious states be brought back into their "proper relationship" with the Union? The victorious North was in a position to dominate the South, but Northern politicians were not united in either resolve or purpose. For over two years after the fighting stopped, there was no coherent Reconstruction policy. Congress and the president struggled with each other, and various factions in Congress had differing views on politics, race, and union. Congress finally won control and dominated the Reconstruction process until Southern resistance and Northern ambivalence led to the end of Reconstruction in 1877. In the years that followed, a "New South" emerged, whose leaders believed the region could be modernized through industrial development. But despite their efforts the South's agricultural sector remained predominant. No economic, political, or social issue in the South could escape the race question. The Jim Crow system created by white southerners succeeded in evading the spirit of the Fourteenth and Fifteenth Amendments, and black hopes for political equality faded. Although enormous changes had taken place, the era left a legacy of continuing racism and sectionalism.

CHAPTER SELF-TEST

After you have read the chapter in the text and done the exercises in the Study Guide, the following self-test can be taken to see if you understand the material you have covered. Answers appear at the end of the Study Guide.

Multiple Choice

Circle the letter of the response which best answers the question or completes the statement.

1. The Thirteenth Amendment to the U.S. Constitution:
   a. declared that the right to vote could not be denied on account of race.
   b. officially ended slavery.
   c. granted "citizenship" to the freedmen.
   d. provided that states could only count three-fifths (60 percent) of their black population when determining how many members they would be given in the U.S. House of Representatives.
   e. opened up the West to homesteading by African Americans.

2. The Fourteenth Amendment to the U.S. Constitution:
   a. declared that the right to vote could not be denied on account of race.
   b. officially ended slavery.
   c. granted "citizenship" to the freedmen.
   d. provided that states could only count three-fifths (60 percent) of their black population when determining how many members they would be given in the U.S. House of Representatives.
   e. opened up the West to homesteading by African Americans.

3. The Fifteenth Amendment to the U.S. Constitution:
   a. declared that the right to vote could not be denied on account of race.
   b. officially ended slavery.

c. granted "citizenship" to the freedmen.
   d. provided that states could only count three-fifths (60 percent) of their black population when determining how many members they would be given in the U.S. House of Representatives.
   e. opened up the West to homesteading by African Americans.

4. Which faction of the Republican party wanted Reconstruction to punish the former Confederacy, disenfranchise large numbers of southern whites, and confiscate the property of leading Confederates?
   a. Moderates.
   b. Conservatives.
   c. Redeemers.
   d. Scalywaggers.
   e. Radicals.

5. Which best describes Congressional reaction to the former Confederate states that had set up new governments under Andrew Johnson's "Presidential Reconstruction"?
   a. They fully accepted all of the states except Georgia and South Carolina, which had elected no blacks to office.
   b. They conditionally accepted all of the states pending the results of local and state elections.
   c. They refused to seat the senators and representatives from the states and set up a committee to investigate and advise on Reconstruction.
   d. They fully accepted all of the states west of the Mississippi River, but required new constitutions in the others.

6. The "Black Codes" were a set of regulations established by:
   a. the Congress to protect the rights of the former slaves to own property and to find employment.
   b. the U.S. Supreme Court to enforce the provisions of the Thirteenth and Fourteenth Amendments to the U.S. Constitution.
   c. the northern states to prevent a massive influx of former slaves from entering their states and seeking homes and jobs.
   d. the southern states to promote white supremacy and to control the economic and social activities of the freedmen.

7. Which of the following, if any, was *not* a provision of the Congressional plan of Reconstruction enacted in early 1867?
   a. Dividing the South into military districts administered by military commanders.
   b. Requiring former Confederate states, as a condition of readmission to the union, to ratify the Fourteenth Amendment to the U.S. Constitution.
   c. Mandating former Confederate states, as a condition of readmission to the union, to hold a constitutional convention and prepare a constitution providing for black male suffrage.
   d. Declaring that each state must present a plan for distributing farmland to or providing jobs for the former slaves.
   e. All of the above were provisions of the Congressional plan of Reconstruction.

8. Critics of native southern whites who joined the Republican Party called them:
   a. carpetbaggers.
   b. whippersnappers.
   c. scalawags.
   d. white camellias.
   e. filibusterers.

9. Which best describes the extent of "Negro rule" in the southern states during reconstruction?
   a. African Americans played a significant political role in several states but never elected a governor or controlled a state legislature.
   b. Some African Americans held local elective offices and a very few were elected to state legislatures but the numbers were politically inconsequential in every state.
   c. In the deep South states where African Americans constituted a majority of the voters due to white disenfranchisement, blacks dominated both houses of the state legislatures and controlled state politics as long as federal troops remained in the South.
   d. African Americans did not actually hold many offices in any state, but they effectively dominated local offices in all but Tennessee and Arkansas through alliances with white Republicans.

10. The key point of contact in the agricultural credit system for most southern farmers, black and white, in the late nineteenth century was:
    a. small-town banks owned by northerners.
    b. large diversified planters.

c. finance companies in the larger cities such as Atlanta and Memphis.
   d. local country store merchants.
   e. mail-order mortgage companies operating out of New York.
11. In the late nineteenth century, the agricultural credit system in the South encouraged farmers to:
    a. rely heavily on cash crops—especially cotton.
    b. diversify away from cotton toward food grains and livestock.
    c. adopt the use of mechanization on increasingly larger farms.
    d. abandon farming and invest in capital-intensive manufacturing enterprises.
12. Ulysses S. Grant's election as President was largely a result of his being:
    a. governor of New York during the postwar economic boom.
    b. a triumphant commanding General of the Union Army.
    c. the popular administrator of the Freedmen's Bureau.
    d. a flamboyant cavalry officer in the western Indian wars.
13. Which of the following, if any, was *not* associated with the "Compromise of 1877"?
    a. Removal of the last federal troops from the South.
    b. Increased federal aid for railroads and other internal improvements.
    c. Appointment of a southerner to the cabinet.
    d. Making Rutherford B. Hayes president.
    e. All of the above are associated with the "Compromise of 1877."
14. Which, of the following, if any, is *not* cited by the text as a reason that Reconstruction failed to accomplish more to promote racial equality in the United States?
    a. Fear that harsh action might lead to resumed military action by the southern states, even though they had been defeated.
    b. Attachment to a states' rights view of the Constitution, even for the rebel states.
    c. Deep respect for private property rights, even for leading Confederates.
    d. Belief in black inferiority by many whites, even northern liberals.
    e. All the above were cited as reasons that Reconstruction failed to accomplish more.

15. The "solid" South refers to the:
    a. work ethic values of southern whites.
    b. courage of Confederate soldiers during the war despite being outnumbered.
    c. steady returns that northern bankers could expect from investment in cotton.
    d. the fact that the Democratic Party could count on the votes of the southern states after Reconstruction.

16. In most southern states, the "Redeemers" or "Bourbons" were typically composed of:
    a. a newly emerging class of merchants, industrialists, railroad developers, and financiers.
    b. essentially the same old planter elite that had dominated antebellum politics.
    c. a coalition of poor working-class whites and blacks.
    d. white farmers who owned small to medium farms.

17. Henry W. Grady was:
    a. the builder of the American Tobacco Company.
    b. an Atlanta editor who became a leading spokesman for the "New South" idea.
    c. the person principally responsible for Birmingham, Alabama, becoming an iron and steel production center.
    d. the governor of South Carolina who was most vociferous in advocating that blacks should migrate from the South to take industrial jobs in the North.

18. Booker T. Washington's principal message to African Americans was that they should:
    a. concentrate on practical, industrial education and work toward adopting the standards of the white middle class.
    b. join in common economic interests with white workers to bring the trade union movement to the South so that the wages would rise for all.
    c. strive first for full voting rights because only political power could bring economic gain.
    d. abandon the South and seek factory jobs in the North where segregation was less of a problem.

19. "Jim Crow" is a nickname for:
    a. white southerners who used violence or intimidation to restrict black activities.
    b. black people who curried favor with whites by acting excessively polite and deferential.
    c. the whole system of laws and customs that kept the races separate in schools, public buildings, housing, jobs, theaters, etc.
    d. black people who pretended to be friendly toward whites but who secretly undermined white interests.
    e. the African American culture of dance, music, food, and religion that grew up after slavery.

20. In *Plessy v. Ferguson* (1896) the U.S. Supreme Court established the general principal that:
    a. states could not prevent blacks from voting just because their grandparents had been slaves.
    b. states could require separate accommodations on trains, in schools, etc., for blacks and whites as long as the accommodations were equal.
    c. Congress could take away a state's seats in the U.S. House of Representatives if the state refused to allow blacks to vote in Congressional elections.
    d. local governments could use zoning and building codes to enforce racial segregation by neighborhood.

True/False

Read each statement carefully. Mark true statements "T" and false statements "F."

1. As bad as the economic and physical situation was for southern blacks in the aftermath of the Civil War, conditions were even worse for the region's white population.
2. The Emancipation Proclamation ended slavery throughout the South in 1863.
3. Republicans were afraid that the quick return of the Southern states to Congress would lead to more Democratic votes, thereby increasing the likelihood that Congress would establish protective tariffs and subsidize railroads.
4. President Lincoln believed that a lenient Reconstruction policy would encourage southern unionists and other southern Whigs to become Republicans and build a stronger party in the South.

5. John Wilkes Booth acted completely on his own in plotting to murder President Lincoln.
6. Characteristics of Andrew Johnson's personality that hampered him as president were that he was too polite and deferential to assume any leadership initiative.
7. The Tenure of Office Act and the Command of the Army Act were passed by Congress to prevent southern states from sending former Confederates to Congress or from having them control the state militia companies.
8. Even though the House's impeachment charges were nominally based on specific "high crimes and misdemeanors," Andrew Johnson was actually convicted by the Senate and removed from the Presidency for petty political reasons.
9. Despite the end of slavery, most black agricultural labor in the South in the late nineteenth century continued to emulate the gang-labor system in which slaves lived in concentrated quarters and worked in groups under the constant supervision of a white field boss suggestive of the prewar overseer.
10. During the period from just before the Civil War to just after Reconstruction, per capita income for African Americans rose significantly while per capita income for whites dropped.
11. In the 1870s, the expanded printing of greenback paper currency was advocated by those, especially debtors, who believed that inflation would help the economy.
12. In the context of Reconstruction, "redeemed" was used to refer to freedmen who had returned to their original slave plantations as workers after running away during or immediately following the war.
13. The Crédit Mobilier was a railroad construction company involved in scandal during the Grant administration.
14. Hamilton Fish was Grant's Secretary of State whose action worsened relations between the United States and Great Britain.
15. Alaska was called "Seward's folly" because of his abortive attempt to sell the territory to the Russian Czar as a method of financing the cost of maintaining troops in the South during Reconstruction.
16. In the period from the end of Reconstruction into the twentieth century, the Democratic Party was the political party of the vast majority of southern whites.

17. In general, the "Redeemer" ("Bourbon") political regimes were inclined to raise taxes to expand services, especially public education.
18. By 1900 the portion of the nation's manufacturing output produced in the South was about three times what it had been on the eve of the Civil War.
19. The portion of southern farmers who were tenants, cash or sharecrop, increased markedly from Reconstruction to 1900.
20. In the period from Reconstruction to 1900, the crop-lien system helped force many southern backcountry farmers in the piney woods and mountains from cash crop commercial farming into a ruggedly independent sort of subsistence farming.
21. By the late 1890s, a significantly smaller portion of southern blacks was allowed to vote than in the late 1860s.

Review Questions

These questions are to be answered with essays. This will allow you to explore relationships among individuals, events, and attitudes of the period under review.

1. Compare and contrast the several plans for Reconstruction: Lincoln's plan, the Wade-Davis Bill, Johnson's Presidential Reconstruction, and the Congressional plan. Consider provisions, motives, goals, and results. What forces and attitudes kept a more radical plan from being adopted?
2. Evaluate the successes and failures of Reconstruction. Given the context of the times, explain what, if anything, could have been done to avoid the failures and expand the successes. What groundwork was laid for the future?
3. Although many changes had occurred by 1900, the South remained an impoverished agricultural region, lagging well behind the rest of the nation. Describe the economic changes in the South, and assess why they were not adequate to bring the old Confederacy into the national mainstream, as some of the region's spokespersons had hoped.
4. Explain the ways in which the Southern white establishment was able to evade the spirit of the Fourteenth and Fifteenth Amendments to the Constitution. What alternative paths of accommodation and resistance did black leaders propose to this rise of Jim Crow?

Chapter Sixteen
The Conquest of the Far West

OBJECTIVES
A thorough study of Chapter 16 should enable you to understand:
1. The cultural characteristics of the varied populations of the region and the conflicts among them.
2. The ways that the western economy evolved toward modern capitalism in terms of mining, cattle raising, and commercial farming.
3. How white culture and federal policy worked to destroy Indian culture in the West.
4. The process by which the West opened to commercial farming and the problems that the farmers faced.

PERTINENT QUESTIONS

The Societies of the Far West (pp. 455–464)
1. Compare and contrast the Pacific Coast Indians with the Pueblos of the Southwest. How did they interact with Spanish, and later Mexican, settlers?
2. What was the most widespread Indian group in the West? What traits did these tribes share, and what was the economic basis of their way of life?
3. Explain the advantages and disadvantages that the Plains Indians had in their conflicts with white settlers. Why did the whites eventually prevail?
4. How did Anglo-American dominance affect the nature of Indian and Hispanic culture in New Mexico from the 1840s to 1900?
5. What factors led to the decline of Mexican-American economic and social dominance in California and Texas? What was the socioeconomic status of most Mexican Americans by the end of the nineteenth century?

6. Up to 1869 in what two fields did the greatest number of Chinese immigrants work? How did employment, residential patterns, and social relations change in the Chinese American community after that point?
7. What led to the increasing Anglo-European hostility toward the Chinese in California? What were the tangible results of this hostility?
8. What led to the late-nineteenth-century boom in migration to the West from the eastern United States and Europe?
9. How did the federal government assist settlers in obtaining western land through the Homestead Act and other laws?
10. Given the rapid political progression from territory to state in most of the West, why did Utah, Arizona, New Mexico, and Oklahoma lag behind?

The Changing Western Economy (pp. 464–470)

11. What was the composition and structure of the labor force in the West? How was it shaped by racial prejudice?
12. Describe the typical pattern of development and decline in the mining regions. What was life like for men and women in the mining camps and towns?
13. Describe the origins, purposes, and practices of the "long drive" and the "open range" cattle industry. What ended this brief but colorful boom?
14. What opportunities opened to women in the West that were not available in the East?

The Dispersal of the Tribes (pp. 470–479)

15. Describe the evolution of basic national Indian policy up to the 1880s. How successful was it for whites? For the Indians?
16. What happened to the great buffalo (bison) herds, and how was Indian life affected by the change?
17. Describe the general pattern of Indian wars from the 1850s to the 1880s. What were the largest and most violent conflicts? Why did whites ultimately prevail?
18. What actions were taken under the Dawes Act, and what basic objective did the federal government hope to achieve by this legislation?

The Rise and Decline of the Western Farmer (pp. 479–484)

19. Describe the building and financing of the transcontinental railroads. What was the impact on the West?
20. What problems not typical of the East did farmers encounter on the Great Plains? What methods and devices helped solve these problems? What problems remained?
21. How were market forces changing the nature of American agriculture in this period? What was the result?
22. What were the three main grievances of the late-nineteenth-century farmer? How were these complaints compounded by psychological factors?

IDENTIFICATION

Identify each of the following, and explain why it is important within the context of the chapter.

1. Taos Rebellion
2. *californios*
3. "coolies"
4. Chinese Exclusion Act
5. polygamy
6. Black Hills
7. vigilantes
8. Indian Territory (Oklahoma)
9. Indian Peace Commission
10. Sand Creek episode
11. Crazy Horse and Sitting Bull
12. George A. Custer
13. Nez Percé
14. Geronimo
15. Wounded Knee incident
16. barbed wire

DOCUMENT

An editorial in the Atlanta *Constitution*, one of the leading newspapers of the postwar South, heralded the completion of the transcontinental railroad in 1896. In light of this and the previous chapter, consider the following questions: How does the editorial reveal the psychological importance of the transcontinental railroad to the American sense of nationhood? How does it show that the railroad would lead to the closing of the far West frontier? What does the writer reveal about Southern jealousy of Northern industrial accomplishment?

> This mammoth enterprise is completed at last. It has no equal in modern history for magnitude, importance, and the energy of its execution. Bold in conception and stupendous in realization, it stands a monument among the monster achievements of the age. It links the oceans with its iron bond. It brings the continents into close social and commercial communion. It nullifies the area of immense distances and overleaps the impediments of boundless wilderness. It pierces savage realms with the probe of civilization. It hitches progress on to the barren domination of the uncultured Indian. It connects the buffalo with the water-fall. With the speed of lightning it transmits the refinements of high polish and the improvements of progressive art and science broadcast over a country that must have remained otherwise a free range of wild forest. It redeems from disuse millions of acres of virgin land, and is the "opening up" [of] a stream of commerce and development that will beneficially inundate one of the magnificent portions of the world.
>
> It is useless to dispute the wonderful spirit of energy and skill that has put this herculean enterprise through. The difficulties have been almost invincible, and the nerve to overcome them has been grand.
>
> But this success has some grave drawbacks concerned with it....It might have been built elsewhere with less money and served the purposes of its construction better....The Southern Pacific route is destined to be the successful road between the two oceans. It is shorter than the one now built, runs through a milder climate, has less obstacles of mountain and river, and can be used all the year round....We regard the Southern Pacific as one of the necessities of Southern effort. It will do more to build up our Southern states than any other one business movement. When we get to be the channel for the stupendous tide of commerce and trade that will surge over the land from the Pacific coast, we will spring into potent importance, and we will absorb and assimilate unreckonable wealth and population. Let us grasp for the huge prize. Let us no longer sit confessed sluggards in contrast with Northern energy. Let us not sit supinely and see our Northern neighbor pick fruits that belong to us legitimately.

Constitution, 12 May 1869, p. 1.

MAP EXERCISE

Fill in or identify the following on the blank map provided.

1. Draw a line indicating the western rim of English-speaking settlement as of 1860. Circle the pockets of such settlement in the Far West.
2. Indicate the area of the Great Plains by means of diagonal lines.
3. Draw lines indicating the general flow of the "long drives."
4. Indicate the Rocky Mountains and the Sierra Nevada-Cascade Range by drawing inverted *V*'s along their positions.

5. Place boxes with dates to indicate the general areas of the gold and silver rushes of 1849, 1858 to 1859, and 1874. Tell what state each strike was in.
6. Draw a line along the route of the first transcontinental railroad. Place a star at the point where the two lines joined. Also draw the routes of subsequent transcontinental railroads.
7. Identify Indian Territory (Oklahoma) with I.T. and the Dakotas with N.D. and S.D.

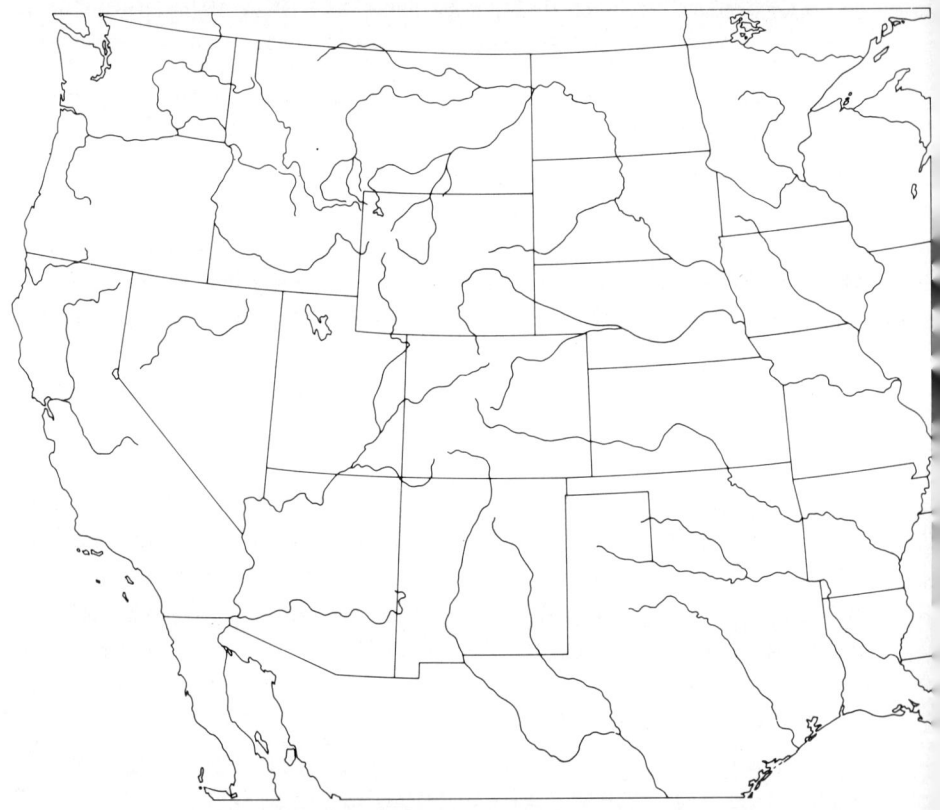

Interpretative Questions

Based on what you have filled in, answer the following. For some of the questions you will need to consult the narrative in your text for information or explanation.

1. Why did the frontier line stop where it did about 1860?
2. How was the pre-Civil War settlement along the Pacific coast isolated from the rest of the nation?

3. Why did the post-Civil War gold and silver rushes involve considerable west-to-east as well as east-to-west migration?
4. What long-term effects did the "cattle kingdom" boom have?
5. Why were the Plains Indians so resentful of the reservations they were provided?
6. What areas of the nation were best served by the first transcontinental railroad? Why was the South resentful?
7. What special challenges did agriculture on the Great Plains present to farmers?

SUMMARY

Far from being empty and unknown, significant parts of what would become the western United States were populated by Indians and Hispanics long before the post-Civil War boom in eastern and European settlement. Even after the waves of white occupation and in the face of significant prejudice from those whites, large numbers of Mexican and Asian Americans continued to live in the West and influence its culture and economy.

White settlement developed in initial boom-and-decline patterns in the three industries that would do much to shape the region in the long run: mining, ranching, and commercial agriculture. Asians, Mexicans, and, to a lesser extent, African Americans provided much of the labor force for these endeavors.

In much of the West, and especially in the plains and the southwest, hostile Indians violently resisted white settlement because it threatened to destroy their culture. Due to better organization and equipment and the force of numbers, whites prevailed in battle and implemented policies designed to destroy tribal identity. Even with the increased access by rail and improved farming techniques, agriculture on the Great Plains was a challenge. Frustrated farmers had more grievances than solutions.

CHAPTER SELF-TEST

After you have read the chapter in the text and done the exercises in the Study Guide, the following self-test can be taken to see if you understand the material you have covered. Answers appear at the end of the Study Guide.

Multiple Choice

Circle the letter of the response which best answers the question or completes the statement.

1. Because the area was arid to semiarid and thought to be unfit for Anglo-European civilization, many early-nineteenth-century Americans called the Far West the:
   a. Trans-Mississippi Wasteland.
   b. Intermountain Barrens.
   c. Prairie Wilderness.
   d. Great American Desert.

2. Indian Territory, to which several eastern Indian tribes including the Cherokees and Creeks were removed, is now the state of:
   a. South Dakota.
   b. Kansas.
   c. Oklahoma.
   d. Wyoming.

3. What happened to the *Californios* who dominated California prior to the gold rush of 1849?
   a. Most died due to epidemic diseases brought in by the miners.
   b. The ones who could speak English adapted well and continued to dominate real estate ownership.
   c. Most emigrated back to Mexico or Arizona.
   d. They lost status and land and were excluded from Anglo-dominated prosperity.

4. Up to 1869, the great majority of Chinese Americans worked in what *two* industries? (Choose two.)
   a. mining (especially gold)
   b. services (domestic work, laundry, etc.)
   c. railroads (especially construction)
   d. retailing (small merchants)

5. Which of the following was *not* a reason for Anglo-American resentment of Chinese immigrants?
   a. They tended to congregate together and maintain Chinese culture.
   b. Some secret societies ("tongs") engaged in crime.
   c. Many of the early female Chinese immigrants had been sold into prostitution.
   d. The Chinese were perceived as lazy slackers who would not work hard.

6. Which of the following was the main flaw in the Homestead Act?
   a. 160 acres was not enough land for grazing and grain farming in the West.
   b. African Americans were prohibited from obtaining land under the Act.
   c. The fees involved in establishing ownership of the land were too costly for most settlers.

7. Which of the following was *not* a state by 1900?
   a. Colorado
   b. California
   c. Nevada
   d. Oklahoma

8. Which type of mining came first as new fields opened?
   a. placer (surface)
   b. quartz (lode)
   c. open pit (blasting)

9. Which of the following states and/or territories did *not* experience significant mining development from the 1850s to the 1880s?
   a. Nevada
   b. Colorado
   c. Kansas
   d. South Dakota
   e. Montana

10. The "long drive" in the open-range cattle industry referred to the process of:
    a. rounding up the cattle from great distances all over the range in the spring for branding.
    b. moving the cattle south to Texas in the winter and north to Colorado, Wyoming, and Montana in the spring to take advantage of the best pasture.
    c. using cattle as oxen to pull covered wagons for settlers seeking homesteads in the West.
    d. herding cattle from the ranges in Texas and other remote areas to the nearest accessible railroad loading point so that the cattle could be shipped to slaughterhouses in the East.

11. The so-called "range wars" of the West were between (choose two letters):
    a. white and black cowboys.
    b. sheep ranchers and cattle ranchers.

c. Hispanics and Anglo landowners.
   d. farmers and ranchers.
12. The federal government agency vested with management of Indian relations and the reservations was the:
    a. Indian Lands Commission.
    b. Native American Administration.
    c. Office of Assimilation and Concentration.
    d. Bureau of Indian Affairs.
13. The two principal Indian chiefs who led the forces that massed in the northern plains in 1875–1876 following the Black Hills gold rush were (choose two letters):
    a. Black Kettle
    b. Sitting Bull
    c. Crazy Horse
    d. Geronimo
    e. Red Eagle
14. The purpose of the Dawes Severalty Act of 1887 was to:
    a. weaken tribes, allot land to individual Indians, and promote assimilation.
    b. geographically disperse the reservations so it would be more difficult for Indian warrior forces to unite.
    c. increase tribal loyalty and reduce violence by allowing chiefs and tribal councils to act autonomously on the reservations.
    d. restore economic viability to the nomadic way of plains Indian live by revitalizing the bison herds.
15. Which of the following was *not* a way that farmers adapted to life on the Great Plains up through the 1890s?
    a. barbed wire fencing
    b. drought-resistant crops
    c. large-scale irrigation
    d. deep wells with windmill-driven pumps

True/False

Read each statement carefully. Mark true statements "T" and false statements "F."

1. As late as 1900, the Far West remained essentially outside America's capitalist economy.
2. Except for warfare, American Indian tribal culture made little distinction between the genders in family and work roles.

3. Although most historians have previously treated the bison (buffalo) as critical to plains Indian culture prior to the 1880s, recent anthropological work has revealed that this is a myth and that the bison was actually relatively unimportant for these tribes.
4. Prior to the arrival of significant numbers of English-speaking settlers, an elite of large landowning Hispanics dominated life in California.
5. A *barrio* was a Mexican-American who cooperated with Anglo settlers and often supervised poor farmworkers.
6. "Coolies" were Chinese indentured servants whose status was close to slavery.
7. In the late nineteenth century, most California residents favored increased Chinese immigration because there was a labor shortage and the Chinese would work for low wages.
8. The Timber Culture Act, Desert Land Act, and Timber and Stone Act provided avenues for westerners to acquire larger tracts of land than were allowed under the Homestead Act.
9. The working class in the American West was racially diversified and stratified.
10. Vigilantes were groups of citizens in mining towns organized to enforce justice in the absence of official legal authority.
11. Prostitution was common in the mining boomtowns.
12. When the "long drive" era began, there was an excess of cattle in Texas, so cowboys drove huge herds to rail centers in Louisiana, especially New Orleans, for shipment to the East.
13. Although the Bureau of Indian Affairs was chronically underfunded and understaffed, the reform-minded whites who ran it established a solid reputation for honesty, efficiency, and sincere concern for the well-being of the native Americans they served.
14. Although small, the Nez Percé tribe was composed of particularly effective warriors who engaged in raids throughout the southern plains until Chief Joseph was finally captured in 1877.
15. The first transcontinental railroad was completed shortly before the beginning of the Civil War, but due to wartime disruption it did not carry much traffic until the end of the 1860s.

Review Questions

These questions are to be answered with essays. This will allow you to explore relationships among individuals, events, and attitudes of the period under review.

1. Explain how the mining, cattle, and farming frontiers followed something of a boom-and-bust pattern. Evaluate the long-term impact of the frontier activities on the development of the West.
2. What was the role of women in the far western mining and railroad towns and on ranches and farms? How did the role change with time?
3. How did white racial, ethnic, and cultural prejudice against Indians, Mexicans, and Asians shape the development of the American West?

Chapter Seventeen
Industrial Supremacy

Objectives

A thorough study of Chapter 17 should enable you to understand:

1. The reasons for the rapid industrial development of the United States in the late nineteenth century.
2. The specific impact of technological innovation in promoting industrial expansion.
3. The role of the individual entrepreneur in the development of particular industries.
4. The changes that were taking place in American business organization.
5. The ways in which classical economics and certain ideas of Darwin were used to justify and defend the new industrial capitalism.
6. The critics of the new industrial capitalism, and the solutions they proposed.
7. The condition of immigrants, women, and children in the work force.
8. The rise of organized labor on a national federated basis.
9. The reasons why organized labor generally failed in its efforts to achieve its objectives.

Pertinent Questions

Sources of Industrial Growth (pp. 487–495)

1. What technological innovations of the late nineteenth century were important for communications and business organization?
2. What impact did the increasingly widespread use of electricity as a source of light and power have on homes and industry?
3. What new methods were developed for the large-scale production of durable steel? Where were the principal American centers of steel production and ore extraction?

4. Describe the beginnings of the oil industry in the United States. What was the main use of petroleum at first?
5. Although the age of the automobile would not fully arrive until the 1910s and 1920s, what developments of the 1890s and early 1900s laid the basis for the later boom?
6. What was the most important change in production technology?
7. How did the rapidly expanding railroads of this era contribute to the expansion of the American economy?
8. What legal and financial advantages does the corporation form of enterprise offer to business and investors?
9. Compare and contrast the vertical and horizontal integration strategies of business combination. Which approaches did Andrew Carnegie and John D. Rockefeller utilize? What "curse" of the business world was consolidation designed to attack?
10. What were the consequences of the consolidation movement?

Capitalism and Its Critics (pp. 495–500)

11. What kept alive the "self-made man" hopes of the American masses? How realistic were those dreams?
12. How did Social Darwinism seem to justify the acquisition of great wealth?
13. Who were the leading proponents of vigorous governmental action to reform industrial society, and what visions did they have?
14. What inspired the increasing resentment of monopoly by many groups?

The Ordeal of the Worker (pp. 500–509)

15. America's new urban working class was drawn primarily from what two groups?
16. Contrast the earlier immigrants to the United States with those who came after the 1880s. What attracted immigrants to the United States?
17. What were the uncertainties and hazards of industrial labor?
18. Why did industry increasingly employ women and children? How were they treated?
19. What was America's first major labor conflict and how did it end? What did it symbolize?
20. Compare and contrast the organization, membership, leadership, and programs of the Knights of Labor and the American Federation of Labor. Why did the AFL succeed, while the Knights disappeared?

21. Compare and contrast the Haymarket affair, Homestead strike, and Pullman strike. On balance, what was their effect on the organized labor movement?
22. What factors combined to help explain why organized labor remained relatively weak before World War I?

IDENTIFICATION

Identify each of the following, and explain why it is important within the context of the chapter.

1. Alexander Graham Bell
2. Thomas A. Edison
3. Guglielmo Marconi
4. Orville Wright and Wilbur Wright
5. Charles Duryea and Frank Duryea
6. Henry Ford
7. Frederick Winslow Taylor
8. Cornelius Vanderbilt
9. J. P. Morgan
10. "middle manager"
11. pool (cartel)
12. trust
13. holding company
14. Herbert Spencer
15. William Graham Sumner
16. "gospel of wealth"
17. Horatio Alger
18. Daniel DeLeon
19. Socialist Labor Party
20. Henry George
21. Edward Bellamy
22. Molly Maguires
23. Samuel Gompers
24. anarchism
25. Eugene V. Debs
26. John P. Altgeld

Document

Read the sections of the text under the headings "Survival of the Fittest" and "The Gospel of Wealth." The great industrialist Andrew Carnegie built his fortune on steel, but he also built a lasting reputation as a philanthropist because he spent millions of dollars on the establishment of libraries. Carnegie's *Gospel of Wealth* was a call for other rich people to share their wealth with the worthy poor. Consider the following questions: How does Carnegie's view exemplify Social Darwinism? What is the essence of Carnegie's argument against socialism? On what social values and assumptions about human nature was the gospel of wealth based?

> The price which society pays for the law of competition, like the price it pays for cheap comforts and luxuries, is also great; but the advantages of this law are also greater still for it is to this law that we owe our wonderful material development, which brings improved conditions in its train. But, whether the law be benign or not, we must say of it as we say of the change in the conditions of men to which we have referred: It is here; we cannot evade it; no substitutes for it have been found; and while the law may be sometimes hard for the individual, it is best for the race, because it insures the survival of the fittest in every department. We accept and welcome, therefore, as conditions to which we must accommodate ourselves, great inequality of environment, the concentration of business, industrial and commercial, in the hands of a few, and the law of competition between these, as being not only beneficial, but essential for the future progress of the race....
>
> Objections to the foundations upon which society is based are not in order, because the condition of the race is better with these than it has been with any others which have been tried. Of the effect of any new substitutes proposed we cannot be sure. The Socialist or Anarchist who seeks to overturn present conditions is to be regarded as attacking the foundation upon which civilization itself rests, for civilization took its start from the day that the capable, industrious workman said to his incompetent and lazy fellow, "If dost not sew, thou shalt not reap," and thus ended primitive Communism by separating the drones from the bees. One who studies this subject will soon be brought face to face with the conclusion that upon the sacredness of property civilization *itself* depends—the right of the laborer to his hundred dollars in the savings bank, and equally the legal right of the millionaire to his millions....
>
> This, then, is held to be the duty of the man of Wealth: First, to set an example of modest, unostentatious living, shunning display or extravagance; to provide moderately for the legitimate wants of those dependent upon him; and after doing so to consider all surplus revenues which come to him simply as trust funds, which he is called upon to administer, and strictly bound as a matter of duty to administer in the manner which, in his judgment, is best calculated to produce the most beneficial results for the community—the man of wealth thus becoming the mere agent and trustee for his poorer brethren, bringing to their service his superior wisdom, experience, and ability to administer, doing for them better than they would or could do for themselves.

Andrew Carnegie, *The Gospel of Wealth* (1889).

Map Exercise

Fill in or identify the following on the blank map provided.

1. Area of the early iron and steel industry.
2. Region of the early petroleum industry.

Interpretative Questions

Based on what you have filled in, answer the following. For some of the questions you will need to consult the narrative in your text for information or explanation.

1. Why did the Pullman railroad strike in the Chicago area disrupt the national transportation system to the extent that it did?
2. What factors combined to make the region from Pittsburgh to Chicago into America's industrial heartland?

Summary

Although some economists place the industrial "takeoff" of America in the years before the Civil War, it was in the three decades following that great conflict that the United States became the world's leading industrial power. A fortunate combination of sufficient raw materials, adequate labor, enviable technological accomplishments, effective business leadership, nationwide markets, and supportive state and national governments boosted America past its international rivals. The industrial transformation had a profound impact on the lives of the millions of workers who made the production revolution possible. Some who were distrustful of industrial power turned toward socialism, others tried to organize workers into powerful unions. But in these early years of industrial conflict, the forces of business usually triumphed.

CHAPTER SELF-TEST

After you have read the chapter in the text and done the exercises in the Study Guide, the following self-test can be taken to see if you understand the material you have covered. Answers appear at the end of the Study Guide.

Multiple Choice

Circle the letter of the response which best answers the question or completes the statement.

1. The two methods of transforming iron into steel that emerged in the 1850s and 1860s were:
   a. the Cyrus-Field method and the air-jet process.
   b. the Bessemer-Kelly method and the open-hearth process.
   c. the Ritty-Scholes method and the molten-pot process.
   d. the Duryea-Thomas method and the ferrous-oxide process.

2. In the nineteenth century, the early petroleum industry concentrated in what states?
   a. Oklahoma, Texas, and Louisiana.
   b. California and Arizona.
   c. New York and New Jersey.
   d. Pennsylvania, Ohio, and West Virginia.
   e. Illinois, Wisconsin, and Michigan.

3. The production of gasoline-powered automobiles began in the United States during the:
   a. 1870s.
   b. 1880s.
   c. 1890s.
   d. 1900s.
   e. 1910s.

4. Frederick Winslow Taylor's theory of "scientific management" advocated:
   a. making the work place pleasant so that workers would have a good attitude and therefore be more productive.
   b. dividing workers into teams and having each team produce the entire product so that the workers would have a sense of pride.
   c. reorganizing the production process by subdividing tasks to speed up production and reduce the dependency on highly skilled workers.
   d. having employees assemble components at home, then bring them to the factory and be paid by the piece.

5. The popularization of mass production by moving assembly line is generally credited to:
   a. Henry Ford and the automobile industry.
   b. Guglielmo Marconi and the radio industry.
   c. the Wright Brothers and the airplane industry.
   d. William S. Burroughs and the adding machine industry.
   e. Charles F. Brush and the street light industry.

6. What legal principle was crucial to the ability of corporations to sell large amounts of stock to investors not directly involved in the business?
   a. sovereign immunity.
   b. limited liability.
   c. joint tenancy.
   d. habeas corpus.
   e. power of attorney.

7. Andrew Carnegie built his dominance in the steel industry by which business integration strategy?
   a. vertical.
   b. horizontal.
   c. angular.
   d. radical.

8. The enormously influential New York City banker who helped perfect the trust and created United States Steel from Carnegie Steel was:
   a. Commodore Vanderbilt.
   b. Gustavus Swift.
   c. Averill Harriman.
   d. John D. Rockefeller.
   e. J. P. Morgan

9. Horatio Alger was famous for his books that:
   a. told of poor boys who found success through hard work, perseverance, and luck.
   b. argued that natural selection and survival of the fittest controlled the economic world as well as the natural world.
   c. proposed the "single tax" on unearned increment property as a panacea for the country's economic problems.
   d. described a utopian social order discovered in the year 2000 by a man who went into a hypnotic sleep in 1889.

10. In the late nineteenth century, the majority of working children were employed in:
    a. railroads.
    b. factories.
    c. agriculture.
    d. mining.
    e. domestic service.

11. The nation's first major national labor conflict was the:
    a. 1868 steel strike.
    b. 1872 coal strike.
    c. 1877 railroad strike.
    d. 1884 textile strike.
    e. 1893 oil strike.

12. The nation's first genuinely national labor organization was the:
    a. National Union of Workers.
    b. Knights of Labor.
    c. American Federation of Labor.
    d. Congress of Industrial Organizations.
    e. Industrial Workers of the World.

13. The leader of the American Federation of Labor in the 1880s and 1890s was:
    a. Terence V. Powderly.
    b. Cyrus McCormick.
    c. Henry Clay Frick.
    d. Samuel Gompers.
    e. Eugene V. Debs.

14. In the mind of middle-class Americans, the code word for the labor radicalism and violence of the 1880s and 1890s was:
    a. communism.
    b. anarchism.

c. socialism.
   d. liberalism.
   e. vigilantism.
15. The *two* major strikes of the 1890s which were marred by violence and which tainted the image of unions in public opinion were the (choose two letters):
   a. Homestead steel strike.
   b. Pinkerton textile strike.
   c. Molly McGuire coal strike.
   d. Pullman railroad strike.
   e. Drake oil strike.

True/False

Read each statement carefully. Mark true statements "T" and false statements "F."

1. The principal use of petroleum in the late nineteenth century was oil for lubrication of machines rather than fuel.
2. Due to overbuilding, the number of miles of railroad track in the United States actually declined from 1880 to 1900.
3. John D. Rockefeller began building Standard Oil by concentrating on the refining stage of the petroleum industry.
4. Although the term "trust" technically referred to a specific form of business organization, the term came to be generally applied to any great economic combination.
5. In the developing economy of the late nineteenth century the majority of the business tycoons personified the "rags to riches" rise to wealth and power.
6. The "Gospel of Wealth" referred to the idea that the rich had a responsibility to use their money to promote social progress.
7. The theory of Social Darwinism argued that great concentrations of wealth in the late nineteenth century violated the principles of evolution and that a great economic collapse was inevitable.
8. Worker frustration with the problems of monopoly led to the formation of the Socialist Labor Party, which elected several congressmen from northeastern urban areas.
9. By the 1890s more women were employed in factories than as domestic workers.
10. Most European immigrants who came to the United States up to the 1880s arrived from northern Europe and the British Isles (Germany, England, Ireland, etc.), but by 1900 southern and east-

ern Europeans (Italians, Poles, Russians, Greeks, Slavs, etc.) dominated.
11. In general, railroads, mining companies, and industrial employers tried to discourage the immigration of workers from Europe.
12. With a very few exceptions, in the period 1870 to 1910 women were prohibited from working in factories.
13. The American Federation of Labor stressed the idea of "one big union" for all workers while the Knights of Labor was a coalition of individual craft unions.
14. Grover Cleveland refused to use federal troops in labor conflicts because he regarded such incidents as state matters.
15. Many European immigrants came to the United States intending to work for a few years to earn some money and then return to Europe.

Review Questions

These questions are to be answered with essays. This will allow you to explore relationships among individuals, events, and attitudes of the period under review.

1. Name the half-dozen main factors that combined to produce America's impressive rise to industrial supremacy and explain how they did so.
2. Both the success-oriented novels of Horatio Alger and the utopian works of Edward Bellamy were bestsellers in late-nineteenth-century America. What might explain the seeming contradiction between Americans' desire to read about how great their country was and their desire to read about how much it needed to improve?
3. The so-called "robber barons" both praised unfettered free enterprise and tried to eliminate competition. How can these apparently conflicting positions be reconciled?

CHAPTER EIGHTEEN
The Age of the City

OBJECTIVES

A thorough study of Chapter 18 should enable you to understand:

1. The patterns and processes of urbanization in late-nineteenth-century America.
2. The changes in the pattern of immigration in the late nineteenth century.
3. The new economic and social problems caused by urbanization.
4. The relationships of both urbanization and immigration to the rise of boss rule.
5. The early rise of mass consumption and its impact on American life, especially for women.
6. The changes in leisure and entertainment opportunities including organized sports, vaudeville, movies, and other activities.
7. The main trends in literature and art during the Gilded Age and early twentieth century.
8. The impact of the Darwinian theory of evolution on the intellectual life of America.
9. The profound new developments in American educational opportunities.

PERTINENT QUESTIONS

The New Urban Growth (pp. 510–521)

1. Compare and contrast rural and urban population growth from 1860 to 1910. What was the attraction of the city, and what were the main sources of urban growth?
2. What sort of jobs did blacks usually hold in cities?
3. How did the typical immigrants of the 1890s and later differ from most of the earlier immigrants?

4. How diverse was the immigration to the United States from 1860–1900?
5. What social institutions and community actions helped facilitate immigrants' adjustment to urban life in America? Which groups adapted especially well economically?
6. What attitudes and actions characterized the assimilation of first- and second-generation European immigrants? How is this process reflected in the Jewish immigrant memory in "American Voices" (page 513)?
7. What groups faced special barriers to success? What groups had advantages?
8. What organizations and laws resulted from the resentment that many native-born Americans felt toward the new immigrants? What effect did the laws have?
9. Compare and contrast the residential patterns of the wealthy and moderately well-to-do urbanites with those of the majority.
10. Describe the evolution of urban transportation technology from omnibus to electric trolley.
11. Describe the urban hazards of fire, disease, and sanitation and the public and private responses to them.
12. What factors contributed to the rise of political machines and their bosses? What were the positive as well as the negative aspects of boss rule in large cities?

Society and Culture in Urbanizing America (pp. 521–528)

13. Describe the changes in income and purchasing power of the urban middle and working classes. Who made the greater gains? Who lagged behind?
14. What changes led to the "new consumerism" for urban dwellers in the late nineteenth and early twentieth century?
15. Compare and contrast the rise of baseball with that of football. What other spectator sports became popular as Americans came to enjoy more leisure time?
16. What were the main sorts of popular entertainment available to urban dwellers of the late nineteenth and early twentieth centuries? How did leisure activities bring people together? What barriers remained?
17. What important changes occurred in journalism and publishing in the decades after the Civil War?

High Culture in the Urban Age (pp. 528–534)

18. What issues did the realist novelists explore? Who were the leading realists.
19. By 1900, what developments in American visual art were becoming evident?
20. How did Darwinism challenge traditional American faith and contribute to the growing schism between urban and rural values?
21. Describe the evolution of free public schooling in the United States. What parts of the nation lagged in education?
22. What government and private actions combined to lead the establishment or significant expansion of universities and colleges after the Civil War?
23. What opportunities for higher education were available to women in this era? What were the distinctive characteristics of the women's colleges, and how did they reflect other changes in women's organizations?

IDENTIFICATION

Identify each of the following, and explain why it is important within the context of the chapter.

1. "immigrant ghettoes"
2. Reform Judaism
3. tenement
4. "skyscraper"
5. William M. Tweed
6. "white collar" workers
7. "chain stores"
8. Cincinnati Red Stockings
9. James A. Naismith
10. Florenz Ziegfeld
11. minstrel shows
12. D. W. Griffith
13. "dime novels"
14. William Randolph Hearst
15. local-color writers
16. modernism
17. pragmatism

18. Carlisle School
19. "land grant" colleges

DOCUMENT

Read the section of the text under the heading "The Urban Landscape," and then read the excerpt below, taken from *How the Other Half Lives* (1890), the famous book by Joseph Riis. Consider the following questions: What comparisons could be made between the poor neighborhood of the late nineteenth century and that of today? What insights on assimilation does Riis offer?

> When once I asked the agent of a notorious Fourth Ward alley how many people might be living in it I was told: one hundred and forty families, one hundred Irish, thirty-eight Italian, and two that spoke the German tongue. Barring the agent herself, there was not a native-born individual in the court. The answer was characteristic of the cosmopolitan character of lower New York, very nearly so of the whole of it, wherever it runs to alleys and courts. One may find for the asking an Italian, a German, a French, African, Spanish, Bohemian, Russian, Scandinavian, Jewish, and Chinese colony. Even the Arab, who peddles "holy earth" from the Battery as a direct importation from Jerusalem, has exclusive preserves at the lower end of Washington Street. The one thing you shall vainly ask for in the chief city of America is a distinctively American community. There is none; certainly not among the tenements....
>
> The once-unwelcome Irishman has been followed in his turn by the Italian, the Russian Jew, and the Chinaman, and has himself taken a hand at opposition, quite as bitter and quite as ineffectual, against these later hordes. Wherever these have gone they have crowded him out, possessing the block, the street, the ward with their denser swarms....
>
> A map of the city, colored to designate nationalities, would show more stripes than the skin of a zebra, and more colors than any rainbow.

Jacob Riis, *How the Other Half Lives.*

MAP EXERCISE

Fill in or identify the following on the blank map provided.

1. Urban population centers of over one-half million (500,000) in 1900.
2. Smaller but more important regional cities: Buffalo; Cleveland; Detroit; Washington, D.C.; Atlanta; New Orleans; Memphis; Minneapolis; Cincinnati; Louisville; Kansas City; Dallas; Houston; Denver; Seattle; San Francisco; and Los Angeles.
3. The area of heaviest industrial concentration.

Interpretative Questions

Based on what you have filled in, answer the following. For some of the questions you will need to consult the narrative in your text for information or explanation.

1. Explain the relationships among railroads, industry, and large cities.
2. In what part of the nation and specifically in what large cities did the bulk of the post-1880 foreign immigrants settle?
3. Within the area indicated by the map as settled, which well-populated region of the country was most lacking in large cities of 100,000 or more? Why?
4. Note that all of the major urban areas of the late twentieth century were already established by 1900. What does this indicate about the maturity of the national economic and transportation system by the turn of the century?

SUMMARY

In the years after the Civil War, America's cities boomed as people left the rural areas of Europe and the United States to seek jobs and other attractions offered by American cities. The cities' rapid growth caused many problems in housing, transportation, and health. Technological attacks on these problems barely kept pace, and city governments often resorted to boss rule to cope. Immigrant groups fought for economic success, but groups that faced strong prejudices found it more difficult to advance than groups that did not. In addition to offering a new consumerism for many residents, the booming cities were places of intellectual ferment and cultural change. Many Americans wanted to prove to skeptical Europeans that the nation had cultural as well as economic accomplishments to admire. At the same time, American art and literature often continued to imitate European models. American culture became more uniform through compulsory education, mass-market journalism, and standardized sports.

CHAPTER SELF-TEST

After you have read the chapter in the text and done the exercises in the Study Guide, the following self-test can be taken to see if you understand the material you have covered. Answers appear at the end of the Study Guide.

Multiple Choice

Circle the letter of the response which best answers the question or completes the statement.

1. Because of rapid growth in the latter nineteenth century, American cities:
   a. protected traditional social and cultural values.
   b. provided services and facilities inadequate to demands.
   c. witnessed the flight of factories and corporate offices to newer, less crowded locations.
   d. supported efficient and honest governments.

2. An important population trend that occurred in the United States from 1860 to 1910 was:
   a. a gradual decline of the rural population.
   b. the mass movement of the urban population from city centers to suburbs.
   c. a population shift from the North to the South.
   d. a faster rate of growth for the cities than for the general population.

3. The movement of blacks from the rural South to industrial cities began during the latter nineteenth century because of the:
   a. poverty and oppression of the South.
   b. prospective professional opportunities in the cities.
   c. abundance of factory jobs in the North for blacks.
   d. lack of racial discrimination in the North.

4. The new immigrants of the latter nineteenth century settled primarily in Eastern industrial cities because they:
   a. lacked the capital to buy land and begin farming in the West.
   b. found immediate employment as unskilled factory workers.
   c. found refuge and camaraderie among fellow nationals there.
   d. all of the above.

5. The formation of ethnic neighborhoods by immigrants in American cities:
   a. tended to reinforce the cultural values of their previous societies.
   b. resulted from discriminatory zoning restrictions.
   c. prevented their identification with and advancement in American society.
   d. intensified a sense of not belonging to a coherent community.

6. Nativist reaction against European immigrants of the latter nineteenth century resulted from all of the following factors *except* the:
   a. arrival of such vast numbers of immigrants.
   b. refusal of most immigrant groups to try to assimilate themselves into American culture.
   c. generalized fears and prejudices against foreigners.
   d. economic concern that immigrant workers would threaten the wages and positions of American workers.

7. Which of the following was *not* a trend contributing to the rise of mass consumption in latter nineteenth century America?
   a. The emergence of ready-made clothing as a basis of the American wardrobe.
   b. The breakup of marketing monopolies held by national chain stores.
   c. The development of canned food and refrigerated railroad cars.
   d. The emergence of great department stores and mail-order houses.

8. The emergence of national press services in the latter nineteenth century contributed most significantly to:
   a. increased salaries for reporters.
   b. standardization of the news product.

c. separation of news from opinions.
   d. a professional identity for American journalists.

9. The role of advertising in American commercial life of the latter nineteenth century increasingly became one of:
   a. stimulating demand and creating new markets.
   b. public information and service.
   c. sponsorship of mass entertainment.
   d. endorsing national cultural values.

10. The theory of evolution:
    a. supported traditional American beliefs about the nature of man and history.
    b. met persistent resistance from middle-class Protestant religious leaders.
    c. gained greater acceptance in rural rather than urban areas.
    d. influenced new ways of thinking in the social sciences.

11. According to the philosophy of pragmatism, modern society should rely for guidance on:
    a. inherited ideals.
    b. scientific inquiry.
    c. moral principles.
    d. religious beliefs.

12. The movement in art (and in other areas of American culture) that rejected heavy reliance on established forms, embraced new ideas, and often glorified the ordinary was called:
    a. genteelism.
    b. realism.
    c. symbolism.
    d. modernism.

13. Which of the following trends in American education did *not* take place in the latter nineteenth century?
    a. The spread of universal free public education.
    b. Passage by states of compulsory attendance laws.
    c. Rapid proliferation of the nation's colleges.
    d. Increased emphasis on the classical curriculum at the university level.

14. Educational opportunities for women expanded in the post-Civil War era as:
    a. states used the Morrill Land Grant Act to create schools for women.
    b. a growing network of women's colleges resulted primarily from philanthropic donations.
    c. most state college systems promoted an ideal of coeducation.
    d. private universities admitted female students in a drive for sexual egalitarianism.
15. The Carlisle School was dedicated to the education of:
    a. women.
    b. Roman Catholics.
    c. American Indians.
    d. African Americans.

True/False

Read each statement carefully. Mark true statements "T" and false statements "F."

1. Urban black males in the late nineteenth century usually held skilled industrial jobs.
2. European immigrants to the United States, especially second- and third-generation individuals, staunchly resisted assimilation into the dominant culture.
3. The political bosses and the machines they operated were usually more popular with the people in the poor and working-class neighborhoods of the large cities.
4. The working class made greater income and lifestyle gains in the late nineteenth century than did the middle class.
5. In the Gilded Age and the early twentieth century, baseball was more important as a college and university sport, and football was mainly played by professionals.
6. Realist novelists tended to explore and write about the seamy side of life.
7. American art around the turn of the century focused mainly on landscape painting that celebrated the natural environment.
8. Darwinism was opposed by all organized Christian religious groups.
9. Because of the lack of private schools available, the South led the nation in the establishment of tax-supported public schools for all children.

10. By granting large amounts of land to state governments, the federal government encouraged states to establish universities and colleges that would emphasize practical learning, especially in agriculture and mechanics.
11. Local-color writers concentrated on the racial issues that troubled America.
12. Minstrel shows laid the foundation for the emergence of serious symphony orchestras in the early twentieth century.
13. D. W. Griffith was a pioneer in the production of motion pictures.
14. Jacob Riis was a journalist whose stories about life in urban slums helped inspire reformers.
15. William Randolph Hearst was the founder of the "reform" movement within Judaism.

Review Questions

These questions are to be answered with essays. This will allow you to explore relationships among individuals, events, and attitudes of the period under review.

1. What factors combined to attract the great masses of people to the cities of America? What were the characteristics of these migrants?
2. Describe the problems created by the stunning pace at which American cities were growing. How well did the institutions of urban life respond to these problems?
3. Much of the serious art and literature of the late nineteenth and early twentieth centuries functioned as social criticism. Was the supposedly realistic criticism based on a balanced view of America's new urban culture?

CHAPTER NINETEEN
From Stalemate to Crisis

OBJECTIVES

A thorough study of Chapter 19 should enable you to understand:

1. The limited role of the federal government and the nature of American party politics in the last third of the nineteenth century.
2. The problems of political patronage in the administrations of Rutherford B. Hayes, James A. Garfield, and Chester A. Arthur that led to the passage of the Pendleton Act.
3. The circumstances that permitted the Democrats to gain control of the presidency in the elections of 1884 and 1892.
4. The origins, purposes, and effectiveness of the Interstate Commerce Act and the Sherman Antitrust Act.
5. The position of the two major parties on the tariff question, and the actual trend of tariff legislation in the 1880s and 1890s.
6. The rise of agrarian discontent as manifested in the Granger movement, the Farmers' Alliances, and the Populist movement.
7. The rise of the silver question from the Crime of '73 through the Gold Standard Act of 1900.
8. The significance of the presidential campaign and election of 1896.

PERTINENT QUESTIONS

The Politics of Equilibrium (pp. 535–544)

1. How well balanced were the two major political parties between the Civil War and the turn of the century—especially from the mid-1870s to the early 1890s?
2. What explains the extraordinary loyalty that voters showed to their political parties in this period?
3. What regional, religious, and ethnic factors distinguished the two major parties?

4. What was the patronage system, and how did it dominate national politics in the 1870s and 1880s?
5. How was James A. Garfield a victim of the spoils (patronage) system?
6. What was the key issue in the 1888 presidential election? How was this campaign different from typical Gilded Age fare? What was done about the issue during the Benjamin Harrison administration? How did the same issue affect the 1890 and 1892 elections?
7. What led to passage of the Sherman Antitrust Act? What practical impact did it have?
8. What caused the demise of the state-based railroad regulation? How was the demise related to the passage of the Interstate Commerce Act?
9. Why was the Interstate Commerce Commission so ineffectual?

The Agrarian Revolt (pp. 544–548)

10. Explain the evolution of purpose and the accomplishments of the Grange. Why did it eventually fail?
11. How did the Farmers' Alliance become transformed into the People's Party?
12. Who was most attracted to Populism? Why did the movement fail to obtain significant labor support?
13. What doomed the possibilities for effective biracial cooperation among Populists?
14. What did the Populists stand for and what were their leaders like? How, according to "Debating the Past" (page 557), have historians differed in their interpretations of Populism?

The Crisis of the 1890s (pp. 548–556)

15. What were the immediate and long-range causes of the Panic of 1893? How serious was the depression that followed?
16. What developments after 1873 led to the coalition of farmers and miners on behalf of silver coinage?
17. Explain the debate over the gold standard. How did it divide the Democratic party?
18. How did the nomination of William Jennings Bryan as the Democratic presidential candidate in 1896 put the Populists in a dilemma? How did they resolve it, and what was the result?
19. Describe the passions of the 1896 campaign. Where did Bryan do well? Why did he lose?

20. How did President William McKinley handle the bimetallism question? What happened during his administration to help resolve the issue?

IDENTIFICATION

Identify each of the following, and explain why it is important within the context of the chapter.
1. "The Gilded Age"
2. Civil War pensions
3. James G. Blaine
4. "rum, romanism, and rebellion"
5. James B. Weaver
6. Granger Laws
7. "Colored Alliances"
8. Coxey's Army
9. 16:1
10. "Crime of '73"
11. "cross of gold"
12. Tom Watson

DOCUMENT

Probably the clearest expression of Populist goals was the Omaha platform of 1892, from which the section below is taken. In light of this document, the text narrative, and the "Debating the Past" section on Populism, consider the following questions: Were the Populist demands reasonable and rational responses to the problems facing the Populist constituency? What elements of socialism can be found in the Populist program? How was the platform designed as an attempt to broaden the appeal of Populism beyond farmers?

We declare, therefore—

First.—That the union of the labor forces of the United States this day consummated shall be permanent and perpetual; may its spirit enter into all hearts for the salvation of the Republic and the uplifting of mankind.

Second.—Wealth belongs to him who creates it, and every dollar taken from industry without an equivalent is robbery. "If any will not work, neither shall he eat." The interests of rural and civil labor are the same; their enemies are identical.

Third.—We believe that the time has come when the railroad corporations will either own the people or the people must own the railroads; and should the government enter upon the work of owning and managing all railroads, we should favor an amendment to the constitution by which all persons engaged in government service shall be placed under a civil-service regulation of the most rigid character, so as to prevent the increase of power of the national administration by the use of such additional government employees.

FINANCE.—We demand a national currency, safe, sound, and flexible, issued by the general government only, a full legal tender for all debts, public and private, and that without the use of banking corporations; a just, equitable, and efficient means of distribution direct to the people, at a tax not to exceed 2 per cent, per annum, to be provided as set forth in the subtreasury plan of the Farmers' Alliance, or a better system; also by payments in discharge of its obligations for public improvements.

1. We demand free and unlimited coinage of silver and gold at the present legal ratio of 16 to 1.
2. We demand that the amount of circulating medium be speedily increased to not less than $50 per capita.
3. We demand a graduated income tax.
4. We believe that the money of the country should be kept as much as possible in the hands of the people, and hence we demand that all State and national revenues shall be limited to the necessary expenses of the government, economically and honestly administered.
5. We demand that postal savings banks be established by the government for the safe deposit of the earnings of the people and to facilitate exchange.

TRANSPORTATION.—Transportation being a means of exchange and a public necessity, the government should own and operate the railroads in the interest of the people. The telegraph and telephone, like the post-office system, being a necessity for the transportation of news, should be owned and operated by the government in the interest of the people.

LAND.—The land, including all the natural sources of wealth, is the heritage of the people, and should not be monopolized for speculative purposes, and alien ownership of land should be prohibited. All land now held by railroads and other corporations in excess of their actual needs, and all lands now owned by aliens; should be reclaimed by the government and held for actual settlers only.

Omaha Platform of the Populist Party, 1892.

Map Exercise

Fill in or identify the following on the blank map provided.

1. The Great Plains, the silver mining regions, and the cotton-tobacco belt.
2. Territories not yet states as of 1896.
3. States carried by Bryan.

Interpretative Questions

Based on what you have filled in, answer the following. For some of the questions, you will need to consult the narrative in your text for information or explanation.

1. Where was the Grange strongest? In what parts of the country did the Populist movement have the most impact? Why?
2. Why were the states carried by Bryan mainly those of the Great Plains, the silver mining regions, and the cotton-tobacco belt? Why did he fail to make inroads in the Midwest and Northeast?

SUMMARY

Close elections and shifting control of the White House and Congress characterized the politics of the period from 1876 to 1900. Regional, ethnocultural, and economic factors helped determine party affiliation, and elections often turned on considerations of personality. But there were real issues, too. Tariff, currency, and civil-service questions arose in almost every election. Discontented farmers in the People's party briefly challenged the Republicans and Democrats, but the two-party system remained intact and the role of the federal government remained limited.

The election of 1896, the great battle between the gold standard and the silver standard, firmly established the Republican party as the majority party in the United States. Agrarian and mining interests were unable to convince voters that currency inflation through the free coinage of silver would lead the nation out of the depression of the 1890s. By fusing with the Democrats, the Populists ended any chance they might have had to become a major force in American politics. By the end of the nineteenth century, business forces had triumphed. They had secured a gold-based currency and a rigorously protective tariff. Efforts to regulate railroads and trusts were halfhearted to begin with and were weakened even further by court decisions.

CHAPTER SELF-TEST

After you have read the chapter in the text and done the exercises in the Study Guide, the following self-test can be taken to see if you understand the material you have covered. Answers appear at the end of the Study Guide.

Multiple Choice

Circle the letter of the response which best answers the question or completes the statement.

1. Which of the following Americans would likely have voted Republican in the latter nineteenth century?
   a. white Southern farmer.
   b. Northern Protestant industrialist.
   c. Catholic immigrant merchant.
   d. poor urban factory worker.

2. Following the Civil War, the leaders of both political parties seemed most concerned with:
   a. resolving the dispute between protectionists and advocates of free trade.
   b. providing inflation of the money supply.
   c. curbing the growing power of big business.
   d. winning elections and controlling patronage.

3. The Sherman Antitrust Act of 1890 was:
   a. passed by a narrow margin after a long and bitter debate in Congress.
   b. immediately successful in halting the trend toward business monopolization.

c. intended by Congress to restructure the economy.
   d. virtually emasculated by hostile court decisions.
4. The Interstate Commerce Act of 1887 provided for:
   a. nominal government supervision of the railroads, designed principally to satisfy the popular clamor for reform.
   b. discrimination in railroad rates between long and short hauls.
   c. an objective standard to determine the extent to which railroad rates were "reasonable and just."
   d. an Interstate Commerce Commission with a clear authority to fix railroad rates.
5. Jacob S. Coxey:
   a. led a march on Washington to protest the depression of the 1890s and to make demands.
   b. organized Farmers' Alliance Chapters across the South and Midwest.
   c. masterminded William McKinley's political career.
   d. wrote dozens of short novels about how millionaires went from "rags to riches."
   e. directed a massive public works program.
   f. advocated a reduction of the tariff.
6. Which of the following groups of the latter nineteenth century would *not* have favored an inflationary policy of "free silver" by the government?
   a. bankers.
   b. silver miners.
   c. farmers.
   d. debtors.
7. Helping William Jennings Bryan win the 1896 Democratic nomination for president was his:
   a. long record of distinguished congressional service.
   b. connection with the urban political machines.
   c. loyal defense of the Cleveland administration.
   d. dramatic "Cross of Gold" speech.
8. In the election of 1896, the Populists:
   a. named their own candidate and thus split the protest vote.
   b. approved William Jennings Bryan but nominated their own vice-presidential candidate.

214 ~ Chapter Nineteen

    c. accepted complete "fusion" with the Democrats.
    d. lost much of their thunder with the adoption of a conservative platform.

9. William Jennings Bryan, in the election of 1896, was the first presidential candidate to:
    a. systematically "stump" every section of the nation.
    b. rely on a "front porch" strategy in meeting the voters.
    c. turn over management of his campaign to a political boss.
    d. raise over $5 million worth of campaign contributions.

10. In politics, "patronage" generally refers to:
    a. the tendency of politicians to talk down to the voters.
    b. the system of fixed bids, kickbacks, and bribes that officeholders took from constituents.
    c. the way that wealthy industrialists controlled the legislators.
    d. the process of awarding government jobs to supporters of the winning party.

11. The key issue debated in the 1888 presidential election campaign was:
    a. monopoly.
    b. tariff.
    c. civil service.
    d. race.

12. The Grange organization was designed to help:
    a. farmers.
    b. industrial workers.
    c. former slaves.
    d. recent immigrants.

13. The so-called "Crime of '73" referred to:
    a. corruption in the Grant administration.
    b. the government decision to stop coining silver.
    c. the creation of the railroad monopoly.
    d. the removal of the barrier to Catholic immigration.

14. The "ratio of 16:1," which was important to the politics of the 1890s, referred to:
    a. the number of poor people for every one middle class person.
    b. the way that southern states counted African Americans for the purposes of determining congressional representation.
    c. the profit that railroads made for each ton carried.
    d. the value of silver compared to the value of gold.

15. The Populists advocated:
    a. abolition of the income tax.
    b. stricter regulation of railroads.
    c. government ownership of all factories.
    d. the end of currency inflation.

True/False

Read each statement carefully. Mark true statements "T" and false statements "F."

1. The Republican party controlled both houses of Congress and the Presidency for all but four years from 1876 to 1896.
2. Electoral turnout of eligible voters in the Gilded Age tended to be lower than it is today.
3. The assassination of William McKinley by an office seeker provided impetus to the passage of the Civil Service Act.
4. In general, Grover Cleveland favored lower tariffs.
5. The Sherman Antitrust Act applied initially only to railroads.
6. The so-called "Granger Laws" provided for state government regulation of railroads.
7. The federal courts often overturned decisions of the Interstate Commerce Commission.
8. The Farmers' Alliance organization provided the foundation from which the Populist Party emerged.
9. There was a separate Farmers' Alliance organization, affiliated with the larger group, for African American farmers.
10. The Populists sought to build ties with industrial workers but were generally unsuccessful in doing so.
11. Some southern Populists tried to build political connections with black farmers, but the efforts did not prove lasting.
12. Among the causes of the Panic of 1893 was the overexpansion of railroad construction.
13. Most industrialized nations of the world recognized *both* gold and silver as backing for their monetary systems.
14. Although the Populists agreed with William Jennings Bryan on the silver issue, they refused to endorse him in 1896 because it would have meant the loss of their identity.
15. In the 1896 election, William Jennings Bryan carried most of his votes from the farming areas of the midwest and mid-Atlantic states.

Review Questions

These questions are to be answered with essays. This will allow you to explore relationships among individuals, events, and attitudes of the period under review.

1. How much policy difference was there between the Republicans and the Democrats in the Gilded Age? What other factors distinguished the parties?
2. Compare and contrast the three major farm groups: the Grange, the Farmers' Alliances, and the Populists. Do you agree with historians who believe that Populism was a reasonable and realistic response to agrarian grievances?
3. In a series of cases, including the *Wabash* case and *United States v. E.C. Knight Company,* the United States Supreme Court severely restricted all efforts to regulate business. What logic did the Court use in these cases, and what effect did the decisions have on congressional action and on business?

Chapter Twenty
The Imperial Republic

OBJECTIVES

A thorough study of Chapter 20 should enable you to understand:

1. The new Manifest Destiny, and how it differed from the old Manifest Destiny.
2. The objectives of American foreign policy at the turn of the century with respect to Europe, Latin America, and Asia.
3. The variety of factors that motivated the United States to become imperialistic.
4. The relationship between American economic interests, especially tariff policy, and developments in Hawaii and Cuba.
5. The causes of the Spanish-American War.
6. The military problems encountered in fighting the Spanish and, subsequently, the Filipinos.
7. The problems involved in developing a colonial administration for America's new empire.
8. The motives behind the Open Door notes and the Boxer intervention.
9. The nature of the military reforms carried out by Elihu Root following the Spanish-American War.

PERTINENT QUESTIONS

Stirrings of Imperialism (pp. 559–565)

1. What intellectual, economic, philosophical, and racial factors helped create a new national mood more receptive to overseas expansionism?
2. What two developments in the late 1880s and mid-1890s demonstrated the increasing interest of the United States in Latin America?

3. Describe Hawaiian society before significant contact with Americans. How did planters and missionaries transform the islands?
4. How did Hawaii gradually get drawn into America's economic and political sphere? Was full annexation inevitable?

War with Spain (pp. 565–574)

5. What were the causes of American involvement in Cuban affairs?
6. What two incidents combined finally to pull the United States into war with Spain?
7. Describe the American plans and preparations for the Spanish-American War. Why was the "Splendid Little War" so short?
8. What role did black soldiers play in the Spanish-American War?
9. Explain how action by the navy's Asiatic and Atlantic squadrons transformed the nature of the War. How was Theodore Roosevelt involved?
10. What happened in the major ground action of the war? How was Theodore Roosevelt involved again?
11. Compare and contrast the development of Cuba and Puerto Rico before the Spanish American War.
12. What arguments were raised for and against imperialism in general and annexation of the Philippines in particular? Why did President McKinley favor annexation? What role did William Jennings Bryan play?

The Republic As Empire (pp. 574–580)

13. Did the Platt Amendment and American actions in Cuba violate the spirit of the ostensible reasons that the United States went to war?
14. Compare and contrast the United States' postwar treatment of Cuba with the relationship that developed with Puerto Rico. What might explain the differences?
15. Was American policy in the Philippine War a repudiation of the ideals that had led the United States to help Cuba secure its independence?
16. How was the Open Door policy calculated to provide maximum commercial and diplomatic advantage at minimum cost? What did the costs turn out to be?
17. What changes from 1900–1903 gave the United States a more modern military establishment?

IDENTIFICATION

Identify each of the following, and explain why it is important within the context of the chapter.

1. Alfred Thayer Mahan
2. G. P. Judd
3. Pearl Habor
4. Queen Liliuokalini
5. Samoa
6. "yellow press"
7. *Cuba Libre*
8. George Dewey
9. Rough Riders
10. Emilio Aguinaldo
11. William Howard Taft
12. Jones Act
13. Chinese "spheres of influence"
14. John Hay
15. Boxer uprising

DOCUMENT

Read the section of the text under the heading "Stirrings of Imperialism." The selection below is taken from an article by Senator Henry Cabot Lodge (R-Mass.) in the March 1895 issue of *Forum* magazine. In the second of his more than thirty years in the Senate, Lodge criticized President Cleveland for his failure to annex Hawaii and then stated his general position on American expansionism. Consider the following questions: What motives for imperialism are reflected in Lodge's article? How would Lodge's argument fit with that of the Social Darwinists? How much of Lodge's dream became reality during his long service in the Senate?

> In the Interests of our commerce and of our fullest development, we should build the Nicaragua Canal, and for the protection of that canal and for the sake of our commercial supremacy in the Pacific we should control the Hawaiian Islands and maintain our influence in Samoa. England has studded the West Indies with strong places which are a standing menace to our Atlantic seaboard. We should have among those islands at least one strong naval station, and when the Nicaragua Canal is built, the island of Cuba, still sparsely settled and of almost unbounded fertility, will become to us a necessity. Commerce follows the flag, and we should build up a navy strong enough to give protection to Americans in every quarter of the globe and sufficiently powerful to put our coasts beyond the possibility of successful attack.

The tendency of modern times is toward consolidation. It is apparent in capital and labor alike, and it is also true of nations. Small states are of the past and have no future. The modern movement is all toward the concentration of people and territory into great nations and large dominions. The great nations are rapidly absorbing for their future expansion and their present defense all the waste places of the earth. It is a movement which makes for civilization and the advancement of the race. As one of the great nations of the world, the United States must not fall out of the line of march.

For more than thirty years we have been so much absorbed with grave domestic questions that we have lost sight of these vast interests which lie just outside our borders. They ought to be neglected no longer. They are not only of material importance but they are matters which concern our greatness as a nation and our future as a great example. They appeal to our national honor and dignity and to the pride of country and of race.

Henry Cabot Lodge, *Forum,* March 1895.

MAP EXERCISE

Fill in or identify the following on the blank map provided.

1. Cuba, Puerto Rico, Hawaii, Samoa, Midway, Guam, Philippines, and Alaska
2. The area of the Venezuelan border dispute
3. The area of the Chinese coast that was divided into European spheres of influence.

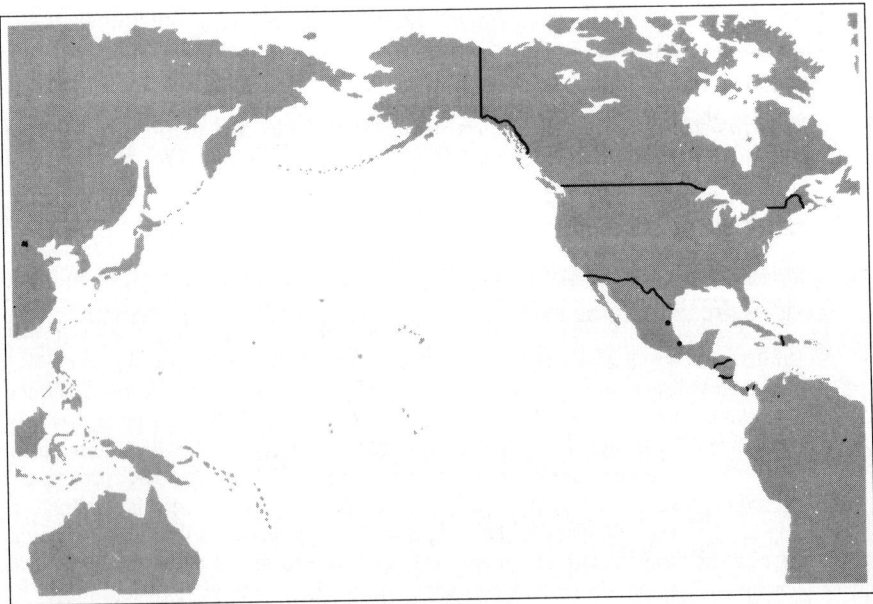

Interpretative Questions

Based on what you have filled in, answer the following. For some of the questions you will need to consult the narrative in your text for information or explanation.

1. Why was the acquisition of Pacific islands so important to American trading and naval interests?
2. How were the annexation of the Philippines and the pronouncement of the Open Door policy related?
3. Why did the United States think its interests were at stake in the Venezuelan border controversy?
4. How did the freeing of Cuba and the acquisition of Puerto Rico secure American hegemony in the Caribbean Sea?

SUMMARY

Turning its interest from the continental United States to the world at large, America in the years after the Civil War fought a war with Spain and acquired a far-flung empire. By 1900, American possessions included Alaska, Hawaii, the Philippines, Puerto Rico, and a string of Pacific islands. In addition, Cuba was essentially an American protectorate. The nation was suddenly a world power with worldwide responsibilities and burdens. The empire had been acquired for economic and philosophical reasons. Expansionism could provide an outlet for a perceived glut of American goods and an arena in which to demonstrate the superiority of Western civilization. To accommodate its new role, the nation had to devise ways to improve its military establishment and govern its overseas territories.

CHAPTER SELF-TEST

After you have read the chapter in the text and done the exercises in the Study Guide, the following self-test can be taken to see if you understand the material you have covered. Answers appear at the end of the Study Guide.

Multiple Choice

Circle the letter of the response which best answers the question or completes the statement.

1. The new "Manifest Destiny" contrasted with the pre-Civil War version in that the new:
   a. was mostly free of the attitudes of racial and ethnic superiority that had characterized the old.
   b. concentrated on lands not geographically adjacent to territory already controlled by the United States.
   c. was patriotically rather than economically motivated whereas the old was steeped in economic exploitation.
   d. tended to involve use of military force whereas such force had been avoided with the old.

2. The renewed American interest in expansionism by the 1890s stemmed partly from the:
   a. restoration of prosperity at home.
   b. fear that Europeans were gaining control of the world and its markets.
   c. resolution of domestic political conflicts.
   d. desire to settle America's frontier regions.

3. The annexation of Hawaii by the United States occurred as a result of:
   a. the request of American missionaries in the 1820s.
   b. negotiation of a treaty with King Kalakaua in 1887.
   c. the overthrow of Queen Liliuokalani by American businessmen in 1893.
   d. passage of a joint resolution by Congress in 1898.

4. The American public was outraged by publication of a letter from Dupuy de Lôme, Spanish minister to Washington, in which he:
   a. described President McKinley as a weak man.
   b. called all North Americans cowardly.
   c. defended Spain's brutal attacks on civilians.
   d. declared that Spain would launch terrorist attacks on the U.S. if the U.S. invaded Cuba.

5. According to the most recent evidence, the sinking of the American battleship *Maine* was probably the result of:
   a. an attack by a Spanish submarine.
   b. contact with a Spanish mine in Havana's harbor.
   c. sabotage by Cuban revolutionaries.
   d. an accidental explosion inside one of the engine rooms.

6. The Spanish-American War was marked by:
   a. a lack of public enthusiasm and military volunteers.
   b. more American lives lost to disease than battle.
   c. efficient mobilization of military supplies and services.
   d. protracted, bloody guerrilla struggles.

7. American capture of Santiago, Cuba, resulted when:
   a. General William R. Shafter ordered his forces to surround the city.
   b. Theodore Roosevelt led the Rough Riders in a reckless charge up Kettle Hill.
   c. members of two black infantry divisions secured San Juan Hill.
   d. the Spanish fleet was destroyed in an attempted escape from the city's harbor by a waiting American squadron.

8. Spain's defeat in the Spanish-American war resulted primarily from:
   a. great numerical superiority by the United States in ships, guns, and military personnel in Cuba.
   b. her own weakness and incompetence.
   c. British intervention on the part of the United States.
   d. the efficient planning and execution of American military strategies.

9. In regard to the Philippine Islands following the war, President McKinley decided to:
   a. annex them as a United States colony.
   b. return them to Spain.
   c. grant them independence.
   d. provide for an international army of occupation.

10. All of the following arguments were made against United States annexation of the Philippines *except* that:
    a. "inferior" Asian races would "pollute" the American population.
    b. defense of the islands would prove costly and entangle America in foreign alliances.
    c. such a move would repudiate American principles of independence and self-reliance.
    d. control of the islands would necessitate American involvement in the Oriental trade.

11. In response to the Philippine insurrection, the United States:
    a. resorted to brutal tactics very similar to those for which it had denounced the Spanish in Cuba.
    b. negotiated a truce with rebel leader Emilio Aguinaldo.

c. spent far less money and effort than had been necessitated by the Spanish-American War.
d. decided to grant the islands immediate independence.

12. The Open Door policy with China was appealing to the United States because it:
    a. won ready approval from European interests with Chinese "spheres of influence."
    b. seemed to allow American trade in China without the need for a military presence or confrontation with other Western powers.
    c. tempered Chinese expansionist impulses.
    d. assured the United States a part of any future dismemberment of China.

13. The Boxer Rebellion was an uprising by:
    a. American sugar growers to take over the government of Hawaii.
    b. Panamanians to win control of the canal zone from Colombia.
    c. Chinese nationalists to expel the "foreign devils" who controlled the country's commerce.
    d. Filipino insurgents to win their independence from the United States.

14. Shortly after the end of the Spanish-American War the U.S. military establishment was:
    a. given a modern command structure.
    b. reduced to a nominal size since the Indians had been pacified and there was no longer a nearby external threat.
    c. restructured, with a shift away from an emphasis on naval power to an increased reliance on infantry forces.
    d. ignored except as a cozy place for ex-war heroes and political patronage.

15. The Platt Amendment had the effect of giving the United States:
    a. significant control over the affairs of Cuba.
    b. ownership of the Panama Canal Zone.
    c. virtually unlimited access to the markets of Japan.
    d. a bigger role in internal European economic affairs.

True/False

Read each statement carefully. Mark true statements "T" and false statements "F."

1. Joseph Pulitzer and William Randolph Hearst, alone among prominent American publishers, disdained sensationalistic report-

ing of the Cuban Revolution of the 1890s as practiced by the nation's "yellow press."
2. The American attack on the Spanish fleet at Manila resulted in the most difficult and bloodiest engagement of the Spanish-American War.
3. Black volunteers were accepted for service in the Spanish-American War and black regiments were used in the American invasion force.
4. United States contact with Hawaii began well before the Civil War.
5. The United States fought a brief naval war with England over the dispute concerning the border of Venezuela.
6. By 1895 almost all the population of Hawaii's main islands was of European ancestry.
7. The main trade commodity between the United States and Cuba was cotton.
8. The Spanish-American War was called the "Splendid Little War" because almost everything went smoothly and efficiently.
9. As assistant secretary of the navy, Theodore Roosevelt worked to keep the scale of the Spanish-American War limited to Cuba and Puerto Rico.
10. The largest ground encounter of the Spanish-American War actually occurred in the Dominican Republic.
11. Emilio Aguinaldo was the principal leader of the Cuban nationalists until he died in a detention camp prior to American intervention.
12. Chinese "spheres of influence" referred to those Pacific Islands, including Samoa, where the United States had interests that were dominated by the Chinese navy.
13. Alfred Thayer Mahan was the key leader of the anti-imperialist movement that tried to prevent U.S. annexation of Hawaii and the Philippines.
14. George Dewey led the American naval force that captured Manila Bay.
15. The Jones Act, which declared Puerto Rico to be a U.S. territory and granted U.S. citizenship to Puerto Ricans, effectively ended all agitation for statehood or independence.

Review Questions

These questions are to be answered with essays. This will allow you to explore relationships among individuals, events, and attitudes of the period under review.

1. Compare and contrast the new and old concepts of Manifest Destiny. Look especially at the economic, philosophical, and racial motives for overseas expansion. Were these factors at work in the older continental expansionism?
2. What hesitations and doubts about imperialism did Americans evince between 1865 and 1898? How did the Spanish-American War change all this?
3. Was the Spanish-American conflict indeed a "splendid little war"? What was splendid about it? What was not so splendid?
4. What parallels can be drawn between America's imperial aspirations and the way white Americans dealt with the American Indian?

Chapter Twenty-One
The Rise of Progressivism

Objectives

A thorough study of Chapter 21 should enable you to understand:

1. The origins of the progressive impulse.
2. The humanitarian reforms of the period, and the role of the church in carrying out the "Social Gospel."
3. The progressive emphasis on scientific expertise, organizational reform, and professionalism.
4. The role of women's groups in promoting reform.
5. The aims and accomplishments of the progressives at the state and local levels.
6. The temperance movement, and its relationship to other progressive reforms.
7. The movement to restrict immigration, and how allowing fewer immigrants was regarded as a reform.
8. The women's suffrage movement and more radical demands for equal rights for women.
9. The progressive attitude toward the consolidation of economic power in corporations.

Pertinent Questions

The Progressive Impulse (pp. 582–590)

1. How did the muckrakers help prepare the way for progressivism?
2. What contribution did the Social Gospel movement make to progressivism?
3. Contrast the Social Darwinist view of society with the progressive vision. How did the settlement house movement in general and Jane Addams in particular illustrate the difference?

4. What distinguished the so-called new middle class? What was the role of expertise and professional organization? Who was usually excluded?
5. In what professions did women dominate? What characteristics did those professions share?

Women and Reform (pp. 590–595)

6. What basic change in the nature of the economy laid the foundation for the emergence of the so-called "new woman"? What were the characteristics of the new woman?
7. What led to the prominence of women in reform movements? How did the women's club movement reflect both the influence of women and the restrictions upon them?
8. What were the principal arguments against the women's suffrage movement, and why did it inspire such passionate antisuffrage sentiments?
9. Explain how the debate over the "sphere" of women shaped the suffrage movement. What shift in emphasis was critical in finally obtaining the vote for women?

The Assault on the Parties (pp. 595–599)

10. Compare and contrast the proponents and opponents of municipal reform.
11. Explain how the commission plan, the city-manager plan, nonpartisanship, at-large elections, and stronger mayors worked together to try to destroy the power of the urban party bosses.
12. What were the basic purposes of the initiative, referendum, recall, and direct primary? How did they work in practice?
13. What was the relationship between the weakening of political parties and the rise of interest groups?

Sources of Progressive Reform (pp. 600–603)

14. What role did labor unions play in progressive reform? Why was the American Federation of Labor not involved at the national level?
15. By what means did some urban political machines, such as Tammany Hall, manage to survive the progressive era?
16. Why were western reformers particularly interested in action at the federal level even though much of the progressive movement focused on state and local legislation? What changes were accomplished?

17. Compare and contrast the ideas of Booker T. Washington with those of W. E. B. DuBois. What was the concrete result of the efforts of DuBois and his allies?

Crusades for Order and Reform (pp. 603–607)

18. Today, antiliquor laws are often thought of as conservative. Why was prohibition regarded as a progressive issue? What forces usually opposed prohibition?
19. Most progressives abhorred the urban disorder resulting from the influx of immigrants, but they differed about the appropriate response to the problem. What were the contrasting approaches? Which one dominated?
20. How did the socialist agenda differ from the typical progressive program? On what issues did the socialists disagree among themselves?
21. Describe the two different progressive approaches to the perceived problem of economic consolidation and centralization. What solutions did advocates of each approach favor?

IDENTIFICATION

Identify each of the following, and explain why it is important within the context of the chapter.

1. Lincoln Steffens
2. Salvation Army
3. Hull House
4. Jane Addams
5. Thorstein Veblen
6. Taylorism
7. social science
8. American Medical Association
9. U.S. Chamber of Commerce
10. National Farm Bureau Federation
11. "Boston marriages"
12. General Federation of Women's Clubs
13. National Association of Colored Women
14. Carrie Chapman Catt and Anna Howard Shaw
15. Alice Paul
16. secret ballot
17. Robert M. La Follette

18. Triangle Shirtwaist Co. fire
19. Niagara Movement
20. Women's Christian Temperance Union
21. Frances Willard
22. eugenics
23. Eugene V. Debs
24. Industrial Workers of the World
25. Louis D. Brandeis

DOCUMENT

Read the section of the text under the subheading "Woman Suffrage." The document below is drawn from a flyer published in 1905 by the Anti-Suffrage Association, based in Albany, New York. The pamphlet was written by noted historian Francis Parkman and was issued several years after his death. Consider the following questions: Why would the emphasis on the "natural" way have been an effective argument against suffrage? To what extent was the suffrage fight a battle among women as well as between men and women? How do Parkman's arguments compare with those who opposed the Equal Rights Amendment? (See Chapters 24 and 32.)

> The man is the natural head of the family, and is responsible for maintenance and order. Hence he ought to control the social and business agencies which are essential to the successful discharge of the trust imposed upon him....
>
> Woman suffrage must have one of two effects. If, as many of its advocates complain, women are subservient to men, and do nothing but what they desire, then woman suffrage will have no other result than to increase the power of the other sex; if, on the other hand, women vote, as they see fit, without regarding their husbands, ... then unhappy marriages will be multiplied and divorces redoubled....
>
> But most women, including those of the best capacity and worth, fully consent that their fathers, husbands, brothers, or friends, shall be their political representatives....
>
> Nothing is more certain than that woman will have the suffrage if they ever want it; for when they want it, men will give it to them regardless of consequences....
>
> Many women of sense and intelligence are influenced by the fact that the woman suffrage movement boasts itself a movement of progress, and by a wish to be on the liberal or progressive side. But the boast is unfounded. Progress, to be genuine, must be in accord with natural law. If it is not, it ends in failure and in retrogression....To plunge [women] into politics, where they are not needed and for which they are unfit, would be scarcely more a movement of progress than to force them to bear arms and fight....
>
> Neither Congress, nor the States, nor the united voice of the whole people could permanently change the essential relations of the sexes. Universal female suffrage,

even if decreed, would undo itself in time; but the attempt to establish it would work deplorable mischief. The question is, whether the persistency of a few agitators shall plunge us blindfold into the most reckless of all experiments; whether we shall adopt this supreme device for developing the defects of women, and demolish their real power to build an ugly mockery instead. For the sake of womanhood, let us hope not....Let us save women from the barren perturbations of American politics. Let us respect them; and, that we may do so, let us pray for deliverance from female suffrage.

Francis Parkman, "Some of the Reasons Against Women's Suffrage" (Albany, N.Y.: Anti-Suffrage Association, 1905).

MAP EXERCISE

Fill in or identify the following on the blank map provided.

1. State known as "the laboratory of progressivism."
2. City in which Hull House was located.
3. Two cities that launched the commission form of municipal government.
4. Two states that did not ratify the Eighteenth Amendment, which established the prohibition of liquor.

Interpretative Questions

Based on what you have filled in, answer the following. For some of the questions you will need to consult the narrative in your text for information or explanation.

1. What led one state to be called the "laboratory of progressivism"? Who was this state's leading progressive?
2. In general, where were settlement houses located and why? What was their function? Why was Hull House the most famous U.S. settlement house?
3. What natural event in what city was the catalyst for the invention of the commission plan of municipal government? Note that both the commission plan and the manager plan began in small southern cities and only spread after they were adopted by larger northern cities. What factors would help explain this pattern?
4. What probably explains why the particular two states failed to ratify the Eighteenth Amendment?

SUMMARY

Convinced that rapid industrialization and urbanization had created serious problems and disorder, progressives shared an optimistic vision that organized private and government action could improve society. Progressivism sought to control monopoly, build social cohesion, and promote efficiency. Muckrakers exposed social ills that Social Gospel reformers, settlement house workers, and other progressives attacked. Meanwhile, increasing standards of training and expertise were creating a new middle class of educated professionals, including many women. The progressives tried to rationalize politics by reducing the influence of political parties in municipal and state affairs. Many of the nation's problems could be solved, some progressives believed, if alcohol were banned, immigration were restricted, and women were allowed to vote. With only scant help from white progressives, African Americans laid the organizational groundwork for attacks on racial discrimination. Other progressives stressed the need for fundamental economic transformation through socialism or through milder forms of antitrust action and regulation.

CHAPTER SELF-TEST

After you have read the chapter in the text and done the exercises in the Study Guide, the following self-test can be taken to see if you understand the material you have covered. Answers appear at the end of the Study Guide.

Multiple Choice

Circle the letter of the response which best answers the question or completes the statement.

1. Progressive reforms were shaped by a belief in the:
   a. need to concentrate power, wealth, and authority for the well-being of the nation.
   b. autonomy of the individual.
   c. laissez-faire orthodoxies of the late nineteenth century.
   d. importance of organization and efficiency.

2. The Social Gospel:
   a. helped bring to progressivism a powerful moral component.
   b. became the dominant philosophy in urban reform.
   c. was dismissed by serious reformers as irrelevant moralization.
   d. was rejected as materialistic by Pope Leo XIII.

3. Most progressive theorists argued that ignorance, poverty, and even criminality resulted from:
   a. a person's "fitness" for survival.
   b. inherent moral or genetic failings.
   c. the workings of divine providence.
   d. the effects of an unhealthy environment.

4. The high value placed by progressives on knowledge and expertise led to the:
   a. justification by middle-class professionals of the existing industrial system.
   b. use of scientific techniques in the study of society and its institutions.
   c. abandonment by managers of the principles of "Taylorism."
   d. rejection of mass-production techniques, such as the assembly line, in favor of highly skilled and trained laborers.

5. Professional roles for women in the early twentieth century were:
   a. widely expanded by custom and law into virtually every field of work.
   b. restricted entirely to the settlement houses and social work.
   c. free of the organizational trends characterizing the male professional world.
   d. most often those involving "helping'" or "domestic" activities traditionally associated with women.

6. Women's clubs formed in the latter nineteenth and early twentieth centuries:
   a. confined their activities to social and cultural activities.
   b. seldom adopted positions on controversial public issues.
   c. overtly challenged the prevailing assumptions about the proper role of women in society.
   d. played an important role in winning passage of state laws regulating conditions of housing and the workplace.

7. To improve municipal government, many urban political reformers favored:
   a. election of mayors and other offices on a nonpartisan basis.
   b. movement of city elections to years of presidential or congressional contests.
   c. election of city councilors by district.
   d. increased power for the city council at the expense of the mayor.

8. Partly in response to progressive political reforms, the:
   a. power of party organizations collapsed.
   b. turnout of eligible voters increased.
   c. influence of special interest groups increased.
   d. influence of party bosses disappeared.

9. By the early twentieth century, the Women's Christian Temperance Union (WCTU):
   a. was widely ridiculed by most progressives as a collection of busybodies and do-gooders.
   b. demanded the complete prohibition of the manufacture and sale of alcoholic beverages.
   c. won substantial support from immigrants and working-class voters.
   d. remained a model of administrative inefficiency and political ineptitude.

10. The sources of greatest immigration to the United States from 1900 to 1920 were:
    a. Ireland and Germany.
    b. Italy and the Austro-Hungarian Empire.
    c. Russia and the Baltic states.
    d. China and Japan.

11. All of the following were movements advocated by many who called themselves progressive era reformers *except:*
    a. eliminating of alcohol from national life.
    b. stopping the flood of immigrants.
    c. winning women the right to vote.
    d. abolishing child labor.
    e. prohibiting workers from joining unions.

12. The advocates of women's suffrage significantly increased their general public support during the Progressive Era when they put increased emphasis on the argument that women's suffrage would:
    a. lead to full social and economic power for women within a generation.
    b. increase political power and office-holding opportunities available to women.
    c. bring more women into the industrial work force thereby countering recession.
    d. enhance the likelihood of the successful enactment of other progressive reform causes.

13. In congressional and presidential circles, the central economic debate of the progressive era was whether the:
    a. unionization of workers should proceed along industrial or craft lines.
    b. capitalistic structure of the system should be replaced by socialism.
    c. government should deal with the trusts through policies of decentralization or regulation.
    d. government should rely primarily upon the tariff or income tax as the major source of revenue.

14. The leading American socialist of the progressive era was
    a. Herbert Croly.
    b. Louis Brandeis.
    c. Alice Paul.
    d. Eugene Debs.

15. Which of the following was a governor and United States senator regarded as a leading progressive?
    a. Chapman Catt
    b. Howard Shaw.
    c. Robert LaFollette
    d. Charles Tammany.

True/False

Read each statement carefully. Mark true statements "T" and false statements "F."

1. "Muckraker" was the nickname given by progressives to politicians who were accused of bribery and corruption.
2. As a general rule, progressive reformers opposed placing governmental power in the hands of nonpartisan, nonelective bureaucrats, who were insulated from electoral politics.
3. The adoption by many American cities of the commission government and city-manager systems of municipal government signaled an attempt to remove municipal government from the corrupting influence of party politics.
4. As a general rule, social Darwinists stressed the role of inherent characteristics and progressives stressed the role of environment in explaining why poor people failed to succeed economically.
5. The settlement house movement led by Jane Addams provided an opportunity for educated women to get together in a rural environment for intellectually stimulating retreats.
6. Professional women who entered the work force during the progressive era tended to be concentrated in the so-called helping professions such as teaching and nursing.
7. The women's club movement provided opportunities for women to exert influence on political issues as well as providing a social outlet.
8. The electoral devices of initiative, referendum, and direct primary were instituted in several states in order to give more political power to the average voter rather than the incumbent legislators.
9. The electoral device known as the "recall" allowed voters to remove an elected officeholder without waiting for the normal end of his term of office.
10. In general, the increasing influence of interest groups during the progressive era strengthened the power of the two political parties.
11. In general, the opposition to prohibition of alcoholic beverages was weakest in the urban areas of the northeastern states.
12. America's entry into World War I and the moral fervor it unleashed helped provide the final push for the adoption of the national prohibition of alcoholic beverages.
13. Booker T. Washington's rhetoric tended to emphasize immediate economic self-improvement rather than long-range social change.

14. The so-called science of eugenics was used by factory reformers to justify improved health and safety conditions and to call for increased education for the workers.
15. Many progressives such as Herbert Croly and Theodore Roosevelt argued that national economic regulation was the best way to deal with the challenges brought forward by the trusts.

Review Questions

These questions are to be answered with essays. This will allow you to explore relationships among individuals, events, and attitudes of the period under review.

1. Consider the "central assumptions" of progressivism identified by the chapter introduction in light of the varying interpretations offered in the "Debating the Past" section (page 608). Was progressivism unified enough to share "central assumptions"?
2. Many progressives professed to believe that government at all levels should be strong, efficient, and democratic so that it could better serve the people. What changes in the structure and operation of government did progressives advocate to achieve these aims? Can the attempts at civil-service reform in the nineteenth century be seen as a precursor of this type of progressive program?
3. To what extent did muckrakers, Social Gospel reformers, settlement house volunteers, social workers, and other experts reflect the central assumptions of progressivism?
4. Explain how progressivism affected women and, conversely, how women affected progressivism.

CHAPTER TWENTY-TWO
The Battle for National Reform

OBJECTIVES

A thorough study of Chapter 22 should enable you to understand:

1. The nature and extent of Theodore Roosevelt's "square deal" progressivism.
2. The similarities and differences between the domestic progressivism of William Howard Taft and of Roosevelt.
3. The conservation issue, and why it triggered the split between Taft and Roosevelt.
4. The consequences of the split in the Republican party in 1912.
5. The differences between Roosevelt's New Nationalism and Wilson's New Freedom.
6. The differences between Woodrow Wilson's campaign platform and the measures actually implemented during his term.
7. The new tone for American foreign policy introduced by Roosevelt, especially in Asia and the Caribbean.
8. The similarities and differences between Taft's and Roosevelt's approach to foreign policy.
9. The reasons for the continuation of American interventionism in Latin America under Wilson.

PERTINENT QUESTIONS

Theodore Roosevelt and the Progressive Presidency
(pp. 610–616)

1. How did Theodore Roosevelt become president?
2. To what extent was Roosevelt a trustbuster? What was Roosevelt's view about how the federal government should deal with economic concentration?
3. What changes did Roosevelt initiate in the traditional role of the federal government in labor disputes?

4. How did Roosevelt's actions in the railroad, medicine, and meat industries illustrate his cautious but progressive approach?
5. What were the two factions within the conservation movement? Toward which side did Roosevelt lean? What was his lasting effect on national environmental policy?
6. How did Roosevelt respond to the Panic of 1907?

The Troubled Succession (pp. 616–620)

7. Contrast the personalities of Theodore Roosevelt and William Howard Taft. What seemed to be Taft's biggest problem?
8. How did Taft manage to alienate progressives on the tariff issue?
9. How did the Pinchot-Ballinger affair drive a wedge between Taft and Roosevelt?
10. Describe the programs that Roosevelt unveiled at Osawatomie, Kansas. How did they go beyond the moderation he had exhibited as president?
11. How did Taft manage to secure the Republican nomination in 1912 despite Roosevelt's obvious popularity?
12. Why did Roosevelt break from the Republicans to form the Progressive Party?

Woodrow Wilson and the New Freedom (pp. 620–624)

13. How did Roosevelt's New Nationalism and Wilson's New Freedom differ from each other?
14. What propelled Wilson to victory in 1912? What roles did Taft and Eugene Debs play in the campaign?
15. How did Wilson influence Congress to pass his legislative program?
16. What was the goal of the Underwood-Simmons tariff? How did it fulfill longstanding Democratic pledges? Why was a graduated income tax needed, as well as the tariff reduction?
17. How did the Federal Reserve Act transform the nation's monetary system?
18. Wilson pushed hard for the Federal Trade Commission Act and gave only lukewarm support to the Clayton Act. What do those actions demonstrate about his ironic move in the direction of New Nationalism?
19. After the initial spate of New Freedom legislation, how and why did Wilson back away from reform? What led him, later in his first term, to advance reform once again?

20. Compare and contrast Wilson's and Roosevelt's actions on racial segregation. What in Wilson's background and political constituency might explain the difference?

The "Big Stick": America and the World, 1901–1917
(pp. 624–632)

21. Explain Roosevelt's distinction between "civilized" and "uncivilized" nations. How did sea power fit into his vision?
22. What was the course of relations between the United States and Japan during Roosevelt's presidency?
23. What were the general and immediate motivations for the proclamation of the Roosevelt Corollary? What pattern of Latin American policy did it establish?
24. Why have many observers questioned the propriety of the methods that the United States used to acquire rights to construct the Panama Canal?
25. What was the central focus of William Howard Taft's foreign policy? What nickname was it given?
26. What actions did Taft and Wilson take toward Nicaragua? (What legacy was left for relations between the United States and Nicaragua?) What other Caribbean areas experienced American intervention?
27. Why did Wilson take sides in the Mexican governmental turmoil? Describe the two interventions and their results.

IDENTIFICATION

Identify each of the following, and explain why it is important within the context of the chapter.

1. Seventeenth Amendment
2. Northern Securities Case
3. Alton B. Parker
4. square deal
5. *The Jungle*
6. J. P. Morgan
7. Robert LaFollette
8. "Bull Moose" party
9. Edward M. House
10. Louis Brandeis
11. Sixteenth Amendment

12. Smith-Lever Act
13. Great White Fleet
14. Pancho Villa
15. John J. Pershing

DOCUMENT

Read the section of the text under the subheading "The Square Deal." Also review earlier parts of the text that discuss the rise of big business and the role of corporate leadership. The following excerpts are from Theodore Roosevelt's First Annual Message, delivered only a few months after he became president. Read the selection and consider the following questions: Does this message reveal an attitude toward trusts consistent with the actions that Roosevelt would undertake as president? How might Roosevelt have reacted to those who called the great industrial leaders "robber barons"? Would this document support the contention that progressivism can best be explained as a reaction to the economic changes of the late nineteenth century? Are Roosevelt's views more consistent with those of Herbert Croly or Louis Brandeis? Does the Republican party of today reflect a similar outlook toward business? Could it be fairly characterized as a "trickle-down" view?

> The tremendous and highly complex industrial development which went on with ever accelerated rapidity during the latter half of the nineteenth century brings us face to face, at the beginning of the twentieth, with very serious social problems. The old laws, and the old customs which had almost the binding force of law, were once quite sufficient to regulate the accumulation and distribution of wealth. Since the industrial changes which have so enormously increased the productive power of mankind, they are no longer sufficient.
>
> The growth of cities has gone on beyond comparison faster than the growth of the country, and the upbuilding of the great industrial centers has meant a startling increase, not merely in the aggregate of wealth, but in the number of very large individual, and especially of very large corporate, fortunes. The creation of these great corporate fortunes has not been due to the tariff nor to any other governmental action, but to natural causes in the business world operating in other countries as they operate in our own.
>
> The process has aroused much antagonism, a great part of which is wholly without warrant. It is not true that as the rich have grown richer the poor have grown poorer. On the contrary, never before has the average man, the wage-worker, the farmer, the small trader, been so well off as in this country at the present time. There have been abuses connected with the accumulation of wealth; yet it remains true that a fortune accumulated in legitimate business can be accumulated by the person specifically benefitted only on condition of conferring immense incidental benefits upon others. Successful enterprise, of the type which benefits all mankind, can only exist if the conditions are such as to offer great prizes as the rewards of success.

The captains of industry who have driven the railway systems across this continent, who have built up our commerce, who have developed our manufactures, have on the whole done great good to our people. Without them the material development of which we are so justly proud could never have taken place....

Moreover, it cannot too often be pointed out that to strike with ignorant violence at the interests of one set of men almost inevitably endangers the interests of all. The fundamental rule in our national life—the rule which underlies all others—is that, on the whole, and in the long run, we shall go up or down together....

The mechanism of modern business is so delicate that extreme care must be taken not to interfere with it in a spirit of rashness or ignorance. Many of those who have made it their vocation to denounce the great industrial combinations which are popularly, although with technical inaccuracy, known as "trusts," appeal especially to hatred and fear. These are precisely the two emotions, particularly when combined with ignorance, which unfit men for the exercise of cool and steady judgment. In facing new industrial conditions, the whole history of the world shows that legislation will generally be both unwise and ineffective unless undertaken after calm inquiry and with sober self-restraint....

All this is true; and yet it is also true that there are real and grave evils, one of the chief being over-capitalization because of its many baleful consequences; and a resolute and practical effort must be made to correct these evils.

There is a widespread conviction in the minds of the American people that the great corporations known as trusts are in certain of their features and tendencies hurtful to the general welfare.

MAP EXERCISE

Fill in or identify the following on the blank map provided. Use the map on page 627 of the text as your source.

1. Mexico, Cuba, Haiti, Dominican Republic, Puerto Rico, Virgin Islands, Nicaragua, Panama, Venezuela, Colombia. (Mark a star on those countries into which the United States intervened militarily. Mark RC on the country to which the Roosevelt Corollary was first applied.)
2. Area of Pancho Villa's raids and General John J. Pershing's intervention.
3. The route of the Panama Canal.

Interpretative Questions

Based on what you have filled in, answer the following. For some of the questions you will need to consult the narrative in your text for information or explanation.

1. Explain the motivation for Theodore Roosevelt's special concern with the Caribbean region. What policy did he formulate in response to his concerns?
2. What were the two possible routes for a Central American canal? What were the advantages and disadvantages of each? Why did the United States settle on the Panamanian choice? Why was Colombia upset?
3. What events inspired U.S. intervention in Nicaragua? Why was the country perceived to be important to American interests?
4. What caused the border strife between the United States and Mexico? What was its result?

SUMMARY

Theodore Roosevelt became president as a consequence of the assassination of William McKinley, but he quickly moved to make the office his own. In many ways, Roosevelt was the preeminent progressive, yet it sometimes seemed that for him reform was more a style than a dogma. Although Roosevelt clearly envisioned a more activist national government, the shifts and contractions embodied in his policies toward trusts, labor, and conservation reflect the complexity and diversity of progressivism. Despite being Roosevelt's handpicked successor, President William Howard Taft managed to alienate Roosevelt and other progressive Republicans by his actions regarding tariffs, conservation, foreign policy, trusts, and other matters. In 1912, Roosevelt decided to challenge Taft for the presidency. When he failed to secure the Republican nomination, Roosevelt formed his own Progressive Party. With the Republicans divided, Woodrow Wilson won the presidency. In actuality, Wilson's domestic program turned out to be much like the one Roosevelt had advocated. In the Caribbean, Wilson continued the pattern of intervention that Roosevelt and Taft had established.

CHAPTER SELF-TEST

After you have read the chapter in the text and done the exercises in the Study Guide, the following self-test can be taken to see if you understand the material you have covered. Answers appear at the end of the Study Guide.

Multiple Choice

Circle the letter of the response which best answers the question or completes the statement.

1. As president, Theodore Roosevelt:
   a. failed to attract significant public attention or devotion.
   b. openly rebelled against the conservative leaders of his party.
   c. advocated reform as a means of protecting American society against more radical challenges.
   d. earned a reputation for the substance, rather than the style, of his leadership.

2. In managing the trusts, Theodore Roosevelt advocated:
   a. government prosecution and breakup of only the largest trusts.
   b. regulation, with government serving as mediator between corporate and public interest.
   c. reversal of the prevailing trend toward economic concentration.
   d. strict enforcement of the Sherman Antitrust Act.

3. In contrast to Roosevelt, William Howard Taft was:
   a. more committed to progressive reform.
   b. insistent upon observing the strict letter of the law.
   c. dynamic and aggressive in personality.
   d. an ardent sportsman and athlete.

4. As president, Taft:
   a. lobbied effectively for reduced tariff rates.
   b. actively supported the insurgent revolt in Congress.
   c. refused to intervene in legislative affairs.
   d. successfully challenged the power of the conservative Old Guard.

5. The election of 1912 offered American voters a choice between:
   a. conservatism and reform.
   b. two brands of progressivism.
   c. socialism and capitalism.
   d. all of the above.

6. Wilson perceived of his role as president as one in which he should:
   a. deal primarily with foreign rather than domestic problems.
   b. delegate most authority to capable subordinates.
   c. guide public demands into legislative realities.
   d. remain above the political squabbles in Congress.

7. In contrast to earlier statements, as President, Woodrow Wilson seemed most supportive of:
   a. vigorous enforcement of the antitrust laws.
   b. additional legislation designed to dismantle the trusts.
   c. creation of a government regulatory agency for big business.
   d. policies to restore a competitive, decentralized economy.

8. The conduct of foreign affairs appealed to Theodore Roosevelt because there the president:
   a. met a lively and spirited debate from Congress.
   b. could exercise power comparatively unfettered.
   c. acted upon concerns of public opinion.
   d. felt more comfortable with his expertise and talents.

9. For Theodore Roosevelt, the definition of a "civilized" nation seemed to depend largely upon its:
   a. ability and willingness to engage in physical combat.
   b. degree of economic development.
   c. historical and cultural accomplishments.
   d. adoption of the Christian religion.

10. The right of the United States to intervene in the domestic affairs of Latin American nations to maintain order was asserted in the:
    a. Monroe Doctrine.
    b. Roosevelt Corollary.
    c. Stimson Doctrine.
    d. Teller Amendment.

11. Which of the following Latin American and/or Caribbean nations were subjected to United States military intervention prior to 1917?
    a. Mexico and Cuba.
    b. Nicaragua and Panama.
    c. Haiti and the Dominican Republic.
    d. all of the above.

12. In Latin America, President Taft sought to:
    a. topple the regimes of military dictators.
    b. extend America's economic investments.
    c. remove all American military troops.
    d. join with European nations in railroad development.

13. The result of Wilson's military intervention in Mexico was:
    a. the capture and execution of Pancho Villa by Mexican authorities.
    b. the establishment of friendly relations with the new Carranza regime.
    c. the successful mediation of the dispute by an international commission.
    d. a lasting Mexican hostility toward the United States.

14. The site chosen for the Panama Canal lay within the boundaries of what country *before* a "revolution" created the nation of Panama?
    a. Colombia.
    b. Nicaragua.
    c. Costa Rica.
    d. Guatemala.

15. The naval force that Roosevelt sent on a world cruise to showcase U.S. strength was nicknamed the:
    a. Big Stick Flotilla.
    b. Bully Squadron.
    c. Yankee Armada.
    d. Great White Fleet.

True/False

Read each statement carefully. Mark true statements "T" and false statements "F."

1. Theodore Roosevelt became president as a result of the assassination of William McKinley.
2. As president, Roosevelt contended that big businesses or trusts were an unnatural occurrence in the economy and that the federal government had the obligation to "bust" them down to a more natural size.
3. By offering to mediate a major coal strike, Roosevelt was moving to take the federal government away from an antilabor stance toward a more neutral approach.
4. Roosevelt opposed the Pure Food and Drug Act and the Meat Inspection Acts because they interfered with the laissez-faire rights of business.
5. The conservation movement was somewhat internally divided between those who stressed the preservation of natural resources and those who stressed managed exploitation of those resources.
6. Roosevelt blamed the Panic of 1907 on bankers and financiers and refused to cooperate with them in any efforts to revive the economy.
7. Roosevelt and William Howard Taft had been long-time rivals in the Republic Party before Taft became Roosevelt's vice president.
8. In the period between the time he left the White House and the outbreak of World War I, Roosevelt drifted away from progressivism and became more and more conservative in his approach to national policy issues.
9. Woodrow Wilson's so-called New Freedom program called for more effort to break up big business combinations than Roosevelt's New Nationalism did.
10. Roosevelt's Progressive Party of 1912 was nicknamed the "Bull Moose" party.
11. As President, Woodrow Wilson advocated a general lowering of the nation's tariff rates.
12. The Federal Reserve Act made individual bank failures less likely but had little effect on the nation's basic circulating currency.
13. Theodore Roosevelt believed that the United States should reduce its world commitments and concentrate instead on domestic reform.

14. William Howard Taft's approach to foreign policy was given the nickname "dollar diplomacy."
15. The United States militarily intervened in Mexican affairs during Woodrow Wilson's administration.

Review Questions

These questions are to be answered with essays. This will allow you to explore relationships among individuals, events, and attitudes of the period under review.

1. In what ways did Theodore Roosevelt transform the role of the presidency and the national government? What specific programs resulted from his vigorous executive leadership?
2. Were the differences between the Taft administration and those of Roosevelt and Wilson more a matter of beliefs and objectives or of personalities and leadership style?
3. Considering Roosevelt's and Wilson's personalities and proposals, what would have happened to domestic reform and foreign relations if Roosevelt had won the Republican nomination in 1912 and become president again?

Chapter Twenty-Three
America and the Great War

Objectives

A thorough study of Chapter 23 should enable you to understand:

1. The background factors and the immediate sequence of events that caused the United States to declare war on Germany in 1917.
2. The contributions of the American military to Allied victory in World War I.
3. The extent of government control of the economy during World War I.
4. Propaganda and the extent of war hysteria in the United States during World War I.
5. The aspirations that the war raised with African Americans and how those hopes were dashed.
6. Woodrow Wilson's successes and failures at Versailles.
7. The circumstances that led the United States to reject the Treaty of Versailles.
8. The economic problems the United States faced immediately after the war.
9. The reasons for the Red Scare, and the resurgence of labor unrest in postwar America.

Pertinent Questions

The Road to War (pp. 633–646)

1. How did World War I begin? (What connection to conflicts in the 1990s are apparent?)
2. Which nations were referred to as the Allies? The Central Powers?
3. What forced President Woodrow Wilson out of his professed stance of true neutrality? To what degree was his decision based on economics?

4. Why did Germany rely on U-boats (submarines)? Why did it back off from the unrestricted use of U-boats early in the war?
5. Before 1917, how did Wilson balance the demands for preparedness and the cries for peace? What effect did his position have on the 1916 election?
6. What key events early in 1917 combined to finally bring the United States fully into World War I?

"War Without Stint" (pp. 638–646)

7. On what aspect of the war did American entry have the most immediate effect? What was the effect?
8. What impact did events in Russia have on the decision of the United States to enter World War I and on the need for American land forces in Europe after entry?
9. On what two methods did the Wilson administration depend to finance the war effort? How did the war cost compare with the typical peacetime budgets of that era?
10. Describe the role of the War Industries Board (WIB) and the National War Labor Board. How successful were they? (What implications did they have for the future of American politics?)
11. What tactics did the Committee on Public Information employ to propagandize the American people into unquestioning support of the war effort?
12. In what ways did the government use the Sedition Act and related legislation to suppress criticism? Who suffered most?
13. How did private acts of oppression supplement the official campaign to suppress diversity and promote unity? Who suffered most?

The Search for a New World Order (pp. 646–650)

14. Into what three major categories did the Fourteen Points fall? Which category was the most important to Wilson? Why?
15. What obstacles did Wilson face in getting the European leaders to accept his approach to peace? What domestic development weakened his position?
16. Which ideals of the Fourteen Points were most directly challenged at Versailles.
17. What victories for his ideals was Wilson able to salvage? Why did he believe that the League of Nations could redeem any specific shortcomings in the Treaty of Versailles?

18. Who were the main opponents of American entry into the League of Nations? What were the two categories of opponents? How much of the blame for the treaty's defeat must be laid on Wilson himself?

A Society in Turmoil (pp. 650–656)

19. What happened to the American economy in the postwar years? Why?
20. What inspired the labor unrest of 1919? What were the most important strikes? What did the wave of strikes reveal about the labor movement?
21. Describe how African American military and industrial contributions during World War I raised black aspirations. How did whites react, and what happened after the war?
22. What led to the string of race riots during and shortly after the war? What were the riots like, and where was the worst episode?
23. What inspired the Red Scare of 1919 to 1920? Was the threat real or imagined?
24. What did the results of the election of 1920 indicate about the mood of the American people?

IDENTIFICATION

Identify each of the following, and explain why it is important within the context of the chapter.

1. "Triple Entente"/"Triple Alliance"
2. Ottoman Empire
3. Archduke Franz Ferdinand
4. *Lusitania*
5. V. I. Lenin
6. American Expeditionary Force (AEF)
7. John J. Pershing
8. Argonne Forest campaign
9. Herbert Hoover
10. Bernard Baruch
11. Eugene V. Debs
12. David Lloyd George
13. Georges Clemenceau
14. Vittorio Orlando
15. Henry Cabot Lodge

16. steel strike of 1919
17. "Great Migration"
18. Marcus Garvey
19. A. Mitchell Palmer
20. Sacco-Vanzetti case
21. "normalcy"

DOCUMENT

Read the subsection of the text entitled "A War for Democracy," paying careful attention to the discussion of the Zimmermann telegram. The following document is the official dispatch in which Walter Hines Page, the American ambassador to Great Britain, informed the State Department that the British had intercepted Germany's invitation to Mexico to join in war against the United States. Unknown to the Germans, the British had broken their diplomatic code. Read the dispatch, and consider the following questions: How did the Zimmermann communication combine with other events early in 1917 to impel the United States to declare war? Why did Germany have reason to believe that Mexico might be receptive to a proposal to wage war against the United States? Why did the British government give a copy of the Zimmermann note to the United States? How does Zimmermann's note reveal that Germany expected the United States to enter the war soon?

> The Ambassador of Great Britain [Walter Hines Page] to the Secretary of State [Robert Lansing]
>
> LONDON, February 24, 1917, 1 P.M.
>
> [Received 8:30 P.M.]
>
> ...British Foreign Secretary Arthur] Balfour has handed me the text of a cipher telegram from [Arthur] Zimmermann, German Secretary of State for Foreign Affairs, to the German Minister to Mexico....I give you the English translation as follows:
>
>> We intend to begin on the 1st of February unrestricted submarine warfare. We shall endeavor in spite of this to keep the United States of America neutral. In the event of this not succeeding, we make Mexico a proposal of alliance on the following basis: make war together, make peace together, generous financial support and an understanding on our part that Mexico is to reconquer the lost territory in Texas, New Mexico, and Arizona. The settlement in detail is left to you. You will inform the President [of Mexico, Venustiano Carranza] of the above most secretly as soon as the outbreak of war with the United States of America is certain and add the suggestion that he should, on his own initiative, invite Japan to immediate adherence and at the same time mediate between Japan and ourselves. Please call the President's attention to the fact that the ruthless employment of our submarines now offers the prospect of compelling England in a few months to make peace.

Signed, Zimmermann.

The receipt of this information has so greatly exercised the British Government that they have lost no time in communicating it to me to transmit to you, in order that our Government may be able without delay to make such disposition as may be necessary in view of the threatened invasion of our territory....

U.S. Department of State, *Papers Relating to the Foreign Relations of the U.S.,* 1917, Supplement 1, The World War (Washington, D.C.: Government Printing Office, 1931), p. 147.

MAP EXERCISE

Fill in or identify the following on the blank map provided.

1. The Allies, the Central Powers, the occupied nations, and the neutrals
2. Paris, Berlin, London, and Vienna.
3. The principal area of submarine warfare.
4. Approximate location of Germany's deepest penetration of France.
5. Approximate location of Germany's deepest penetration of Russia.
6. Approximate location of the armistice line.

Interpretative Questions

Based on what you have filled in, answer the following. On some of the questions you will need to consult the narrative in your text for information or explanation.

1. What two nations bore the brunt of the western front fighting within their borders? What nation suffered the most on the east? How did this affect the peace negotiations?
2. Why was the ocean war so crucial in bringing the United States into the war?
3. What geographic and naval advantages did Great Britain have in sea warfare? How did Germany try to counter these advantages and how successful was it?

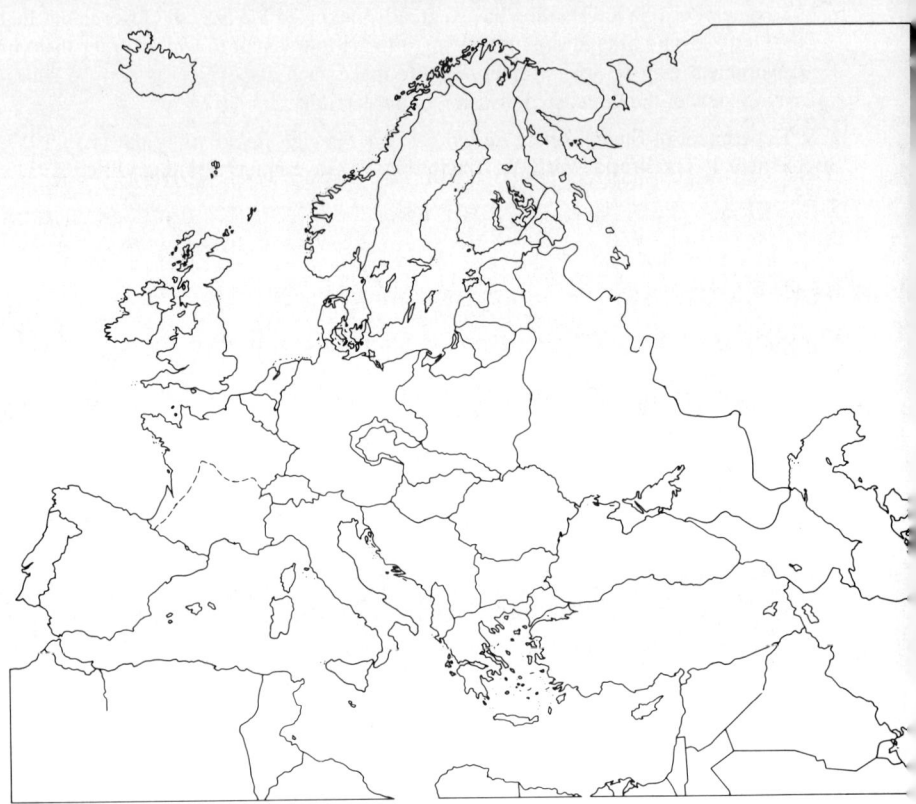

Summary

Following two and a half years of pro-Allied "neutrality," the United States entered World War I because of economic and cultural factors as well as German submarine warfare. The armies and civilians of Europe had already suffered mightily by the time the United States finally entered. American forces, initially at sea and then on land, provided the margin of victory for the Allies. To mount its total effort, the United States turned to an array of unprecedented measures: sharply graduated taxes, conscription for a foreign war, bureaucratic management of the economy, and a massive propaganda and antisedition campaign. The war effort at home and overseas seemed to offer new opportunities for black Americans, but most of their hopes were dashed after the war. President Woodrow Wilson formulated American war aims in his famous Fourteen Points, but he was unable to convince either Europe or the United States to fully accept them as the basis for peace. By 1920, the American people, tired from nearly three decades of turmoil, had repudiated Wilson's precious League of Nations in favor of an illusion called "normalcy."

CHAPTER SELF-TEST

After you have read the chapter in the text and done the exercises in the Study Guide, the following self-test can be taken to see if you understand the material you have covered. Answers appear at the end of the Study Guide.

Multiple Choice

Circle the letter of the response which best answers the question or completes the statement.

1. Americans responded to the outbreak of the Great War in 1914 with a conviction that the conflict:
   a. would be quickly and peacefully resolved.
   b. would remain a limited war.
   c. had little to do with them.
   d. required their immediate intervention.

2. Which of the following nations was *not* a member of the Central Powers in World War I?
   a. Germany.
   b. The Austro-Hungarian Empire.
   c. The Ottoman Empire.
   d. Russia.

3. President Wilson protested German violations of American neutrality more harshly than British violations because:
   a. he admired the British and instinctively favored their cause.
   b. a profitable trade was resulting between the United States and the Allies.
   c. German violations cost American lives.
   d. all of the above.

4. In the Zimmermann telegram, Germany:
   a. notified the United States it would begin unrestricted submarine warfare on February 1, 1917.
   b. offered Russian revolutionists aid for a plot to overthrow the czarist regime.

c. proposed to Mexico a military alliance in the event of war between Germany and the United States.
d. offered aid to German-Americans for plans of industrial sabotage.

5. After the Bolshevik Revolution in November, 1917, the new Russian government, led by V. I. Lenin:
   a. negotiated a hasty peace with the Central Powers.
   b. negotiated secret treaties with the Allied Powers to divide the postwar spoils.
   c. supplied the necessary troops which would guarantee Allied success.
   d. called for creation of a world government to maintain international peace and security.

6. Members of the American Expeditionary Force (AEF) played a crucial role in the fighting at:
   a. the Marne.
   b. Verdun.
   c. the Somme.
   d. the Argonne forest.

7. In mobilizing the American economy for war, the War Industries Board:
   a. divided the country geographically, setting up local defense councils in each region.
   b. operated with incredible success and efficiency.
   c. worked to restrict private power and limit corporate profits.
   d. established a mutually beneficial alliance between government and the private sector.

8. During World War I, German-Americans suffered all of the following forms of abuse *except:*
   a. a campaign to purge society of all things German.
   b. the loss of jobs.
   c. the loss of homes and internment in camps.
   d. physical harassment and beatings.

9. Woodrow Wilson's Fourteen Points:
   a. included specific formulas for the implementation of national self-determination.
   b. specifically addressed the needs of the new Soviet government in Russia.

c. reflected his belief that the world as a whole was capable of just and efficient government.
d. attracted the strong, enthusiastic support of the Allied leaders.

10. Wilson's most notable triumph at the Paris Peace Conference was the:
    a. impartial mediation and settlement of colonial claims.
    b. creation of a League of Nations.
    c. establishment of national self-determination for all Europeans.
    d. obstruction of demands for punitive damages from the defeated Central Powers.

11. Wilson's cross-country tour to arouse support for the Treaty of Versailles:
    a. generated enough enthusiasm and popular support to pressure the Senate into ratification.
    b. exhausted Wilson and precipitated a serious stroke.
    c. convinced Wilson to accept significant changes in the treaty's language.

12. During World War I and the aftermath, Herbert Hoover established a reputation as:
    a. a great military tactician and adviser.
    b. an efficient administrator and true humanitarian.
    c. a creative public relations expert and propagandist.
    d. an apologist for German aggression and atrocities.

13. Which of the following was *not* one of the three principal negotiators who joined Woodrow Wilson at the Versailles Conference?
    a. David Lloyd George.
    b. Vittorio Orlando.
    c. Georges Clemenceau.
    d. Bernard Baruch.

14. The catch phrase used by Warren Harding in the 1920 campaign to communicate that the people wanted to put the turmoil of the war years behind them was:
    a. "search for stability."
    b. "return to normalcy."
    c. "seeking for security."
    d. "calling for calm."

15. The so-called "Great Migration" of World War I and the years before and after involved the movement of:
    a. Asian Americans from the West Coast to the rest of the nation.
    b. Hispanics from Mexico into the American Southwest.

c. African Americans from the rural south to the urban north.
d. poor white farmers to California.

True/False

Read each statement carefully. Mark true statements "T" and false statements "F."

1. The "Central Powers" of World War I included Germany, the Ottoman Empire (Turkey), and the Austro-Hungarian Empire.
2. At the time of its sinking by German submarine the British Ocean liner *Lusitania* was carrying munitions as well as passengers.
3. Woodrow Wilson's victorious presidential campaign in 1916 was significantly aided by his pledge that the United States would enter World War I on the allied side if he were reelected.
4. The episode involving the intercepted telegram from Arthur Zimmermann concerned German relations with Mexico.
5. In World War I, Russia started out on the Allied side but joined Germany in fighting the allies after the communists took over and renamed the Russian Empire the Union of Soviet Socialist Republics.
6. The United States Congress seriously considered instituting a military draft during World War I but decided not to when volunteer enlistments provided enough soldiers.
7. The biggest defeat of American ground forces in World War I was in the Argonne Forest.
8. In order to keep support for the war high, the federal government choose to raise all extra funds by selling war bonds rather than raising taxes.
9. As President Wilson's principal economic adviser during World War I, Bernard Baruch favored corporate volunteerism rather than central direction by a government board.
10. Government actions during World War I resulted in a significant increase in labor union membership between 1917 and 1919.
11. Unlike France and Great Britain, where opposition to the war was treated harshly, the United States allowed dissidents to speak and operate freely without supervision or harassment.
12. The majority of Wilson's Fourteen Points concerned his aspirations for postwar European boundaries and self-determination for the people of the Austro-Hungarian and Ottoman Empires.

13. Wilson's Fourteen Points contained proposals for an alliance of Western European powers against the newly-created Soviet Union.
14. When Wilson traveled to Paris for the peace conference, he visited several European cities and encountered considerable public hostility toward his idealistic ideas for peace.
15. In the United States Senate the leader of the opposition to Wilson, the treaty, and the League of Nations was Henry Cabot Lodge.

Review Questions

These questions are to be answered with essays. This will allow you to explore relationships among individuals, events, and attitudes of the period under review.

1. Was American involvement in World War I inevitable? What forces worked to maintain neutrality? What forces propelled the country away from neutrality and into full belligerency?
2. Describe the suffering that the Great War visited on Europe. Why is it said that the United States emerged from the war as "the only real victor"?
3. What "surprises" did America face as the reality of "war without stint" unfolded? How did the American people respond to them? What long-term legacies came from these responses?
4. Despite his tumultuous reception by the peoples of Europe and the generally favorable response he received on his tour in the western United States, Wilson faced troublesome opposition from both European statesmen and the United States senators. Why did he encounter such intransigence? Did he respond in a rational and politically effective way?

Chapter Twenty-Four

The New Era

OBJECTIVES

A thorough study of Chapter 24 should enable you to understand:

1. The reasons for the industrial boom in the 1920s after the initial period of economic readjustment following World War I.
2. The nature and extent of labor's problems.
3. The plight of the American farmer.
4. The changes in the American way of life and American values in the 1920s in the areas of consumerism, communications, religion, and the role of women.
5. The effects of Prohibition on American politics and society.
6. The reasons for xenophobia and racial unrest in the 1920s.
7. The debacle of the Harding administration.
8. The probusiness tendencies of the Republican administration in the 1920s.

PERTINENT QUESTIONS

The New Economy (pp. 657–663)

1. Outline the causes of the economic boom of the 1920s. What impact did the spectacular growth of the automobile industry have on related business activities?
2. What was the "New Era" trend in business organization? What sort of firms were less likely to consolidate?
3. What were the elements of "welfare capitalism"? Did the average worker truly benefit?
4. To what extent was the lag in union membership due to the unions themselves? What were the other causal factors?
5. How did the African Americans, Hispanics, and Asians fare with labor unions?

6. What national group composed the largest number of immigrants in the 1920s? Where did they concentrate, and how were they treated?
7. What caused the big drop in farm prices and income in the 1920s? Explain how parity was designed to solve the problem. What happened to parity?

The New Culture (pp. 663–670)

8. Describe the new urban consumer society. How did advertising help shape it?
9. How did newspaper chains, mass-circulation magazines, movies, and radio serve as unifying and nationalizing forces in America?
10. How did the image of the "new professional woman" compare with reality for most working women?
11. What new attitudes toward motherhood, sex, and leisure developed in the 1920s, especially among middle-class women? Was the new woman mostly a figure of myth?
12. What social forces combined to disenchant many intellectuals? What did these people attack? Who were the main attackers?

A Conflict of Cultures (pp. 670–676)

13. What more basic conflict in society did the controversy over the "noble experiment" of prohibition come to symbolize? What were the results of prohibition?
14. Explain the changes in immigration laws brought about by the National Origins Act and subsequent legislation. What ethnic groups were favored?
15. What helped resurrect the Ku Klux Klan in the 1920s? Whom did the Klan target for its rage? How influential was it?
16. Compare and contrast the views of the religious modernists and fundamentalists. How did Darwinism and the Scopes trial symbolize the conflict between the two? How has the conflict persisted?
17. How were the cultural tensions of the 1920s reflected in the Democratic party?

Republican Government (pp. 676–679)

18. What features of President Warren G. Harding's personal background led to his political repudiation? What was the biggest of the various Harding-era scandals?
19. Contrast the personal lives of Harding and Calvin Coolidge. Did their politics and policies differ as much as their personalities?

20. What approach did Harding take toward taxes and the Federal budget?
21. Why did Herbert Hoover push so strongly for the creation of trade associations?

IDENTIFICATION

Identify each of the following, and explain why it is important within the context of the chapter.

1. "normalcy"
2. American Plan
3. "pink collar" jobs
4. Issei/Nisei
5. barrios
6. KDKA
7. "behaviorists"
8. Margaret Sanger
9. "flapper"
10. Equal Rights Amendment
11. H. L. Mencken
12. Sinclair Lewis
13. "Harlem Renaissance"
14. Langston Hughes
15. "wets" and "drys"
16. Leo Frank case
17. ACLU
18. Alfred E. Smith
19. Andrew Mellon

DOCUMENT

Read H. L. Mencken's obituary for Calvin Coolidge, noting his contempt for politics and his sarcasm concerning Coolidge's lack of aggressiveness. Mencken's iconoclastic style was extremely popular with young intellectuals; but, in fact, his *American Mercury* was not a mass-circulation magazine, and Mencken's comments reached a relatively small portion of the general public.

> In what manner he would have performed himself if the holy angels had shoved the Depression forward a couple of years—this we can only guess, and one man's hazard is as good as another's. My own is that he would have responded to bad times precisely as he responded to good ones—that is, by pulling down the blinds, stretching

his legs upon his desk, and snoozing away the lazy afternoons....He slept more than any other President, whether by day or by night. Nero fiddled, but Coolidge only snored....Counting out Harding as a cipher only, Dr. Coolidge was preceded by one World Saver and followed by two more. What enlightened American, having to choose between any of them and another Coolidge, would hesitate for an instant? There were no thrills while he reigned, but neither were there any headaches. He had no ideas, and he was not a nuisance.

H. L. Mencken, *American Mercury,* April 1933.

MAP EXERCISE

Fill in or identify the following on the blank map provided. Use the maps in the text as your sources.

1. Locate and label the following cities: Boston, New York, Philadelphia, Chicago, Nashville, Atlanta, Birmingham, Memphis, Dallas-Fort Worth, Denver, Seattle, San Francisco, Los Angeles.
2. Circle the region of the nation that was most heavily urbanized as of 1920.
3. Shade in the states that Al Smith carried in the election of 1928.

Interpretative Questions

Based on what you have filled in, answer the following. For some of the questions you will need to consult the narrative in your text for information or explanation.

1. To what extent was the new consumerism and change in communication related to increasing urbanization in the United States?
2. Why did Al Smith carry states in such different regions—the urban Northeast and the more rural South? Why did he not carry as much of the South as a Democrat of that period normally would have?

SUMMARY

Through the mid-1920s, America enjoyed unparalleled prosperity fueled by a great boom in automobiles and related businesses. Many people believed that the progressive ideal of an efficient, ordered society was at hand. The boom, however, masked problems. The prosperity was not equitably distributed through society; many workers and farmers were left out, and, as usual, racial and ethnic minorities were excluded from most economic benefits. The new ways forged by economic and technological advancement brought an unprecedented cultural nationalism, but they also aroused serious conflicts as both intellectuals and traditionalists attacked elements of the New Era culture. Presidents Harding and Coolidge, despite their contrasting styles, personified the pro-business policies of the Republican party, which dominated American politics throughout the 1920s.

CHAPTER SELF-TEST

After you have read the chapter in the text and done the exercises in the Study Guide, the following self-test can be taken to see if you understand the material you have covered. Answers appear at the end of the Study Guide.

Multiple Choice

Circle the letter of the response which best answers the question or completes the statement.

1. America's economic boom in the 1920s resulted from the:
   a. debilitation of Europe after World War I.
   b. rapid pace of technological innovations.
   c. expansion of the automobile industry.
   d. all of the above.

2. The industry that seemed *least* affected by a trend toward consolidation in the 1920s was:
   a. steel.
   b. automobiles.
   c. cotton textiles.
   d. public utilities.

3. Which of the following was *not* provided by the "welfare capitalism" of the 1920s?
   a. economic benefits for some workers.
   b. company unions or workers councils.
   c. real control over workers' fates

4. Most American workers in the 1920s:
   a. received wage increases that were proportionately below the increases in corporate profits.
   b. became increasingly militant and committed to unionization as the means for improving their position.
   c. experienced sufficient increases in their standard of living to place them in the middle class.

5. The plight of the American farmers in the 1920s resulted most directly from the:
   a. failure of agriculture to adapt to changing technology.
   b. depleted fertility of the land.
   c. inability of American agriculture to service an expanded European market.
   d. overproduction by American farmers.

6. By the 1920s, most working women in America:
   a. were college graduates.
   b. entered professional fields.
   c. attempted to combine marriage and careers.
   d. were employed in nonprofessional, low-paying jobs.

7. Many American artists and intellectuals of the 1920s felt alienated by modern American society for all of the following reasons *except* its:
   a. obsession with materialism.
   b. outmoded, straight-laced morality.
   c. lack of idealism.
   d. emphasis on individualism.

8. Immigration to the United States was restricted in the 1920s on the basis of:
   a. religion.
   b. national origin.
   c. special skills or talents.
   d. need for political asylum.

9. Which of the following characteristics did *not* apply to President Warren G. Harding?
   a. good looks and geniality.
   b. polished speaking style.
   c. aggressive leadership.
   d. party regularity.

10. Like Harding, Calvin Coolidge:
    a. was tolerant of corruption among his cronies.
    b. had a loose, debauched lifestyle.
    c. took a passive, conservative approach to the presidency.
    d. had been a major congressional leader before taking executive office.

11. As Commerce Secretary for much of the 1920s, Herbert Hoover advocated:
    a. vigorous enforcement of antitrust legislation.
    b. voluntary business cooperation through trade associations.
    c. government-sanctioned collusion among manufacturers.
    d. the establishment of government relief programs.

12. Al Smith, Democratic presidential nominee in 1928, gained his strongest support at the party convention from:
    a. rural Southern delegates.
    b. "dry" delegates from all regions.
    c. northeastern urban delegates.
    d. midwestern small-town delegates.

13. A method of mass communication that was totally new to the 1920s was:
    a. popular magazines.
    b. radio.
    c. television.
    d. daily newspapers.

14. After World War I, the revived Ku Klux Klan dedicated itself to:
    a. defending what it considered to be traditional values.
    b. promoting the ideal of racial integration.
    c. secularizing American society.
    d. helping southern European immigrants adapt to America.

15. The Scopes trial of 1925:
    a. illustrated the power of business corporations.
    b. personified intellectual alienation.
    c. symbolized religious conflict between fundamentalists and modernists.
    d. solidified the open-shop concept.

True/False

Read each statement carefully. Mark true statements "T" and false statements "F."

1. The Democratic Party of the 1920s consisted of a diverse coalition of interests that often faced internal conflicts.
2. The "American Plan" was a nickname given by corporate leaders to the "open shop" concept, which held that no worker could be required to join a union to get or keep a job.
3. The economic sector most responsible for the prosperity of the 1920s was agriculture.
4. During the 1920s, the trend toward business consolidation that had begun in the 1890s began to slow.
5. During the 1920s, membership in labor unions declined significantly compared to the World War I years.
6. The concept of "parity" for agricultural prices was designed to make sure that farmers earned at least the cost of producing the products.
7. During the 1920s, advertising expanded rapidly and advertisers were increasingly trying to identify their products with a modern lifestyle.

8. "Flapper" was the nickname given during 1920s to women who tried to hold on to traditional female roles and who criticized the "wild" ways of the youth of the decade.
9. H. L. Mencken and Sinclair Lewis were among the authors whose writings were harshly critical of the dominant middle-class values of the 1920s.
10. The New York City-based flourishing of African-American culture in the 1920s was given the nickname "Gotham Revival."
11. Support for the prohibition of liquor was strongest in the provincial, largely rural, Protestant-dominated areas of the country.
12. The effect of the Immigration Act of 1921 and the National Origins Act of 1924 was to increase foreign immigration, especially Asian immigration, following the restrictive period around World War I.
13. In the 1920s, the Ku Klux Klan grew rapidly in some midwestern states as well as in the South.
14. Within American Protestantism, the so-called "modernists" tended to be urban, middle-class people who attempted to adapt religion to the teachings of modern science and secular society.
15. The Republican administrations of the 1920s achieved significant reductions in taxes on corporate profits, personal incomes, and inheritances.

Review Questions

These questions are to be answered with essays. This will allow you to explore relationships among individuals, events, and attitudes of the period under review.

1. Many people gained from the boom of the New Era, and others fell through the economic cracks. But the prosperity was widespread enough to usher in a modern consumer society. Who gained? Who did not? What were the main elements of the national consumer-based society?
2. One of the questions that has troubled historians concerns the legacy of progressivism. Looking at the 1920s, would you say that progressive thought had died or had triumphed? Why?
3. Impressions of the 1920s vary, according to which vision one accepts—that of members of the ruling elite, such as Andrew Mellon and Herbert Hoover; of the disenchanted, such as H. L. Mencken; of evangelicals such as Billy Sunday; or of the blacks in the Harlem Renaissance. Briefly describe each of those visions,

and tell how one or several capture the real significance of the decade.

CHAPTER TWENTY-FIVE
The Great Depression

OBJECTIVES

A thorough study of Chapter 25 should enable you to understand:

1. The relationship between the stock market crash and the subsequent Great Depression.
2. The causes of the Depression and the reasons for its severity.
3. The problems of unemployment and the inadequacy of relief.
4. The particular problems of farmers in the Dust Bowl.
5. The impact of the Depression on minorities.
6. The impact of the Depression on working women and the American family.
7. The reflection of the economic crisis in American culture.
8. President Herbert Hoover's policies for fighting the Depression.

PERTINENT QUESTIONS

The Coming of the Depression (pp. 680–684)

1. What caused the stock market boom to get so out of hand, and why did the stock market collapse?
2. Which two industries were most responsible for the New Era prosperity and hence substantially to blame for the Great Depression when they slumped? Why did these and other industries have trouble selling accumulated inventory?
3. What impact did international trade and debt factors have on the American economy? What role did U.S. tariff policy play?
4. What happened to the banking system early in the Depression? What role did the Federal Reserve system play?

The American People in Hard Times (pp. 684–694)

5. Describe the extent of unemployment. How effective were local, state, and private relief agencies in meeting the ravages of widespread unemployment?
6. Compare and contrast the impact of the Great Depression on blacks, Hispanics, and Asians with its impact on whites. What demographic shifts occurred in this period?
7. What effect did the Depression have on the role of women in general and black women in particular?
8. How did American families adjust to the pressures of the hard times?
9. What sort of fare dominated radio, movies, and popular literature in the 1930s?
10. How much allure did such radical movements as communism and socialism have for Americans in the 1930s? What was the "Popular Front" approach and what happened to it?

The Ordeal of Herbert Hoover (pp. 694–701)

11. What were Herbert Hoover's first approaches to combating the Depression? How effective were they?
12. What were the results of Hoover's agricultural policy?
13. What was Hoover's new approach to the Depression in the spring of 1931? What caused his shift in emphasis?
14. What impact did Hoover's handling of the Veterans' Bonus March have on his popularity?
15. What made Franklin Roosevelt such an attractive presidential candidate for the Democrats? Why did he win the 1932 election?
16. How did Roosevelt react to Hoover's demands for policy pledges during the desperate winter of 1932–1933?

IDENTIFICATION

Identify each of the following, and explain why it is important within the context of the chapter.

1. Dow Jones Industrial Average
2. "Dust Bowl"
3. "Okies"
4. Scottsboro case
5. Dale Carnegie
6. Farm Security Administration Photographers

7. Erskine Caldwell
8. Richard Wright
9. John Steinbeck
10. Will Hays
11. Abraham Lincoln Brigade
12. Norman Thomas
13. Southern Tenant Farmers Union
14. Hawley-Smoot Tariff
15. "Hoovervilles"
16. Reconstruction Finance Corporation
17. Farmers Holiday Association

DOCUMENT

The years 1932 and 1933 were the hardest of the Great Depression. Even normally conservative, business-oriented *Fortune* magazine was convinced that extraordinary measures were necessary in the face of the collapse of existing relief agencies and the inadequacy of the $300 million Emergency Relief Act. The excerpt below is from *Fortune*'s September 1932 issue. Consider the following questions: Why were existing relief programs so inadequate? Why is it especially significant that a business-minded publication like *Fortune* would, in the autumn of 1932, stress the magnitude of the crisis and the failure of the response? What do you suppose the writer meant by the statement "One does not talk architecture while the house is on fire...."?

> There can be no serious question of the failure of those methods. For the methods were never seriously capable of success. They were diffuse, unrelated, and unplanned. The theory was that private charitable organizations and semi-public welfare groups, established to care for the old and the sick and the indigent, were capable of caring for the casualties of a worldwide economic disaster. And the theory in application meant that social agencies manned for the service of a few hundred families, and city shelters set up to house and feed a handful of homeless men, were compelled by the brutal necessities of hunger to care for hundreds of thousands of families and whole armies of the displaced and the jobless. And to depend for their resources upon the contributions of communities no longer able to contribute, and upon the irresolution and vacillation of state legislatures and municipal assemblies long since in the red on their annual budgets. The result was the picture now presented in city after city and state after state—heterogeneous groups of official and semiofficial and nonofficial relief agencies struggling under the earnest and untrained leadership of the local men of affairs against an inertia of misery and suffering and want they are powerless to overcome....
>
> One does not talk architecture while the house is on fire and the tenants are still inside. The question at this moment is the pure question of fact. Having decided at

last to face reality and do something about it, what is reality? How many men are unemployed in the U.S.? How many are in want? *What are the facts?*

The following minimal statements may be accepted as true—with the certainty that they underestimate the real situation:

1. Unemployment has steadily increased in the U.S. since the beginning of the depression and the rate of increase during the first part of 1932 was more rapid than in any other depression year.
2. The number of persons totally unemployed is now at least 10 million.
3. The number of persons totally unemployed next winter will, at the present rate of increase, be 11 million.
4. Eleven million unemployed means better than one man out of every four employable workers.
5. This percentage is higher than the percentage of unemployed British workers registered under the compulsory insurance laws (17.1 percent in May 1932, as against 17.3 percent in April and 18.4 percent in Jan.) and higher than the French, the Italian, and the Canadian percentages, but lower than the German (43.9 percent of trade unionists in April 1932) and the Norwegian.
6. Eleven million unemployed means 27,500,000 whose regular source of livelihood has been cut off.
7. Twenty-seven and a half million without regular income includes the families of totally unemployed workers alone. Taking account of the numbers of workers on part time, the total of those without adequate income becomes 34 million, or better than a quarter of the entire population of the country.
8. Thirty-four million persons without adequate income does not mean 34 million in present want. Many families have savings. But savings are eventually dissipated and the number in actual want tends to approximate the number without adequate income. How nearly it approximates it now or will next winter no man can say. But it is conservative to estimate that the problem of next winter's relief is a problem of caring for approximately 25 million souls....

Such, broadly speaking, are the facts of unemployment relief in the late summer of 1932. Ahead, whether the depression "ends" this fall or not, is the problem of caring for some 25 million souls through what may prove to be one of the most difficult winters of the republic's history. Behind are three years of muddled purpose, insufficient funds, and unscientific funds, and unscientific direction. Across the threshold lies a new federal policy and a formal acceptance of the issue.

Fortune, September 1932.

MAP EXERCISE

Fill in or identify the following on the blank map provided. Use the map on page 700 of the text as your source.

1. States carried by Hoover
2. States carried by Roosevelt

Interpretative Questions

Based on what you have filled in, answer the following. For some of the questions you will need to consult the narrative in your text for information or explanation.

1. Why did the nation so thoroughly reject Herbert Hoover? What was expected from Roosevelt?
2. What parts of the country that were normally reliably Republican voted for Roosevelt in 1932? What does that signify about the seriousness of the Depression?

SUMMARY

In October 1929, the stock market's overinflated values collapsed, and the Great Depression began. Its causes were complex, and its consequences were enormous. In a few short years, the 2 percent unemployment rate of the 1920s had become the 25 percent rate of 1932. The nation's political institutions were not equipped to respond. The task overwhelmed local and private relief efforts. President Herbert Hoover's tentative program of voluntary cooperation, big-business loans, and limited public works was activist by old standards but inadequate to the challenge. American tariffs and war-debt policy aggravated international economic problems and thereby added to domestic woes. Although the suffering of Americans, especially blacks, Asians, and Hispanics, was great, most citizens clung to traditional values and resisted radical solutions. With veterans marching, farmers protesting, and millions not working, Franklin Delano Roosevelt won the presidency.

CHAPTER SELF-TEST

After you have read the chapter in the text and done the exercises in the Study Guide, the following self-test can be taken to see if you understand the material you have covered. Answers appear at the end of the Study Guide.

Multiple Choice

Circle the letter of the response which best answers the question or completes the statement.

1. The Great Depression of the 1930s affected the nation more profoundly than any prior economic crisis because it:
   a. occurred unexpectedly and without warning.
   b. began with a dramatic stock market crash.
   c. affected virtually everyone.
   d. resulted in widespread civil strife.

2. The stock market boom of the late 1920s rested primarily upon the:
   a. maintenance of high interest rates by stockbrokers.
   b. widespread speculative mania of American investors.
   c. increased earning power of American corporations.
   d. economic support of J. P. Morgan and Company.

3. There was a serious lack of diversification in the American economy of the 1920s, with prosperity excessively dependent upon what two industries?
   a. Oil and steel.
   b. Railroads and public utilities.
   c. Radio and motion pictures.
   d. Construction and automobiles.

4. The profits generated by America's economic expansion in the 1920s:
   a. went disproportionately to the producers rather than potential consumers.
   b. lifted a great majority of the families in America above a minimum subsistence level.
   c. created a consistently expanding market for consumer goods.
   d. led corporations to neglect the expansion of capital facilities.

5. American banks of the 1920s:
   a. had most of their assets in agricultural land.
   b. protested tight regulations of the Federal Reserve System.
   c. invested wisely in the stock market.
   d. often made unwise loans and failed to maintain adequate reserves.

6. The international credit structure collapsed by the early 1930s to a great extent because:
   a. Germany defaulted on reparations payments it owed to the United States.
   b. the United States forgave the debts of the Allied Powers.
   c. high American tariffs restricted Europeans ability to repay their loans.
   d. European demand for American goods increased too rapidly.

7. The industrial cities of the Northeast and Midwest in the early 1930s:
   a. largely escaped the high rates of unemployment burdening the nation as a whole.
   b. lacked sufficient resources and understanding to provide the necessary relief for unemployed workers.
   c. combined the efforts of private charities and local public relief systems to ensure adequate food and housing for all unemployed workers.
   d. convinced state governments of the need for establishment of a permanent welfare system.

8. American farmers faced all of the following problems during the 1930s *except:*
   a. an inability to produce enough food to feed Americans.
   b. one of the worst droughts in the history of the nation.
   c. a steady loss of land through mortgage foreclosures or evictions.
   d. creation of a Dust Bowl in a large area of the South and Midwest.

9. For black Americans, the Depression:
   a. actually reduced the average income gap between white and black families.
   b. mitigated white attitudes of racism and discrimination.
   c. weakened their commitment to and drive for economic and political equality.
   d. intensified problems and created special hardships.
10. Perhaps the most effective documentation of rural poverty in the 1930s came from:
    a. fact-finding commissions of the national government.
    b. a group of photographers employed by the Farm Security Administration.
    c. the powerful instruments of popular culture—radio and the movies.
    d. the academic fields of sociology and anthropology.
11. Thousands of disillusioned members left the American Communist party as a result of the:
    a. formation of the Abraham Lincoln brigade for intervention in the Spanish Civil War.
    b. signing of a nonaggression pact in 1939 between the Soviet Union and Nazi Germany.
    c. party's defense of extreme and violent tactics to achieve racial justice.
    d. party's refusal to engage actively in the organization and promotion of unions.
12. In response to the Depression, President Herbert Hoover called for a program of:
    a. voluntary cooperation among leaders of business, labor, and agriculture.
    b. massive and permanent federal public works projects.
    c. substantial government cutbacks to ensure a balanced budget.
    d. tax increases and tariff reductions.
13. The Hawley-Smoot tariff of 1930:
    a. put tariff rates completely in the hands of the presidentially appointed Tariff Commission.
    b. provoked foreign governments to enact trade restrictions of their own in reprisal.
    c. helped expand the market for American agricultural goods.
    d. rendered industrial products more affordable to American farmers.

14. Hoover's use of the United States army to clear the "Bonus Army" out of Washington D.C.:
    a. increased congressional support for the immediate payment of a bonus to veterans of World War I.
    b. enhanced his reputation as a defender of law and order.
    c. confirmed his image as aloof and insensitive to the distress around him.
    d. offered proof of the growing and dangerous threat of radicalism in America.

15. Immediately prior to becoming President Franklin D. Roosevelt served as:
    a. U.S. Senator from Iowa well known for holding hearings on problems in the banking industry.
    b. Secretary of State well known for leading the isolationist movement.
    c. Speaker of the U.S. House of Representatives well known for supporting organized labor.
    d. Governor of New York well known for a positive program of government assistance early in the depression.

True/False

Read each statement carefully. Mark true statements "T" and false statements "F."

1. The stock market reached its lowest point of the depression era in late 1929 and then gradually inched back up, finally reaching 1928 levels by mid-1932.
2. Most economic historians contend that one important cause of the Great Depression was that the economy lacked diversification and too much of the prosperity had depended on automobiles and construction.
3. Most economic historians believe that one important cause of the Great Depression was the U.S. decision early in the 1920s to forgive the debts that France and Great Britain owed to U.S. banks for loans taken out during World War I.
4. In 1932, during the presidential campaign, unemployment in the United States stood at about ten percent.
5. Thousands of "Okies" and other families from the "dust bowl" region migrated to California in the 1930s.

6. During the Great Depression several hundred thousand African Americans left the industrial cities of the North to return to their agriculturally-based families in the South.
7. In general, the economic crisis of the Great Depression gave strength to the idea that a woman should not hold a job outside the home if her husband was employed.
8. Black women in the South suffered massive unemployment because many families cut back on domestic help during the Great Depression.
9. In general, American social values apparently changed relatively little in response to the Depression. Rather, many people responded to hard times by redoubling their commitment to familiar ideas and goals.
10. From 1935 through 1938 the American Communist Party adopted a "Popular Front" strategy that called for cooperation with other antifascist groups.
11. President Herbert Hoover's first response to the Great Depression was to issue optimistic statements and meet with business leaders in an attempt to restore public confidence in the economy.
12. President Hoover tried to help American farmers by raising tariffs on agricultural products from foreign farms.
13. The Reconstruction Finance Corporation (RFC) was used by Hoover to create massive numbers of government-funded "make work" jobs for the unemployed.
14. President Hoover's sagging popularity revived significantly in response to his support of the demands of the so-called Veterans' Bonus Marchers.
15. Franklin Roosevelt's presidential campaign avoided mention of economic grievances, preferring instead to focus on easily understood cultural issues such as prohibition, immigration, and women's rights.

Review Questions

These questions are to be answered with essays. This will allow you to explore relationships among individuals, events, and attitudes of the period under review.

1. List and explain the five factors that the text identifies as having been principally responsible for causing the Great Depression and making it so severe.

2. On what causes of the Great Depression did Herbert Hoover place emphasis? How did that shape his response?
3. What did the Depression mean to typical Americans in terms of standard of living and lifestyle? What groups suffered especially? Why? How did basic American social and political values stand up to the economic crisis?

CHAPTER TWENTY-SIX
The New Deal

OBJECTIVES

A thorough study of Chapter 26 should enable you to understand:

1. The series of emergency measures designed to restore confidence that were enacted during the first 100 days.
2. The New Deal programs for raising farm prices and promoting industrial recovery.
3. The first federal efforts at regional planning.
4. The New Deal program for reforming the financial system.
5. The federal relief programs and Social Security.
6. The political pressures from both the left and the right that caused Franklin Roosevelt to move in new directions from 1935 on.
7. The changes in organized labor during the New Deal period.
8. The effects of the Court-packing scheme, and the recession of 1937 and 1938, on Roosevelt and the New Deal.
9. The impact of the New Deal on minorities and women.
10. The lasting significance of the New Deal to the American economy and political system.

PERTINENT QUESTIONS

Launching the New Deal (pp. 702–711)

1. What sort of relationship did President Roosevelt develop with the press and the public?
2. Why was banking the new president's number-one order of business? What was done immediately and later in the New Deal?
3. What did the Economy Act of 1933 reveal about Roosevelt's fundamental economic philosophy?
4. What was the principal feature of New Deal farm policy? How well did it work? Which farmers were served best? Who was left out?

5. Describe the goals and concepts of the National Recovery Administration (NRA). Why was it less than fully successful? How did it end?
6. What were the goals and concepts of the Tennessee Valley Authority (TVA)? How well did it meet them?
7. What assumptions and values underlay the early relief programs of the Federal Emergency Relief Administration (FERA) and the Civil Works Administration (CWA)? How was the Civilian Conservation Corps (CCC) different?

The New Deal in Transition (pp. 711–721)

8. Who led the conservative attack on Roosevelt in 1934 and 1935? How did the president react?
9. How successful were the Socialists and Communists in exploiting the unrest caused by the Depression?
10. Briefly characterize the ideas of Huey Long, Francis Townsend, and Charles E. Coughlin. Who was probably most important among them? How did Roosevelt respond?
11. What 1935 legislative initiatives signaled the emergence of the Second New Deal? To what extent were these acts reactions to political agitation and court rulings?
12. Compare and contrast craft unionism and industrial unionism. What caused the split between the AFL and the CIO?
13. Why did organized labor become more militant in the 1930s? How did the Wagner Act help? In what industries did unions make especially significant gains?
14. What programs did the Social Security Act provide for? Why does the text call it "the most important single piece of social welfare legislation in American history"?
15. Describe the Works Progress Administration (WPA) and its accomplishments. How did it go beyond traditional public-works programs?
16. What were the elements of the New Deal-Democratic political coalition that propelled Roosevelt to victory in 1936?

The New Deal in Disarray (pp. 721–724)

17. What was Roosevelt's objective in the "Court-packing" plan? What were the political repercussions of the episode?

18. What seems to have been the main cause of the 1937 recession? What economic notion appeared to be supported by the recession and the administration's response to it?

Limits and Legacies of the New Deal (pp. 724–729)

19. What did the New Deal offer to African Americans? What did it not provide? What role did Eleanor Roosevelt play?
20. What new direction in Indian policy did the Roosevelt administration take? What were the results of the new policy?
21. What pushed the New Deal toward a greater role for women? What held it back?
22. Describe the impact the New Deal had on the West. Why was it greater than on other sections of the nation?
23. Drawing from the "Debating the Past" section (page 730), compare and contrast how historians have evaluated the New Deal. Which view tends to predominate today?

IDENTIFICATION

Identify each of the following, and explain why it is important within the context of the chapter.

1. "fireside chats"
2. "bank holiday"
3. Twenty-first Amendment
4. Harry Hopkins
5. American Liberty League
6. John L. Lewis
7. sit-down strike
8. Frances Perkins
9. Alf M. Landon
10. "Black Cabinet"
11. John Collier
12. Grand Coulee Dam

The New Deal created many "alphabet agencies," several of which still exist today. Explain the purpose of each of the following.

1. Federal Deposit Insurance Corporation (FDIC)
2. Securities and Exchange Commission (SEC)
3. Agricultural Adjustment Administration (AAA)
4. Rural Electrification Administration (REA)

5. National Recovery Administration (NRA)
6. Public Works Administration (PWA)
7. Tennessee Valley Authority (TVA)
8. Civilian Conservation Corps (CCC)
9. National Labor Relations Board (NLRB)
10. Works Progress Administration (WPA)

DOCUMENT

In the campaign of 1932, Franklin Roosevelt revealed little of what would become the New Deal. And during the interregnum of 1932 and 1933, he refused to announce the specifics of his program. In fact, some of his campaign speeches were so conservative that New Dealer Marriner Eccles later commented that they sometimes "read like a giant misprint in which Roosevelt and Hoover speak each other's lines." By March 1933, however, although he may not yet have known where he was headed, Roosevelt knew where he was going to start. The most quoted line of his first inaugural address was his famous dictum that "the only thing we have to fear is fear itself." The following excerpts are from later in the speech where he acknowledged the severity of the crisis and outlined his proposed course of action. Read the selection, and consider the following questions: How were Roosevelt's experiences as a member of the wartime Wilson administration reflected in his approach to the Depression? What values of the progressive era did the Roosevelt program embody? How many of the promised programs were implemented during the first two years of the New Deal? How many worked as intended?

> In such a spirit on my part and on yours, we face our common difficulties. They concern, thank God, only material things. Values have shrunken to fantastic levels; taxes have risen; our ability to pay has fallen; government of all kinds is faced by serious curtailment of income; the means of exchange are frozen in the currents of trade; the withered leaves of industrial enterprise lie on every side; farmers find no market for their produce; the savings of many years in thousands of families are gone.
>
> More important, a host of unemployed citizens face the grim problem of existence, and an equally great number toil with little return. Only a foolish optimist can deny the dark realities of the moment....
>
> There must be an end to a conduct in banking and in business which too often has given to a sacred trust the likeness of callous and selfish wrongdoing.
>
> Small wonder that confidence languishes, for it thrives only on honesty, on honor, on the sacredness of obligations, on faithful protection, on unselfish performance; without them it cannot live.

Restoration calls, however, not for changes in ethics alone. This nation asks for action, and action now.

Our greatest primary task is to put people to work. This is no unsolvable problem if we face it wisely and courageously.

It can be accomplished in part by direct recruiting by the government itself, treating the task as we would treat the emergency of a war, but at the same time, through this employment, accomplishing greatly needed projects to stimulate and reorganize the use of our natural resources.

Hand in hand with this, we must frankly recognize the overbalance of population in our industrial centers and, by engaging on a national scale in a redistribution, endeavor to provide a better use of the land for those best fitted for the land.

The task can be helped by definite efforts to raise the values of agricultural products and with this the power to purchase the output of our cities.

It can be helped by preventing realistically the tragedy of the growing loss, through foreclosure, of our small homes and our farms.

It can be helped by insistence that the Federal, State and local governments act forthwith on the demand that their cost be drastically reduced.

It can be helped by the unifying of relief activities which today are often scattered, uneconomical and unequal. It can be helped by national planning for and supervision of all forms of transportation and of communication and other utilities which have a definitely public character.

There are many ways in which it can be helped, but it can never be helped merely by talking about it. We must act, and act quickly.

Finally, in our progress toward a resumption of work we require two safeguards against a return of the evils of the old order; there must be a strict supervision of all banking and credits and investments; there must be an end to speculation with other people's money, and there must be provision for an adequate but sound currency.

MAP EXERCISE

Fill in or identify the following on the blank map provided. Use the narrative in the text and the maps in the back of the text as your sources.

1. Approximate route of the Tennessee River from source to the Ohio River.
2. Note the states affected by the Tennessee River and its smaller tributaries not shown on the map.

Interpretative Questions

Based on what you have filled in, answer the following. For some of the questions you will need to consult the narrative in your text for information or explanation.

1. What development in the utility industry sparked the final approval of the TVA concept? What impact did TVA have on the industry?
2. How did the TVA benefit the region? What were its limitations?
3. Why did the New Deal fail to embark on any other regional projects of the magnitude of the TVA?

SUMMARY

Franklin D. Roosevelt was bound by traditional economic ideas; but unlike Herbert Hoover, Roosevelt was willing to experiment and was able to show compassion. During the first two years of his New Deal, the groundwork was laid for a new relationship between government and the economy. Roosevelt sought temporary relief for the desperate unemployment plus long-term recovery and reform for industry and finance. Not everything worked, and the Depression was not stopped, but Roosevelt got the country moving again. In 1935, frustrated and facing pressures from all sides, Roosevelt launched a new set of programs, which sometimes is called the Second New Deal. The new programs were less conciliatory to big business and more favorable to the needs of workers and consumers than were those of the New Deal of 1933. Roosevelt was swept to reelection in 1936 by a new coalition of workers, blacks, and liberals. Soon, however, Roosevelt's political blunders in the Supreme Court fight and congressional purge effort combined with growing conservative opposition to halt virtually all New Deal momentum. The legacy of the New Deal was a more activist national government poised to serve as the broker among society's various interests.

CHAPTER SELF-TEST

After you have read the chapter in the text and done the exercises in the Study Guide, the following self-test can be taken to see if you understand the material you have covered. Answers appear at the end of the Study Guide.

Multiple Choice

Circle the letter of the response which best answers the question or completes the statement.

1. The New Deal resulted in all of the following *except* the:
   a. beginnings of a modern welfare system.
   b. extension of federal regulation over new areas of the economy.
   c. birth of the modern labor movement.
   d. full end of the Great Depression.

2. Much of Roosevelt's success in restoring public confidence in government can well be attributed to his:
   a. consistent application of clear-cut philosophies to social and economic problems.
   b. optimistic and ebullient personality.
   c. refusal to engage in press conferences.
   d. explicit public demonstration of how a man could overcome physical paralysis.

3. Roosevelt's most immediate concern as President was the:
   a. public panic caused by the bank failures.
   b. collapse of agriculture.
   c. problem of widespread unemployment.
   d. deflationary spiral which had crippled business.

4. The Twenty-first Amendment, ratified in 1933, repealed the:
   a. progressive income tax.
   b. poll tax, literacy test, and other discriminatory voting restrictions.
   c. prohibition on the manufacture and sale of alcoholic beverages.
   d. "quota system" of immigration limitations.

5. The New Deal program that was most effective in improving the lives of many farmers was a program to:
   a. provide payments for increased production.
   b. help irrigate and reclaim marginal lands for cultivation.
   c. provide loans for resettlement.
   d. make electric power available through utility cooperatives.

6. Which of the following provisions was *not* included in the National Industrial Recovery Act of 1933?
   a. trade association agreements on pricing and production.
   b. loans by the national government to railroads, banks, and insurance companies.
   c. legal protection to the right of workers to form unions and engage in collective bargaining.
   d. a major program of public works designed to pump needed funds into the economy.

7. The Supreme Court declared the National Industrial Recovery Act unconstitutional because it:
   a. improperly delegated legislative power to the president and interfered with intrastate commerce.
   b. favored big business and encouraged monopoly.
   c. raised prices excessively while suppressing wage increases.
   d. allowed poorly written codes without adequate means of administration or enforcement.

8. The Tennessee Valley Authority (TVA):
   a. received strong support from the nation's utility companies.
   b. suffered as a result of the collapse of the electrical utility empire of Samuel Insull.
   c. was intended to serve as a agent for comprehensive redevelopment of the entire region.
   d. converted the Tennessee Valley into one of the most prosperous regions of the country.

9. The Roosevelt Administration instituted all of the following financial actions and reforms except:
   a. inspection of banks before their reopening after the "bank holiday."
   b. establishment of the Federal Deposit Insurance Corporation (FDIC).
   c. transfer of control over interest rates from the Federal Reserve Board to Congress.
   d. establishment of the Securities and Exchange Commission (SEC) to police the stock market.

10. The result of right-wing criticism of the New Deal was to:
    a. significantly undermine Roosevelt's political strength.
    b. push Roosevelt to work more closely with conservative forces.
    c. convince Roosevelt that conciliation of big business would not work for him and move him toward more liberal legislation.
    d. drive Roosevelt into the arms of radical and semiradical advisers.

11. According to the flamboyant Louisiana politician Huey Long, the national government could end the Depression by:
    a. providing federal pensions for the elderly.
    b. actions to remonetize silver, issue additional greenbacks, and nationalize the banking system.
    c. ending its "dictatorial" policies and attacks on free enterprise.
    d. taxing the rich and sharing the wealth with others through income redistribution.

12. The National Labor Relations Act of 1935 sponsored by Senator Robert F. Wagner of New York:
    a. specifically outlawed "unfair practices" by which employers had fought unionization.
    b. offered fewer protections than had been provided by Section 7(a) of the National Industrial Recovery Act.
    c. was enthusiastically supported by President Roosevelt from the beginning of consideration.
    d. was declared unconstitutional by the Supreme Court on the grounds that the Congress could only regulate interstate commerce.

13. A significant social development of the 1930s due to a great extent to action by the national government was:
    a. the elimination of legally enforceable racial discrimination and segregation in jobs and housing.
    b. the emergence of the powerful American trade union movement.
    c. the creation of a movement dedicated to the expansion of women's rights.
    d. an increasing rate of marriage and a subsequent "baby boom."

14. The Congress of Industrial Organization (CIO) had the intent of:
    a. organizing workers into a given union on the basis of their specific skill regardless of the worker's industry—e.g. welders.
    b. organizing workers into a given union on the basis of the specific industry in which they worked regardless of the worker's skill—e.g. automobile workers.

c. converting factories into "profit-sharing" cooperative enterprises.
d. eliminating the older, more conservative American Federation of Labor (AFL).

15. The United Auto Workers (UAW) gained union recognition from General Motors in 1937 after:
    a. staging a series of controversial but successful sit-down strikes.
    b. winning public sympathy following the brutal "Memorial Day Massacre" of peaceful demonstrators by police.
    c. gaining a federal court order to force company recognition.
    d. the company decided to relent rather than risk a costly strike at a time of economic recovery.

True/False

Read each statement carefully. Mark true statements "T" and false statements "F."

1. President Franklin D. Roosevelt held frequent informal press conferences and won the respect and friendship of most reporters.
2. The area of the economy that President Roosevelt first concentrated on was banking.
3. The principal feature of New Deal agricultural policy was that it provided direct income supplements to farmers rather than trying to increase prices and thereby indirectly raise farm income.
4. The Agricultural Adjustment Act turned out to be more beneficial to sharecroppers and tenant farmers than it was to landowning farmers.
5. The basic idea of the National Recovery Administration (NRA) was that in exchange for the federal government's relaxing of antitrust laws, corporations would make concessions such as recognizing the right of workers to organize unions and establishing a minimum wage.
6. The U.S. Supreme Court ruled the legislation creating the NRA void because Congress had unconstitutionally delegated legislative power to the president.
7. The series of dams and related facilities built by the Tennessee Valley Authority virtually eliminated flooding in the region and brought electricity to thousands of people who had not had it before.
8. The New Deal tried to revive the lagging stock market by removing the regulatory restrictions that had hampered brokers in the 1920s.

9. The Civilian Conservation Corps, which housed young men in semimilitary camps and put them to work on such projects as tree planting and park development, was President Roosevelt's favorite relief program.
10. President Roosevelt's supporters organized the "Liberty League" to counter those who argued that Roosevelt was moving the nation toward socialism.
11. Senator Huey P. Long of Louisiana gathered a national following by arguing that a massive, across-the-board tax cut would rapidly stimulate the economy and end the depression faster than the spending programs that Roosevelt advocated.
12. In the so-called Second New Deal beginning in 1935, President Roosevelt's proposals were generally more conservative in an attempt to placate big business.
13. The concept of "industrial unionism" is that all the workers in a particular industry, e.g. automobiles, should belong to one union rather than joining specific craft unions, e.g. welders.
14. The Works Progress Administration (WPA) not only provided work for traditional manual laborers, it also provided government-supported jobs for intellectual and creative workers such as writers, artists, musicians, and actors.
15. As a consequence of the New Deal the allegiance of most African-American voters switched from the Republican Party to the Democratic Party.

Review Questions

These questions are to be answered with essays. This will allow you to explore relationships among individuals, events, and attitudes of the period under review.

1. Which of Roosevelt's early New Deal programs illustrate his willingness to experiment with bold, innovative ideas? Which of his actions show his hesitation and attachment to conventional values?
2. What forces caused Roosevelt to launch his so-called Second New Deal programs in 1935? How did he steal the thunder from some of his most vocal opponents?
3. Compare the impact of the Depression on blacks, Hispanics, and Native Americans with its consequences for the typical white American.

4. What specific programs and general approaches formed the important political legacy of the New Deal?

CHAPTER TWENTY-SEVEN
The Global Crisis, 1921–1945

OBJECTIVES

A thorough study of Chapter 27 should enable you to understand:

1. The new directions of American foreign policy in the 1920s.
2. The effects of the Great Depression on foreign relations.
3. The pattern of Japanese, Italian, and German aggression that eventually led to World War II.
4. The factors that led to the passage of neutrality legislation in the 1930s.
5. The specific sequence of events that brought the United States into the War.

PERTINENT QUESTIONS

The Diplomacy of the New Era (pp. 733–737)

1. What was accomplished by the Washington Conference?
2. What circular pattern of international finance was created by the Dawes Plan? What was the result?
3. How did Hoover change U.S policy toward Latin America?
4. How did the Hoover administration deal with Japanese expansionism? How effective was the approach?

Isolationism and Internationalism (pp. 737–742)

5. How did Roosevelt break with Hoover on the matter of economic relations with Europe?
6. In what ways did the Good Neighbor policy of Roosevelt build on Hoover's Latin American policy?
7. What ideas and developments fed isolationist sentiment in the first half of the 1930s? What was Roosevelt's position?
8. Taken as a whole, what were the basic provisions and central purpose of the Neutrality Acts of 1935, 1936, and 1937?

9. What German moves and diplomatic failures led to the start of World War II in Europe?

From Neutrality to Intervention (pp. 742–747)

10. How did Roosevelt manage to aid Great Britain in 1939 and 1940 by modifying the "cash and carry" principle and establishing "lend-lease"?
11. What naval developments led the United States to the brink of war in Europe?
12. What events in Asia brought Japan into conflict with the United States?
13. Why could the attack on Pearl Harbor be considered a tactical victory but a political blunder by the Japanese?

IDENTIFICATION

Identify each of the following, and explain why it is important within the context of the chapter.

1. Henry Cabot Lodge
2. isolationism
3. Charles Evans Hughes
4. Kellog-Briand Pact
5. Benito Mussolini
6. National Socialist (Nazi) Party
7. diplomatic relations with the Soviet Union
8. Francisco Franco
9. *Panay* incident
10. "appeasement"
11. *blitzkrieg*
12. America First Committee
13. Henry A. Wallace
14. Wendell Willkie
15. Atlantic Charter
16. Hideki Tojo

DOCUMENT

Read the section in the text entitled "The Rise of Isolationism," paying careful attention to the discussion of the investigations chaired by Senator Gerald P. Nye (R-N.D.). The following statements were made in May 1935 by Nye and Senator Bennett Champ Clark (D-Mo.), a member of

Nye's committee, before a "Keep America Out of War" meeting at Carnegie Hall in New York City. Also on the program was Representative Maury Maverick (D-Tex.), another isolationist. Read the statements and consider the following questions: Was it really the sale of munitions that led America into World War I? Why might a 1935 audience have been especially receptive to charges that bankers were responsible for war? How successful were Nye, Clark, and others in enlisting the "overwhelming body of public sentiment" for neutrality legislation? If Roosevelt had strictly followed the spirit of the neutrality legislation, could American entry into World War II have been avoided?

SENATOR GERALD P. NYE (R-N. D.)

[The investigations of the Senate Munitions Committee have not been in vain;] truly worthwhile legislation will be forthcoming to meet the frightful challenge.

Out of this year of study has come tremendous conviction that our American welfare requires that great importance be given to the subject of our neutrality when others are at war.

Let us be frank before the next war comes as Wilson was frank after the last war was over.

Let us know that it is sales and shipments of munitions and contraband, and the lure of profits in them that will get us into another war.

If Morgan and the other bankers must get into another war, let them do it by enlisting in the Foreign Legion. That's always open.

SENATOR BENNETT CHAMP CLARK (D-MO.)

In these resolutions [calling for neutrality legislation] we propose that American citizens who want to profit from other people's war shall not be allowed again to entangle the United States.

We appeal to you to lend your efforts to the creation of an overwhelming body of public sentiment to bring about the firm establishment of that policy. The time for action is due and past due.

New York times, 28 May, 1935. Copyright © 1935 by The New York Times Company. Reprinted by permission.

MAP EXERCISE

Fill in or identify the following on the blank maps provided. Use the text and the maps on pages 750, 753, and 766 as your sources.

1. Label the following: Japan, Manchuria, Pearl Harbor (Hawaii), Indochina.
2. Label the following: Soviet Union, Poland, Germany, Austria (incorporated into Germany), Czechoslovakia, Great Britain,

Denmark, Norway, Netherlands, Belgium, France, Italy, and Spain.
3. Shade the areas that Germany and Italy controlled at the farthest extent of Axis control in Europe and north Africa.
4. Shade the areas that Japan controlled at its extent of farthest advance in World War II.

Interpretative Questions

Based on what you have filled in, answer the following. For some of the questions you will need to consult the narrative in your text for information or explanation.

1. How was Great Britain isolated during the height of Axis conquest?
2. Why was Germany initially concerned with avoiding a two-front war? Why did the United States aid the Soviet Union after the German invasion?
3. How did the Japanese expansion in Asia threaten U.S. interests?

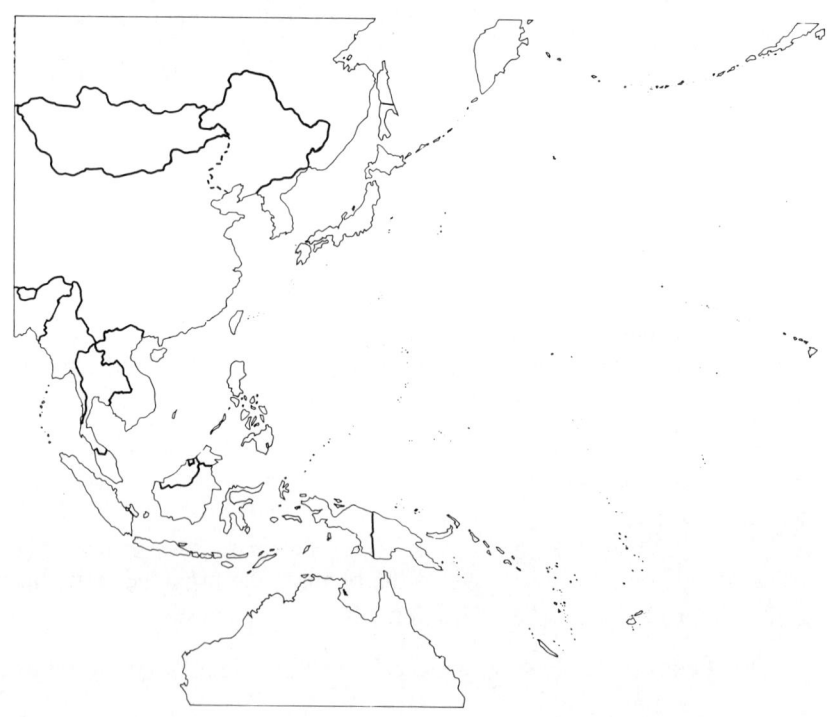

SUMMARY

After World War I, the United States avoided international commitments but not international contact. Relations with Latin America improved; but in Asia and Europe, crises were brewing. The initial American reaction to the aggressive moves of Italy, Germany, and Japan was one of isolationism. Anxious to avoid involvement in another world war, the United States passed a series of Neutrality Acts; but as the Axis aggressors became bolder, Roosevelt eased the nation closer and closer to war. The attack on Pearl Harbor blew away all isolationist remnants, and the nation entered World War II determined and unified.

CHAPTER SELF-TEST

After you have read the chapter in the text and done the exercises in the Study Guide, the following self-test can be taken to see if you understand

the material you have covered. Answers appear at the end of the Study Guide.

Multiple Choice

Circle the letter of the response which best answers the question or completes the statement.

1. Throughout the 1920s, the makers of American foreign policy attempted to:
   a. win ratification of the Treaty of Versailles.
   b. promote U.S. membership in the League of Nations.
   c. retreat from international events and renew the traditional policy of isolationism.
   d. expand America's role and interests in world affairs without assuming burdensome responsibilities.

2. At the Washington Conference of 1921, the United States sought negotiation of a treaty to:
   a. prevent a naval arms race in the Pacific Ocean.
   b. restructure the Open Door policy in China, allowing spheres of influence to separate nations.
   c. entice Japan to surrender colonial control over Korea.
   d. sanction Japanese dominance in East Asia.

3. The Kellog-Briand Pact of 1928, which "outlawed" war, suffered a fatal weakness in that it:
   a. contained a built-in expiration date.
   b. denied Germany the opportunity to join.
   c. lacked effective means of enforcement.
   d. involved only France and the United States.

4. According to the Dawes Plan of 1924, the United States would:
   a. scale down the amount of war debts owed by the former Allies to the United States.
   b. provide loans to Germany, enabling it to pay reparations to Britain and France.
   c. reduce tariff rates, allowing trading partners to increase exports and thus earn needed funds to repay debts.
   d. double its investments in Latin America, providing modern facilities to weaken the appeal of revolutionary groups in that region.

5. Official recognition of the Soviet regime in Russia by the American government in 1933 resulted in:
   a. an increased understanding and appreciation of the theories of communism by most Americans.
   b. plans by which the Soviet Union and the United States intended to contain expansion by fascist governments.
   c. significantly increased sales of American manufactured goods inside the Soviet Union.
   d. relatively little change in the mutual mistrust which had characterized Soviet-American relations in the past.

6. According to the Neutrality Acts of 1935-1937,
   a. American citizens could travel only on American ships.
   b. no American arms could be sold to any belligerents.
   c. military goods could be sold on a cash-and-carry basis only.
   d. military goods could be sold to "victims" but not to "aggressors."

7. The "appeasement" of Hitler at the Munich Conference consisted of allowing German annexation of:
   a. the Rhineland.
   b. Austria.
   c. the Sudentenland.
   d. Czechoslovakia.

8. Following the Nazi *blitzkrieg* of western Europe, Roosevelt used presidential authority to circumvent the Neutrality Act by:
   a. imposing a "moral embargo" on arms sales to Russia.
   b. seeking additional defense expenditures from Congress.
   c. trading American destroyers for rights to build bases on British territory in the Western Hemisphere.
   d. inaugurating the first peacetime military draft in American history.

9. In 1939, following the start of World War II in Europe, Congress:
   a. declared war on Germany and Italy.
   b. allowed the United States to sell arms to belligerents on a "cash and carry basis."
   c. directed the President to give weapons to the French and British and to transport them on U.S. ships.
   d. passed a Neutrality Act prohibiting the United States from having any economic contact with any belligerent nation.

10. The America First Committee was:
    a. an isolationist lobby that included such prominent Americans as Charles Lindberg.
    b. a British organization working to convince the American public that the United States should enter the war to help England.
    c. a group within the German high command that tried to convince Hitler that he could not win unless he came to a truce with the Soviet Union and concentrated his efforts on the United States.
    d. an association of World War I veterans who lobbied Congress to significantly increase appropriations for the military so that America would be prepared for war.

11. The "lend-lease" program:
    a. placed "voluntary" U.S. troops under British command at British Empire outposts so that Great Britain could concentrate more troops in the European theater.
    b. allowed the United States to rent naval bases on Atlantic and Pacific islands from Great Britain "to provide for the mutual defense of the seas."
    c. funneled borrowed money indirectly to the "joint Atlantic war effort" through an elaborate arrangement involving banks in New York, Toronto, and London.
    d. provided a mechanism for President Roosevelt to get armaments to any nation "vital to the defense of the United States," mainly Great Britain, if the nation would promise to return the armaments after the crisis.

12. By the summer of 1941, U.S. naval vessels in the north Atlantic were:
    a. conducting "search and destroy" missions against German submarines.
    b. escorting supply ships to England with orders to fire "on sight" at German submarines.
    c. prohibited from sailing into the "war zone" which extended 500 nautical miles from the coast of the British Isles.
    d. allowed to use long-range guns to provide "artillery support" for British commando operations in northern France.

13. In the August 1941 Atlantic Charter, President Roosevelt and Prime Minister Winston Churchill:
    a. decided that as soon as Nazi submarines were controlled in the Atlantic military forces should make the defeat of Japan in the Pacific the "highest priority."
    b. announced a set of *de facto* war aims with "common principles" that called for the "final destruction of the Nazi tyranny."
    c. resolved to defeat Germany as quickly as possible because they regarded the Soviet Union as "a greater threat to world self determination."
    d. agreed that the British would have principal responsibility for "command and control" in the European theater and that the United States would have it in Asia.

14. The militant Japanese Prime Minister and leader of the so-called war party was General:
    a. Hirohito.
    b. Yamamoto.
    c. Kamikaze.
    d. Tojo.

15. Militarily, the most significant U.S. loss in the attack on Pearl Harbor was the:
    a. sinking of eight battleships.
    b. sinking or disabling of four aircraft carriers.
    c. delay in obtaining a congressional declaration of war because of the demoralizing of the American public.
    d. delay in declaring war on Germany because of all the immediate anger focusing on Japan.

True/False

Read each statement carefully. Mark true statements "T" and false statements "F."

1. Rather than being a pure isolationist, Senator Henry Cabot Lodge wanted the United States to exert its influence internationally but in a way that reflected U.S. interests and virtues and avoided obligations to other nations.
2. Secretary of State Charles Evans Hughes was the key figure in resisting efforts to significantly reduce the size of the American military establishment after World War I.

3. The Dawes Plan of international finance granted France and Britain a moratorium on payment of war debts to the United States as long as Germany remained unable to make timely war reparations payments to them.
4. Herbert Hoover tried to improve U.S. relations with Latin America by declining to intervene militarily in the affairs of the neighboring nations.
5. When Japan invaded northern Manchuria and territories even deeper into China in 1931–1932, President Hoover cooperated with the League of Nations in imposing economic sanctions against Japanese aggression.
6. President Roosevelt's "Good Neighbor" policy extended the approach of nonintervention that President Hoover had begun.
7. A major reason that the United States decided in 1933 to extend diplomatic recognition to the Soviet Union was that many Americans regarded Russia as a fertile source for trade expansion.
8. One point feeding isolationist sentiment in the 1930s was the Nye Committee charge that war profiteers in banking and industry had pressured the United States to enter World War I.
9. In the Spanish Civil War, Hitler and Mussolini supported Francisco Franco while the governments of France, Great Britain, and the United States provided assistance to the republican cause.
10. The *Panay* incident brought the United States and Japan close to war in 1937 when an American battleship accidentally sank a Japanese patrol boat.
11. In the Munich accords of 1938, the French and British agreed to accept the German demands in Czechoslovakia in return for Hitler's promise to expand no further.
12. The generally acknowledged "beginning of World War II" came with the German *blitzkrieg* against France and the low countries in June 1940.
13. Agricultural Secretary Henry A. Wallace, President Roosevelt's choice for vice president in 1940, was unpopular with many Democrats because he was perceived as too liberal and too controversial.
14. In the 1940 election, Republican nominee Wendell Willkie took a strong stance against President Roosevelt's policy of assisting France and Great Britain without actually entering the war.
15. The U.S. Congress declared war on Germany and Italy *before* those nations could declare war on the United States.

Review Questions

These questions are to be answered with essays. This will allow you to explore relationships among individuals, events, and attitudes of the period under review.

1. How isolationist was the United States in the 1920s? Was the dual policy of economic penetration and arms limitation an effective approach?
2. Compare and contrast the American reactions to World Wars I and II. Explain the relationship between attitudes toward World War I and the isolationist sentiment and neutrality legislation of the 1930s.
3. How close to full involvement in World War II was the United States prior to the attack on Pearl Harbor? Was full entry likely?

CHAPTER TWENTY-EIGHT
America in a World at War

OBJECTIVES

A thorough study of Chapter 28 should enable you to understand:

1. The efforts of the federal government to mobilize the nation's economy for war production.
2. The effects of American participation in the war on the Depression and the New Deal.
3. The changes that wartime involvement brought for women and racial and ethnic minorities and for regional development.
4. The contribution of the U.S. military to victory in North Africa and Europe.
5. The contribution of the U.S. military to victory in the Pacific and Asia.

PERTINENT QUESTIONS

War on Two Fronts (pp. 748–754)

1. What was the strategy toward Japan early in the war? What two naval and air victories stemmed the Japanese tide?
2. What did the North African and Italian offensives accomplish? How did the Soviet Union regard these efforts?
3. How did the United States react to the Holocaust? Why did the United States not do more to save the Jews?

The American People in Wartime (pp. 754–765)

4. As the war ended the Depression, what changes in income distribution and composition of the labor force became evident?
5. What section of the nation benefited most economically from the war? Why?
6. How did labor unions fare during the War?

7. What efforts did the national government make to regulate production, labor, and prices during the war?
8. How was World War II financed?
9. Describe the demographic changes, economic gains, and military role of blacks in the war. What tensions resulted?
10. Describe the contributions American Indians made to the war effort? What impact did the war have on federal Indian policy?
11. How did the war effort affect Mexican Americans?
12. How were the women who filled war jobs treated? What obstacles did they face? What long-term consequences for the role of women in society and the work force were foreshadowed by the wartime experience?
13. How were Japanese Americans treated? Why did they suffer more than German Americans? What was done to atone for the treatment?
14. What impact did the war have on the various programs of the New Deal?

The Defeat of the Axis (pp. 765–772)

15. Describe the Normandy invasion and the liberation of France. What role did air power play in preparing for the assault?
16. What role did Soviet forces play in the final defeat of Germany?
17. Why did the United States decide to use the atomic bomb against Japan? Was it a wise decision?

IDENTIFICATION

Identify each of the following, and explain why it is important within the context of the chapter.

1. Douglas MacAuthur
2. Chester Nimitz
3. George C. Marshall
4. Dwight D. Eisenhower
5. Office of Price Administration (OPA)
6. A. Philip Randolph
7. Congress of Racial Equality (CORE)
8. *braceros*
9. "zoot suiters"
10. "Rosie the Riveter"
11. Issei and Nisei

12. Thomas E. Dewey
13. Harry S. Truman
14. Dresden raid
15. Battle of the Bulge
16. Chiang Kai-shek
17. Battle of Leyte Gulf
18. Iwo Jima
19. Okinawa
20. kamikaze
21. Manhattan Project
22. Hiroshima and Nagasaki

DOCUMENT

Read the section of the text under the heading "African-Americans and the War," paying careful attention to the discussion of the March on Washington movement, the establishment of the Fair Employment Practices Commission (FEPC), and the formation of the Congress of Racial Equality (CORE). The following excerpt is from a magazine article that A. Philip Randolph wrote after the FEPC was organized but before CORE was born. Consider the following questions: Could Randolph's remarks be interpreted as a threat that American blacks might not support the war efforts unless they received assurances of better treatment? Was his description of the plight of blacks in the military and in defense plants accurate? Was Randolph right in saying that racial tension in American was worth "many divisions to Hitler and Hirohito"?

> Though I have found no Negroes who want to see the United Nations[s][1] lose this war, I have found many who, before the war ends, want to see the stuffing knocked out of white supremacy and of empire over subject peoples. American Negroes, involved as we are in the general issues of the conflict, are confronted not with a choice but with the challenge both to win democracy for ourselves at home and to help win the war for democracy the world over.
>
> There is no escape from the horns of this dilemma. There ought not to be escape. For if the war for democracy is not won abroad, the fight for democracy cannot be won at home. If this war cannot be won for the white peoples, it will not be won for the darker races.
>
> Conversely, if freedom and equality are not vouchsafed the peoples of color, the war for democracy will not be won. Unless this double-barreled thesis is accepted and applied, the darker races will never whole-heartedly fight for the victory of the United Nations. That is why those familiar with the thinking of the American Negro have sensed his lack of enthusiasm, whether among the educated or uneducated, rich or poor, professional or nonprofessional, religious or secular, rural or urban, North, South, East, or West.

That is why questions are being raised by Negroes in church, labor union, and fraternal society; in poolroom, barbershop, schoolroom, hospital, hairdressing parlor, on college campus, railroad, and bus. One can hear such questions asked as these: What have Negroes to fight for? What's the difference between Hitler and that "cracker" Talmadge of Georgia?[2] Why has a man got to be Jim-Crowed to die for democracy? If you haven't got democracy yourself, how can you carry it to someone else?

What are the reasons for this state of mind? The answer is: discrimination, segregation, Jim Crow. Witness the Navy, the Army, the Air Corps; and also government services at Washington. In many parts of the South, Negroes in Uncle Sam's uniform are being put upon, mobbed, sometimes even shot down by civilian and military police, and, on occasion, lynched. Vested political interests in race prejudice are so deeply entrenched that to them winning the war against Hitler is secondary to preventing Negroes from winning democracy for themselves. This is worth many divisions to Hitler and Hirohito.[3] While labor, business, and farm are subjected to ceilings and floors and not allowed to carry on as usual, these interests trade in the dangerous business of race hate as usual.

When the defense program began and billions of the taxpayers' money were appropriated for guns, ships, tanks, and bombs, Negroes presented themselves for work only to be given the cold shoulder. North as well as South, and despite their qualifications, Negroes were denied skilled employment. Not until their wrath and indignation took the form of a proposed protest march on Washington, scheduled for July 1, 1941, did things begin to move in the form of defense jobs for Negroes. The march was postponed by the timely issuance (June 25, 1941) of the famous Executive Order No. 8802 by President Roosevelt. But this order and the President's Committee on Fair Employment Practice, established thereunder, have as yet only scratched the surface by way of eliminating discriminations on account of race or color in war industry. Both management and labor unions in too many places and in too many ways are still drawing the color line.

[1] The United Nations was the official name for the Allies. After the war, the name was used for the new international organization.
[2] Eugene Talmadge, racist governor of Georgia.
[3] Emperor of Japan.

Survey Graphic, November 1942.

MAP EXERCISE

Fill in or identify the following on the blank maps provided. Use the maps on pages 750, 753, and 766 of the text as your source.

1. Label the major belligerents, and indicate after the name whether the nation was Axis (AX) or Allied (AL). Circle the areas under Axis control.
2. Indicate by the arrows the main American (AM) and British (GB) thrusts against the enemy in North Africa.

3. Label Normandy, Paris, and Berlin, and draw an arrow indicating the approximate line of advance of the Allied forces on the western front.
4. Label Stalingrad, and draw an arrow indicating the approximate line of advance of the Russian forces on the eastern front.
5. Label Japan, China, Manchuria, Burma, Indochina, Australia, Hawaii, the Philippines, Iwo Jima, and Okinawa.
6. Draw a light circle to indicate the approximate extent of the Japanese advance at its peak. Draw a darker circle around the area under Japanese control at the time the first atomic bomb was dropped.

Interpretative Questions

Based on what you have filled in, answer the following. For some of the questions you will need to consult the narrative in your text for information or explanation.

1. How was Great Britain isolated during the height of Axis conquest?
2. Why was Allied control of North Africa considered so important?
3. Compare the Allied advance in World War II with that in World War I. (See the Map Exercise in Chapter 23.) Why did France and Russia suffer the most in both wars?
4. Why was the encircling of Japan the most effective strategy for the Allies in the Pacific?

SUMMARY

The United States entered World War II ideologically unified but militarily ill-prepared. A corporate-government partnership solved most of the production and manpower problems, and the massive wartime output brought an end to the Great Depression. Labor troubles, racial friction, and social tensions were not absent, but they were kept to a minimum. Roosevelt and the American generals made the decision that Germany must be defeated first, since it presented a more serious threat than Japan. Gradually American production and American military might turned the tide in the Pacific and on the western front in Europe. The key to victory in Europe was an invasion of France that would coincide with a Russian offensive on the eastern front. Less than a year after D-Day, the war in Europe was over. In the Pacific, American forces—with some aid from the British and Australians—first stopped the Japanese advance, and then went on the offensive. The strategy for victory moved Allied forces progressively closer to the Japanese homeland. Conventional bombing raids pulverized Japanese cities, and American forces were readied for an invasion that the atomic bomb made unnecessary.

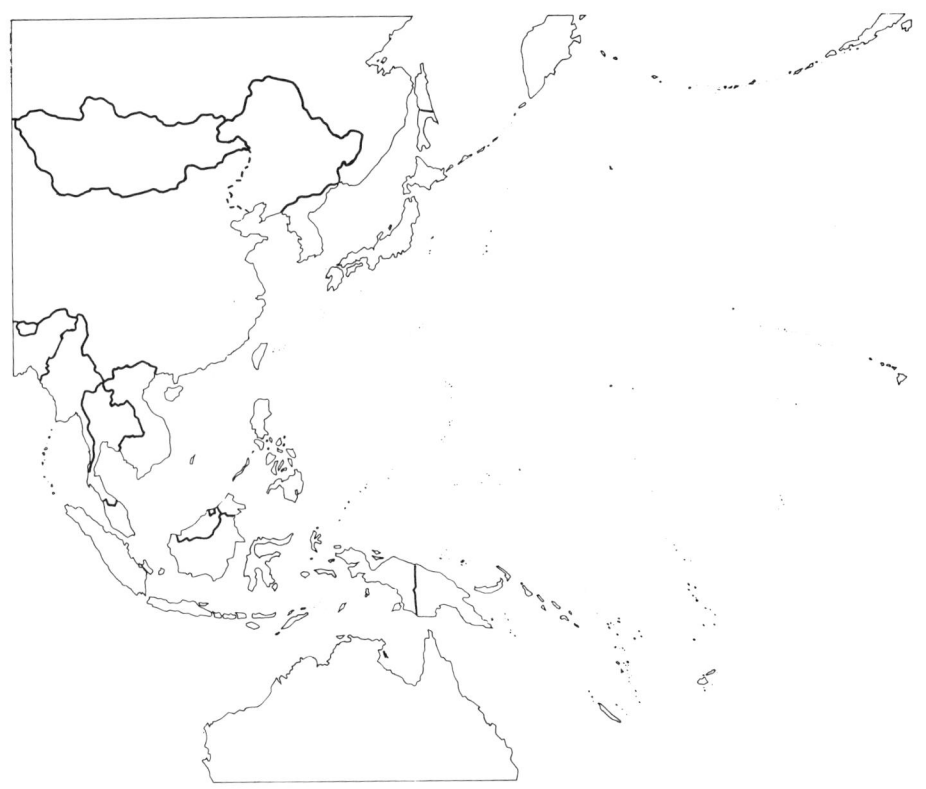

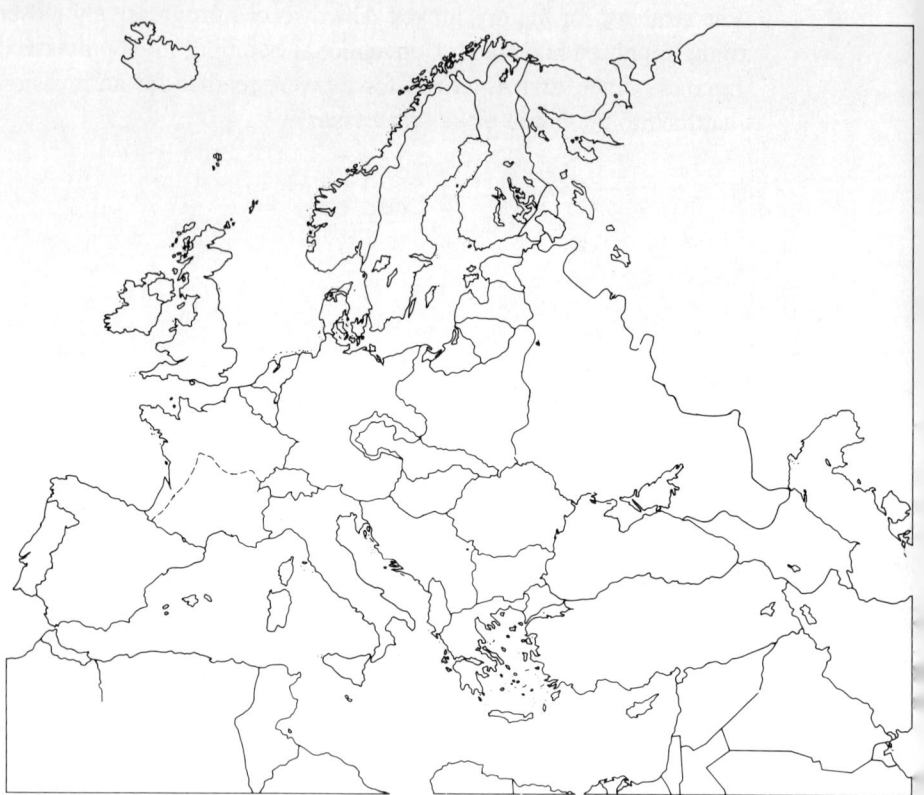

Chapter Self-Test

After you have read the chapter in the text and done the exercises in the Study Guide, the following self-test can be taken to see if you understand the material you have covered. Answers appear at the end of the Study Guide.

Multiple Choice

Circle the letter of the response which best answers the question or completes the statement.

1. The Battle of Coral Sea:
   a. led to Japanese possession of Hong Kong.
   b. represented the first important victory of the Allies in the Pacific, stopping the Japanese southern offensive.

c. enabled the United States to regain control of the central Pacific region.
   d. resulted in the Japanese takeover of the Dutch East Indies.

2. Rather than proceed with early plans for the invasion of France, American military leaders:
   a. agreed to Russian demands for establishment of a "second front" in Italy.
   b. agreed to British arguments to "soften" the edges of the Nazi empire with an offensive in northern Africa.
   c. concentrated almost exclusively on the war in the Pacific.
   d. decided an invasion of Europe should begin in Greece.

3. Before a successful regrouping by General George S. Patton, American forces in North Africa suffered a serious setback at:
   a. Tobruk.
   b. the Kasserine Pass.
   c. Algiers.
   d. Casablanca.

4. Hitler's eastern offensive was shattered with his failure to capture the Russian stronghold of:
   a. Leningrad.
   b. Moscow.
   c. Kiev.
   d. Stalingrad.

5. The United States government responded to reports of the Holocaust, the Nazi campaign to exterminate European Jews, by:
   a. attempted bombings of concentration camp crematoria and railroad lines.
   b. limiting its attention at the time to the larger military goal of winning the war.
   c. admitting into the United States large numbers of Jewish refugees.
   d. transporting large numbers of Jewish refugees to Palestine.

6. The most profound immediate economic impact of World War II upon America was a(n):
   a. end to the decade-long problems of unemployment, depression, and industrial sluggishness.
   b. substantial reduction of the federal deficit with increased tax rates and revenues.

c. tremendous increase in personal spending as workers used higher wages for newly available consumer goods.
d. further imbalance in the nation's distribution of wealth.

7. African-American spokesman A. Philip Randolph threatened a massive march on Washington by blacks in the summer of 1941 to protest:
   a. the violent race riot in Detroit which had left twenty-five blacks dead.
   b. racial segregation in theaters and restaurants.
   c. racial segregation and limited assignments for blacks in the armed forces.
   d. discrimination against black workers in wartime industries.

8. For American women, wartime America provided:
   a. an increased and liberating role in the work force.
   b. reduced opportunities for marriage and motherhood.
   c. greater family stability with declining incidence of marital separation and divorce.
   d. government programs designed to address social concerns such as child care and juvenile crime.

9. In 1942 over 100,000 Japanese-Americans were "interned" in government "relocation centers" because of:
   a. the revelation of Japanese sabotage at Pearl Harbor.
   b. their refusal to allow their young men to serve in U.S. military forces.
   c. racial animosity toward a people that many Americans held in contempt.
   d. an order by the Supreme Court upon news of a plotted Japanese invasion of California.

10. The Allied movement toward Germany from the west met the last serious German resistance at the:
    a. raid on Dresden.
    b. Battle of the Bulge.
    c. Battle of Saint-Lô.
    d. capture of Cologne.

11. The invasion at Normandy, June 6, 1944,
    a. occurred approximately at the narrowest part of the English Channel.
    b. involved U.S. soldiers only since British troops were pinned down in northern Italy.

c. took about two months to dislodge German forces from the Normandy coast.
   d. was preceded by intensive bombardment of German fortifications and paratrooper drops behind the lines.
12. The allied raid on Dresden, Germany:
   a. involved the use of incendiary bombs that killed over 100,000 people.
   b. was carried out by "Free French" commandos who liberated several thousand concentration camp survivors.
   c. was the first to demonstrate the effectiveness of unmanned guided missiles.
   d. diverted German attention so that Soviet forces could enter Berlin.
13. The leader of the nationalist Chinese forces allied with the United States in World War II was:
   a. Mao Zedong.
   b. Sun Yat-sen.
   c. Chou En-lai.
   d. Chiang Kai-shek.
   e. Lao Chungking.
14. The Battle of Leyte Gulf resulted in:
   a. the sinking of two American attack carriers and thus a significant delay in the invasion of the Philippines.
   b. a change in American strategy from reliance on battleships to more emphasis on lighter, faster ships such as destroyers and cruisers.
   c. severe damage to the British Pacific fleet from Hong Kong and thereby entrenched Japanese control of the Chinese mainland.
   d. a major American victory and a serious crippling of the Japanese navy in the largest naval engagement in history.
15. The "Manhattan Project" was the name given to the:
   a. intensive U.S. activities to develop an atomic bomb.
   b. consortium of Wall Street banks and investment firms that underwrote U.S. war bonds.
   c. top secret group that broke German and Japanese military codes and kept Allied commanders aware of Axis plans.
   d. effort to recruit experienced civilian corporate executives to work for the federal government's War Production Board.

True/False

Read each statement carefully. Mark true statements "T" and false statements "F."

1. Other than Pearl Harbor, the two greatest Japanese victories in World War II came in the Battles of Coral Sea and Midway.
2. The Soviet Union complained about the North African campaign because they believed that it had delayed a major second front in Europe by tying up American and British resources.
3. Because of the horror of the Holocaust, the American and British command officers decided to make the liberation of Nazi concentration camps a higher priority than achieving the quickest possible end of the war.
4. The most profound impact of World War II on American economic life was finally to end the Great Depression, virtually wiping out unemployment.
5. Because of "no-strike" pledges and government arbitration rules, labor union membership declined during World War II.
6. In order not to slow down the economic recovery associated with the war effort, President Roosevelt and Congress decided to finance the war effort almost entirely by war bond drives without increasing income taxes.
7. During World War II, A. Philip Randolph was the administrator of the Office of Price Administration (OPA).
8. During World War II, the term *braceros* applied to Mexican workers who were allowed into the United States for a limited time to work at a specific job.
9. The nickname often applied to women who took wartime industrial jobs was "Homefront Hannah."
10. The domestic Japanese internment program during World War II moved virtually all Issei (first generation, unnaturalized) to camps but did not move Nisei (naturalized or native-born) unless they were the minor children of Issei.
11. During World War II, President Roosevelt himself indicated that political emphasis should shift away from domestic reform, declaring that "Dr. New Deal" should give way to "Dr. Win-the-War."
12. The Normandy Invasion came in the spring of 1944, and Paris was liberated from Nazi control by the end of that summer.
13. In January of 1945, the Soviet Union captured Poland and made peace with Nazi Germany, so the United States and Britain had to carry the bulk of the burden of conquering Berlin.

14. The relatively easy conquest of Iwo Jima and Okinawa by naval and marine forces indicated that the Japanese military had nearly lost the means and will to resist.
15. President Harry Truman's decision to drop atomic bombs on Japan was probably inevitable since as U.S. Senator he had been chairman of the congressional committee that oversaw the atomic bomb development project.

Review Questions

These questions are to be answered with essays. This will allow you to explore relationships among individuals, events, and attitudes of the period under review.

1. Many of the broad strategy and social decisions of World War II are still debated. Describe the key issues involved in the Germany-first decision, the second-front debate, the Japanese-American internment, and the dropping of the atomic bombs. Were the right decisions made?
2. United States-Soviet relationships were tense throughout World War II despite the fact that the Soviets were on the Allied side. What issues caused those tensions? How important was the Eastern Front to the outcome of the war in Europe?

Chapter Twenty-Nine
America and the Cold War

OBJECTIVES

A thorough study of Chapter 29 should enable you to understand:

1. The background of United States relations with the Soviet Union before World War II.
2. The extent of collaboration between the United States and the Soviet Union during World War II, and the differences of view that developed between the two nations concerning the nature of the postwar world.
3. The meaning of the doctrine of the containment, and the specific programs that implemented the concept.
4. The problems of postwar readjustment in the United States, especially controlling inflation.
5. The nature of the Fair Deal, its successes and failures.
6. The significance of China's becoming communist to American foreign policy in Asia.
7. The circumstances that led to United States participation in a "limited" war in Korea.
8. The reaction of American public opinion to President Harry Truman's handling of the "police action" in Korea, including his firing of General Douglas MacArthur.
9. The nature and extent of American fears of internal communist subversion during the early Cold War years.

PERTINENT QUESTIONS

Origins of the Cold War (pp. 773–778)

1. Describe the legacy of mistrust between the Soviet Union and the United States up to World War II. How did the world view of the United States differ from that of the Soviets and the British?

2. What were the accomplishments of the Casablanca and Teheran conferences?
3. How did the Yalta Conference deal with the Polish and German questions? What differing views of the conference did the Soviets and Americans hold?
4. What was the basic United Nations plan that was agreed to at Yalta?

The Collapse of the Peace (pp. 778–785)

5. Compare and contrast the attitudes toward Stalin and the Soviet Union of Franklin Roosevelt and Harry Truman. How did Potsdam reveal the difference?
6. How did the situation in China affect U.S. policy toward Japan?
7. Explain the Truman Doctrine and containment. What future pattern was established?
8. What motives lead to the Marshall Plan? How successful was it?
9. How did the National Security Act of 1947 reorganize the administration of national security? What agencies were created?
10. Why did Stalin blockade Berlin? How did the United States respond, and what resulted?
11. What was the fundamental agreement central to the North Atlantic Treaty Organization (NATO)? How did the Soviet Union respond?
12. What events of 1949 thrust the Cold War into a new and seemingly more dangerous stage?

America after the War (pp. 785–790)

13. What factors combined to keep the United States from experiencing another depression after the war? What economic challenges did the nation face?
14. How did President Truman respond to the coal and railroad strikes in 1948?
15. How did reconversion affect the many women and minorities who had taken war-related jobs?
16. What was the Fair Deal? Why was it initially unsuccessful?
17. What strategy did Truman use to win the presidential election despite problems within the party?
18. What were the successes and failures of Truman's reform agenda after 1948?

The Korean War (pp. 790–795)

19. What caused the Korean War? How did it turn into a stalemate?
20. Why did Truman dismiss Douglas MacArthur? Why was the decision so controversial?
21. What social and economic effects did the Korean War have in America?

The Crusade Against Subversion (pp. 795–800)

22. Describe the factors that combined to create the anticommunist paranoia that led to the rise of Joseph McCarthy. How does the "American Voice" of Whittaker Chambers (page 796) reflect this mood?
23. How did Joseph McCarthy exploit the existing mood of hysteria? What sort of tactics did he use in his attacks on alleged subversion?
24. What personalities and policies led to the Republican victory in the presidential election of 1952?

IDENTIFICATION

Identify each of the following, and explain why it is important within the context of the chapter.

1. Dumbarton Oaks
2. reparations
3. Chiang Kai-shek
4. Mao Zedong
5. George F. Kennan
6. hydrogen bomb
7. Formosa (Taiwan)
8. Atomic Energy Commission (AEC)
9. NSC-68
10. GI Bill of Rights
11. Taft-Hartley Act
12. "right-to-work" laws
13. "Dixiecrat" Party
14. Thomas E. Dewey
15. Syngman Rhee
16. House Un-American Activities Committee
17. Hollywood blacklist

18. Alger Hiss
19. J. Edgar Hoover
20. McCarran Internal Security Act
21. Julius and Ethel Rosenburg
22. Adlai Stevenson
23. Dwight D. Eisenhower
24. Richard M. Nixon

DOCUMENT

Read the section of the chapter under the heading "The Containment Doctrine," paying special attention to the discussion of the Truman Doctrine. The following is an excerpt from the March 12, 1947, speech in which Truman proclaimed the doctrine. He later remembered this program as "the turning point in America's foreign policy." Consider the following questions: What were the implications of a president unilaterally issuing what was, in essence, a treatylike commitment? Was the speech based on a false dichotomy between communist and "free" peoples? What in the speech foreshadows the economic containment approach of the Marshall Plan? Does American foreign policy continue to be based on the assumptions of containment and the Truman Doctrine?

> I am fully aware of the broad implications involved if the United States extends assistance to Greece and Turkey, and I shall discuss these implications with you at this time.
>
> One of the primary objectives of the foreign policy of the United States is the creation of conditions in which we and other nations will be able to work out a way of life free from coercion. This was a fundamental issue in the war with Germany and Japan. Our victory was won over countries which sought to impose their will, and their way of life, upon other nations.
>
> The peoples of a number of countries of the world have recently had totalitarian regimes forced upon them against their will. The Government of the United States has made frequent protests against coercion and intimidation, in violation of the Yalta Agreement, in Poland, Rumania, and Bulgaria....
>
> At the present moment in world history nearly every nation must choose between alternative ways of life. The choice is too often not a free one.
>
> One way of life is based upon the will of the majority, and is distinguished by free institutions, representative government, free elections, guarantees of individual liberty, freedom of speech and religion, and freedom from political oppression.
>
> The second way of life is based upon the will of a minority forcibly imposed upon the majority. It relies upon terror and oppression, a controlled press and radio, fixed elections, and the suppression of personal freedoms.
>
> I believe that it must be the policy of the United States to support free peoples who are resisting attempted subjugation by armed minorities or by outside pressures.

I believe that we must assist free peoples to work out their own destinies in their own way.

I believe that our help should be primarily through economic and financial aid, which is essential to economic stability and orderly political processes.

The world is not static and the status quo is not sacred. But we cannot allow changes in the status quo in violation of the Charter of the United Nations by such methods as coercion, or by such subterfuges as political infiltration. In helping free and independent nations to maintain their freedom, the United States will be giving effect to the principles of the Charter of the United Nations....

Should we fail to aid Greece and Turkey in this fateful hour, the effect will be far reaching to the West as well as to the East. We must take immediate and resolute action....

The seeds of totalitarian regimes are nurtured by misery and want. They spread and grow in the evil soil of poverty and strife. They reach their full growth when the hope of a people for a better life has died.

We must keep that hope alive.

The free peoples of the world look to us for support in maintaining their freedoms.

If we falter in our leadership, we may endanger the peace of the world—and we shall surely endanger the welfare of our own Nation.

Great responsibilities have been placed upon us by the swift movement of events.

I am confident that the Congress will face these responsibilities squarely.

MAP EXERCISE

Fill in or identify the following on the blank map provided. Use the map on page 783 of the text as your source.

1. Label all the countries.
2. Locate Berlin on the large map and show the approximate dividing line on the inset.
3. Label the Warsaw Pact nations.
4. Label the NATO nations.

Interpretative Questions

Based on what you have filled in, answer the following. For some of the questions you will need to consult the narrative in your text for information or explanation.

1. Why was the form of government in Poland such a difficult issue to resolve? What sort of Polish state emerged?
2. Why was Germany divided? Why was Berlin divided even though it lay in the Russian zone? What was behind the decision of the United States, Great Britain, and France to merge their zones into a single nation?

3. Explain the policy of the Truman Doctrine. What was to be contained? Where? What developments were the catalyst for Truman's promulgation of the policy? What was the economic manifestation of the idea?
4. Why was the Soviet Union so suspicious of the West and so insistent on control of East Germany and the nations along the Soviet border? Were the Soviet concerns justified?

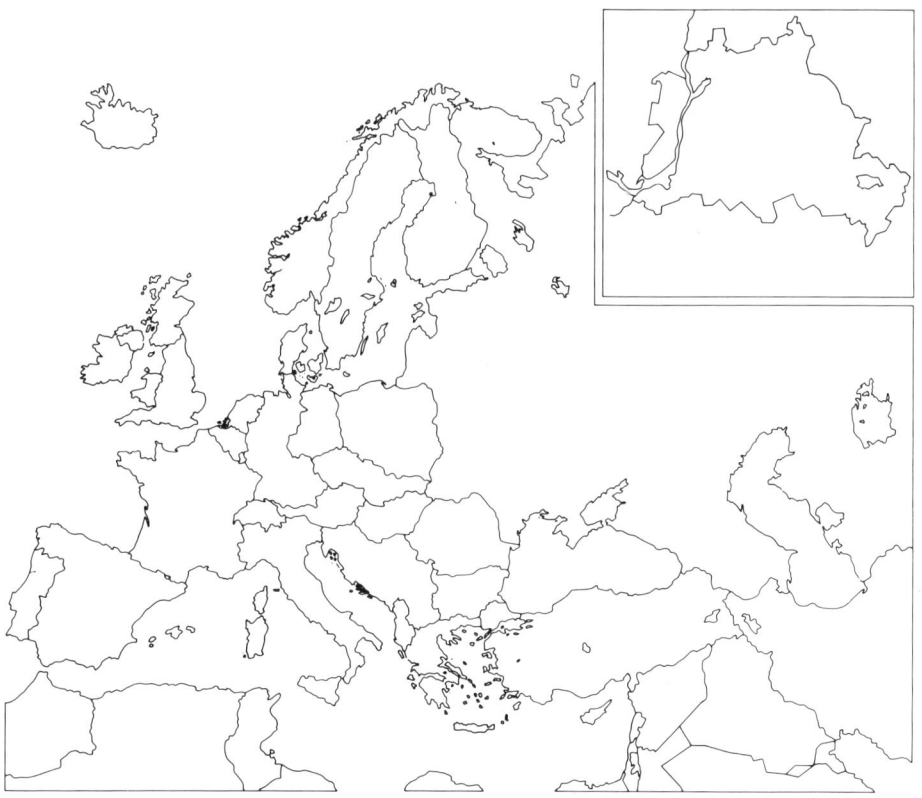

Summary

The mutual hostility between the United States and the Soviet Union grew out of ideological incompatibility and concrete actions stretching back to World War I and before. The alliance of convenience and necessity against Germany temporarily muted the tensions, but disagreement over the timing of the second front and antagonistic visions of postwar Europe pushed the two nations into a "cold war" only a few months after the victory over the Axis. The Cold War was marked by confrontation and the fear of potential military conflict. The United States vowed to contain communism by any means available.

Meanwhile, the American people, exhausted from a decade and a half of depression and war, turned away from economic reform. They were worried about the alleged Soviet threat in Europe, especially after the Soviet Union exploded its own atomic bomb in 1949. They were dismayed by the communist victory in China and perplexed by the limited war in Korea. Many Americans latched onto charges of domestic communist subversion as an explanation for the nation's inability to control world events. No one exploited this mood more effectively than Joseph McCarthy.

CHAPTER SELF-TEST

After you have read the chapter in the text and done the exercises in the Study Guide, the following self-test can be taken to see if you understand the material you have covered. Answers appear at the end of the Study Guide.

Multiple Choice

Circle the letter of the response which best answers the question or completes the statement.

1. According to the so-called "postrevisionist" view of some historians, the Cold War was principally the result of:
   a. aggressive Soviet policies of expansion in the postwar years.
   b. an American commitment to maintaining an "open door" for American trade in world markets.
   c. America's use of its nuclear monopoly to attempt to threaten and intimidate the Soviet Union.
   d. natural, predictable, and perhaps inevitable tensions and conflicts of interest between the world's two most powerful nations.

2. An issue on which basic disagreement remained for the Big Three at the Yalta Conference in February, 1945, one which led to only a vague compromise, was the:
   a. structure and elections for a postwar Polish government.
   b. need for Soviet participation in the war against Japan.
   c. return of some territory that the Soviet Union lost in the 1904 Russo-Japanese War.
   d. representation and powers of Security Council members in a United Nations.

3. According to the text, the Yalta accords represented a:
   a. fair and impartial settlement of the major postwar issues.
   b. general set of loose principles that sidestepped the most decisive issues.
   c. mutual acceptance of the idea of an "open" Europe.
   d. virtual "sellout" to Soviet demands for domination of Eastern Europe.

4. Unlike Roosevelt, President Truman:
   a. insisted that the Russians could be persuaded to bargain.
   b. viewed Stalin as an essentially reasonable man.
   c. used a surface geniality to disguise his diplomatic intentions.
   d. believed in patient negotiations rather than confrontation.
   e. considered the Soviet Union fundamentally untrustworthy and viewed Stalin with suspicion.

5. Upon the eruption of a full-scale civil war in China between the forces of Chiang Kai-shek and Mao Zedong, the United States:
   a. sought a third, alternative faction to support.
   b. tried to reach an accommodation with Mao.
   c. continued to pump money and weapons to Chiang.
   d. dismissed the government of Chiang as hopelessly incompetent and corrupt.

6. The Truman Doctrine committed the United States to a policy of:
   a. containing any attempt of communist expansion.
   b. appeasing the Soviet Union.
   c. initiating movements of national liberation in Greece and Turkey.
   d. overthrowing existing communist regimes.

7. The North Atlantic Treaty Organization (NATO) alliance:
   a. led to a quick reduction of America's military influence in Europe.
   b. spurred the Soviet Union to create the Warsaw Pact, an alliance with the communist governments in Eastern Europe.
   c. was not ratified by the United States Senate until after the Korean War.
   d. was composed of all the nations that had opposed Germany in World War II.

8. The Cold War took on a new tone in 1949 as a result of what *two* developments? (Choose two letters.)
   a. Soviet refusal to pull their occupation forces out of Iran.
   b. Victory of communist forces in mainland China.

c. Communist overthrow of the pro-Western government in Greece.
   d. Successful explosion of atomic weapons by the Soviet Union.
   e. The reunification of North and South Korea.

9. Representing a shift in foreign policy, the 1950 National Security Council report known as NSC-68 suggested:
   a. a massive airlift of supplies to break the communist blockade of West Berlin.
   b. United States assistance to Marshall Josip Broz Tito and the "unaligned" communist state of Yugoslavia.
   c. that the United States must take the initiative in resisting the expansion of communism in any location.
   d. creation of a defensive military alliance between the United States and the democratic nations of Western Europe.

10. The primary economic problem for the United States in the immediate years following World War II was:
    a. serious inflation caused by heavy consumer demand and the lifting of wartime controls.
    b. return of recession with the cancellation of wartime contracts.
    c. unemployment caused by soldiers flooding the labor market.
    d. labor unrest and strikes protesting massive layoffs.

11. President Harry S Truman's "Fair Deal" contained all of the following proposals *except:*
    a. expansion of Social Security benefits.
    b. significant tax reductions.
    c. federal aid to education.
    d. public housing and slum clearance projects.

12. The Labor-Management Relations Act of 1947, better known as the Taft-Hartley Act, outlawed the:
    a. closed shop, a workplace in which no one could be hired without first being a member of a union.
    b. union shop, a workplace in which workers must join a union after being hired.
    c. creation of open shops by passage of state "right-to-work" laws.
    d. stoppage of a strike by a presidential call for a "cooling-off" period.

13. The Taft-Hartley Act:
    a. was effectively killed by President Truman's veto.
    b. destroyed the political power of the labor movement.

c. speeded the process of unionization in the South.
   d. represented a conservative backlash against New Deal reforms.
14. One of the factors contributing to Truman's stunning upset victory in the election of 1948 was:
   a. a serious splintering of the Republican party into conservative and progressive factions.
   b. Truman's charge that the Republican-controlled Congress was "do-nothing, good-for-nothing."
   c. Truman's decision to conduct a quiet, reserved, statesmanlike campaign.
   d. Truman's shift from a liberal to a conservative stance on domestic issues.
15. The United States was able to win United Nations support for South Korea in the Korean War because the:
   a. war represented a clear case of aggression by North Korea.
   b. Security Council feared an expanded influence in Korea of the new communist government in China.
   c. Soviet Union was boycotting the Security Council at the time.
   d. United Nations had pledged itself to the creation of a unified, independent, and democratic Korea.

True/False

Read each statement carefully. Mark true statements "T" and false statements "F".

1. At the Teheran Conference in November 1943, despite some tension and unresolved issues, Roosevelt and Stalin established a cordial personal relationship and the Soviet Union agreed to enter the war in the Pacific after the end of hostilities in Europe.
2. At the Yalta Conference Stalin, Churchill, and Roosevelt agreed to the basic plan for the United Nations which included a Security Council with permanent membership for the United States, Great Britain, France, China, and the Soviet Union.
3. The Communist victory in China in 1949 increased U.S. resolve to keep Japan economically weak so that the Japanese would not be tempted to renew aggression against China.
4. The specific conflict that inspired President Truman to issue the "Truman Doctrine" involved a dispute between Poland and Hungary.

5. The NSC-68 report was suppressed by President Truman because it pointed out the high cost of containment and suggested that an arms race would delay economic recovery.
6. Shortly after World War II there was a sharp rise in labor unrest marked by major strikes in the automobile, electrical, steel, and coal industries.
7. When Chiang Kai-shek and his forces fled to the island of Formosa (Taiwan), the United States officially recognized Mao Zedong's regime as the government of mainland China.
8. The United States originally offered to include the Soviet Union and its eastern European satellites in the Marshall Plan for economic recovery.
9. Stalin blockaded access to Berlin so as to pressure the United States, Britain, and France to merge their zones of occupation into one unit as West Germany.
10. President Truman's "Fair Deal," including the Taft-Hartley Act, was designed mainly as a conservative reaction to the reforms of the New Deal.
11. After President Truman's unexpected victory in 1948, Congress quickly passed most of his "Fair Deal" agenda.
12. Congress passed the "right to work" bill in order to guarantee work to any American unable to find a job, but it was killed by a Truman veto.
13. The Korean War began in 1950 when military forces of the communist North invaded the pro-Western South.
14. The investigations by the House Un-American Activities Committee (HUAC) exposed convincing evidence that communist agents had thoroughly infiltrated the U.S. Department of State during World War II while the United States was officially allied with the Soviet Union against Germany.
15. Congress passed the McCarran Internal Security Act in order to prevent Sen. Joseph McCarthy from extending his "red scare" hearing to the army.

Review Questions

These questions are to be answered with essays. This will allow you to explore relationships among individuals, events, and attitudes of the period under review.

1. The United States hotly protested Stalin's actions in Poland, East Germany, and the rest of Eastern Europe as a violation of the

"one world" principle of the Atlantic Charter and a departure from the agreements reached at Yalta and Potsdam. Aside from pushing for creation of the United Nations, did American policy actually abide by its own principles, or was it just as much based on national self-interest as the Soviet Union's?

2. Explain how the Truman Doctrine, the Marshall Plan, NATO, support for Chiang Kai-shek, and the Korean War were based on the policy of containment. What did that policy concede to the Soviets? How did NSC-68 refine the doctrine? What geopolitical realities limited American options in Asia and Eastern Europe?

3. What general factors made the United States susceptible to the anticommunist paranoia of 1947 to 1953? What activities fanned the fury and paved the way for the rise of Joseph McCarthy?

4. Was the Cold War, as some historians have argued, an almost unavoidable conflict?

CHAPTER THIRTY
The Affluent Society

OBJECTIVES

A thorough study of Chapter 30 should enable you to understand:

1. The strengths and weaknesses of the economy in the 1950s and early 1960s.
2. The problems faced by the "other America."
3. The changes in the American lifestyle in the 1950s.
4. The significance of the Supreme Court's desegregation decision.
5. The characteristics of Dwight D. Eisenhower's middle-of-the-road domestic policy.
6. The new elements of American foreign policy introduced by Secretary of State John Foster Dulles.
7. The rationale for the initial United States involvement in Vietnam.
8. The causes and results of the 1956 Suez crisis.
9. The sources of United States difficulties in Latin America.
10. The reasons for new tensions with the Soviet Union toward the end of the Eisenhower administration.

PERTINENT QUESTIONS

Abundance and Society (pp. 803–814)

1. What caused the low unemployment rate and the great growth in GNP from 1945 to 1960? How widespread was the prosperity?
2. What factors combined to stimulate the rapid population expansion and economic growth that characterized the American West in the post-World War II era?
3. What major advances in benefits did the major labor unions obtain in the late 1940s and 1950? What challenges did the labor movement face?
4. Describe the increasing consumerism of the postwar period. What role did consumer credit play?

5. What was the appeal of suburbia? What was family life like for the typical middle-class white suburbanite? How did suburbia reflect the nation's class and racial divisions?
6. To what extent did television function as a force for cultural uniformity in the 1950s and 1960s? How did it alienate some people at the same time?
7. How did the United States react to the launching of *Sputnik?*
8. How did many writers of the 1950s reflect the growing tensions between an organized, bureaucratic society and the tradition of individualism?

The Other America (pp. 814–817)

9. What was the extent of "hard core" poverty in the otherwise prosperous nation?
10. Why was so much of rural America still mired in poverty as late as 1960?
11. Describe the process that led to large pockets of poverty-stricken minorities in northern and southwestern cities. Why did so many of these people remain poor at a time of growing national affluence?

The Rise of the Civil Rights Movement (pp. 817–820)

12. How did the political power structure of the Deep South states respond to the *Brown v. Board of Education* ruling? What was the result?
13. What was the importance of the Montgomery, Alabama, bus boycott?
14. What philosophy shaped the approach of Martin Luther King, Jr., to civil rights protest? How did he become the principal leader and symbol of the movement?

Eisenhower Republicanism (pp. 820–823)

15. From what segment of society did President Dwight Eisenhower draw most of the members of his administration? How did these men and women differ from their 1920s counterparts of similar background?
16. Contrast Eisenhower's attitude toward new social legislation with his approach to existing programs.
17. What led to the demise of Senator Joseph McCarthy and the end of the Red Scare?

Eisenhower, Dulles, and the Cold War (pp. 823–828)

18. Why did John Foster Dulles move the United States toward the policy of massive retaliation?
19. How did the Korean War end?
20. Describe Ho Chi Minh's background, motives, and sources of support in his defeat of the French?
21. For what did the Geneva Accords of 1954 provide?
22. Why was the United States so committed to friendliness and stability in the Middle East? How was this approach implemented in Iran?
23. What led to the Suez Crisis of 1956? What position did the United States take?
24. What led to increasing animosity toward the United States on the part of many Latin Americans? What did the Guatemalan incident reveal about American intentions?
25. What led to Fidel Castro's rise in Cuba? How did the United States deal with his new regime?
26. What did the Hungarian Revolution and the U-2 incident reveal about the nature of the United States-Soviet relationship in the late 1950s and into 1960?

IDENTIFICATION

Identify each of the following, and explain why it is important within the context of the chapter.

1. "baby boom"
2. Los Angeles
3. AFL-CIO
4. Benjamin Spock
5. Jonas Salk vaccine
6. "astronauts"
7. "beatniks"
8. Michael Harrington
9. "juvenile delinquency"
10. "massive resistance"
11. Earl Warren
12. White Citizens' Councils
13. Little Rock Central High School
14. Rosa Parks

15. Southern Christian Leadership Conference (SCLC)
16. Federal [Interstate] Highway Act of 1956
17. Ngo Dinh Diem
18. Gamal Abdel Nasser
19. Nikita Khrushchev
20. "military-industrial complex"

DOCUMENT

Read the section of the text headed "France, America, and Vietnam," paying close attention to the discussion of how the United States got involved in Southeast Asia. The following document is from the so-called *Pentagon Papers,* a classified Defense Department study of the Vietnam conflict up to 1967. The study was leaked to the press in 1971 amid considerable controversy, including a landmark Supreme Court decision on freedom of the press. The massive report details American involvement in Indochina stretching back into World War II. The study clearly indicates that the government consistently misled Congress and the American people about the extent of American involvement and the gravity of the situation. This document is an excerpt from an official National Security Council (NSC) statement of policy approved by President Truman on June 25, 1952, two years before the fall of Dien Bien Phu. Read the document, and consider these questions: How might the Korean experience have shaped NSC thinking? Was the United States really defending the "free world" in Vietnam, or was it protecting its own interests and pursuing an obsession with fighting communism whatever its source? Was the Geneva agreement really doomed from the beginning?

OBJECTIVE

1. To prevent the countries of Southeast Asia from passing into the communist orbit, and to assist them to develop the will and ability to resist communism from within and without and to contribute to the strengthening of the free world.

GENERAL CONSIDERATIONS

2. Communist domination, by whatever means, of all Southeast Asia would seriously endanger in the short term, and critically endanger in the longer term, United States security interests.

    a. The loss of any of the countries of Southeast Asia to communist control as a consequence of overt or covert Chinese Communist aggression would have critical psychological, political and economic consequences. In the absence of effective and timely counteraction, the loss of any single country would probably lead to relatively swift submission to or an alignment with communism by the remaining countries of this group. Furthermore, an alignment with communism of the rest of Southeast Asia and India, and in the longer term, of the Middle East (with the probable exceptions of at least Pakistan and Turkey) would in all probability progressively follow. Such widespread alignment would endanger the stability and security of Europe.

b. Communist control of all of Southeast Asia would render the U.S. position in the Pacific offshore island chain precarious and would seriously jeopardize fundamental U.S. security interests in the Far East.

c. Southeast Asia, especially Malaya and Indonesia, is the principal world source of natural rubber and tin, and a producer of petroleum and other strategically important commodities. The rice exports of Burma and Thailand are critically important to Malaya, Ceylon and Hong Kong and are of considerable significance to Japan and India, all important areas of free Asia.

d. The loss of Southeast Asia, especially of Malaya and Indonesia, could result in such economic and political pressures in Japan as to make it extremely difficult to prevent Japan's eventual accommodation to communism....

3. The danger of an overt military attack against Southeast Asia is inherent in the existence of a hostile and aggressive Communist China, but such an attack is less profitable than continued communist efforts to achieve domination through subversion. The primary threat to Southeast Asia accordingly arises from the possibility that the situation in Indochina may deteriorate as a result of the weakening of the resolve of, or as a result of the inability of the governments of France and of the Associated States to continue to oppose the Viet Minh rebellion, the military strength of which is being steadily increased by virtue of aid furnished by the Chinese Communist regime and its allies.

MAP EXERCISE

Fill in or identify the following on the blank map provided. Use the map on page 844 and the narrative in your text as your source.

1. Identify and label the following countries: Cuba and Guatemala.
2. Identify and label the following U.S. interests: Florida, Panama Canal Zone, Puerto Rico.

Interpretative Questions

Based on what you have filled in, answer the following. For some of the questions you will need to consult the narrative in your text for information or explanation.

1. Why was the United States so concerned about the ideology of those in control of Guatemala in 1954? What action did the United States take?
2. What was the pre-1959 U.S. relationship with Cuba? How did the U.S. reaction to Fidel Castro evolve?

SUMMARY

From the late 1940s through the 1950s, the United States experienced continued economic growth and low unemployment. Most of the nation participated in the prosperity and agreed about the beneficence of American capitalism. Only a few intellectuals questioned the rampant consumerism and the values of the growing corporate bureaucracies. Those who lived in the "other America" of rural and core-city poverty were generally ignored by the affluent and the intellectuals. The politics of the period, symbolized by President Eisenhower, the cautious war hero, reflected the popular contentment. Blacks, inspired by the *Brown* school desegregation decision, began the protests that would bring the civil rights revolution of the 1960s. Locked into a policy of containment and a rigidly dualistic world view, the United States was less successful in its overseas undertakings. Despite a string of alliances, an awesome nuclear arsenal, and vigorous use of covert operations, the nation often found itself unable to shape world events to conform to American desires.

CHAPTER SELF-TEST

After you have read the chapter in the text and done the exercises in the Study Guide, the following self-test can be taken to see if you understand

the material you have covered. Answers appear at the end of the Study Guide.

Multiple Choice

Circle the letter of the response which best answers the question or completes the statement.

1. America's economic prosperity in the 1950s was fueled by:
   a. increased public funding of schools, housing, veteran's benefits, welfare, and interstate highways.
   b. the continuation of military spending at almost wartime levels.
   c. the "baby boom" and rapid expansion of the suburbs.
   d. all of the above.
   e. none of the above.

2. The prosperity of the 1950s was accompanied by:
   a. a significant decrease in defense spending.
   b. continued corporate mergers and formation of conglomerates.
   c. a much more equitable distribution of corporate profits.
   d. the survival and renewal of the family farm.

3. All of the following trends marked the American labor movement of the 1950s *except:*
   a. the merger of the AFL and CIO to create the giant federation, the AFL-CIO.
   b. a leveling off of membership caused in part by the growing shift of workers from blue-collar to white-collar jobs.
   c. noticeably greater success in organizing new workers than in winning benefits for workers already organized in strong unions.
   d. signs of corruption and indifference among some labor leaders as the unions themselves became wealthy, powerful bureaucracies.

4. According to many social observers, American culture in the 1950s seemed dominated by:
   a. a restless search by individuals for identity and purpose.
   b. a quest for economic and political justice within the United States.
   c. an absorption with consumer goods by a growing middle class.
   d. an isolationist desire to avoid international affairs or commitments.

5. Life in suburbia was especially attractive to many American families in the 1950s because in contrast to the central cities the suburbs provided:
   a. variety and excitement in lifestyles and entertainment.
   b. harmonious racial integration in neighborhoods and schools.
   c. greater opportunities for attending cultural facilities such as symphonies and museums.
   d. larger, safer, and more private homes.

6. Which region of the United States experienced the most dramatic change as a result of economic growth in the period from World War II to about 1960?
   a. South.
   b. North.
   c. East.
   d. West.
   e. Midwest.

7. According to Dr. Benjamin Spock, the highly regarded child care expert of the late 1940s and 1950s, women could become better mothers by:
   a. fulfilling their career and professional goals.
   b. staying home and focusing on the needs of their children.
   c. sharing the role of parenting more equally with the fathers.
   d. working to supplement income and increase family purchasing power.

8. During the 1950s, the television industry:
   a. actually affected only a very small percentage of the total population.
   b. served to encourage individuality and an independence in values and beliefs among members of the white middle class.
   c. served primarily as a culturally unifying force since millions of Americans viewed standard fare.
   d. failed to attract enough interest from commercial advertisers to be financially successful.

9. The United States accomplished which of the following feats *before* the Soviet Union? (Choose one or more letters as appropriate.)
   a. Launching a satellite into outer space.
   b. Sending a manned satellite into outer space.

c. Initiating a manned orbit of the globe.
d. Landing men on the surface of the moon.
e. None of the above.

10. In *The Organization Man* (1956), William H. Whyte, Jr. indicated the most important trait for a worker in a bureaucracy was:
    a. a reliance on individual initiative.
    b. a willingness to be candid.
    c. an ability to "get along."
    d. a talent for creativity.
    e. a willingness to change careers and companies frequently.

11. The principal message of the "beats" (or beatniks), young poets and writers of the 1950s:
    a. criticized the sterility and conformity of American life and culture.
    b. warned of the dangers of international communism.
    c. offered a romantic and nostalgic vision of the past.
    d. urged rededication by politicians to the American dream.

12. Michael Harrington's *The Other America* (1962) captured the nation's attention by focusing on:
    a. technological advances.
    b. the continuing problem of poverty.
    c. future political prospects.
    d. the network of organized crime.
    e. working women.

13. The *Brown v. Board of Education* decision of 1954:
    a. was strongly endorsed by President Eisenhower.
    b. bitterly divided the justices of the Supreme Court.
    c. provided a specific timetable and guidelines for school integration.
    d. encountered strong opposition and delay tactics throughout the South.

14. The arrest of Rosa Parks in Montgomery, Alabama, led to a boycott by blacks of the city's:
    a. lunch counters.
    b. department stores.
    c. bus lines.
    d. public schools.
    e. court system.

15. In domestic affairs, President Dwight D. Eisenhower:
    a. worked to expand government's involvement in and control of the economy.
    b. exercised strong personal leadership to pass his social agenda through Congress.
    c. expanded public development of natural resources through TVA-type projects.
    d. permitted the survival, and sometimes the expansion, of the social programs that were already in place when he took office.

True/False

Read each statement carefully. Mark true statements "T" and false statements "F."

1. From 1945 to 1960 the American economy grew significantly because of rapid population growth, but the growth was misleading because the economy was actually declining in real per capita dollars.
2. In 1955 the American Federation of Labor (AFL) and the Congress of Industrial Organizations (CIO) split due to philosophical differences and did not reunify until the early 1980s.
3. In the 1950s, the Levittown development near New York City symbolized the rapid postwar growth of suburban, single-family-house neighborhoods.
4. By the late 1950s televisions had become, according to one report, more common than refrigerators in American homes.
5. The Russian launching of the space satellite *Sputnik* before the U.S. had launched its own satellite alarmed Americans and led not only to an increased focus on the nation's space program but also to increased emphasis on science education in the schools.
6. Although the *Brown v. Board of Education of Topeka* decision on school integration was not popular with most white southerners, most states and school districts bowed to pressure from the Eisenhower administration and implemented the ruling within about three years.
7. The incident that thrust Martin Luther King, Jr., into prominence as a leader of the civil rights movement was the black boycott of the segregated bus system in Montgomery, Alabama.
8. The president of General Motors Company who declared that "what was good for our country was good for General Motors,

and vice versa," became Secretary of Defense for President Eisenhower.
9. Although President Eisenhower was a Republican who remained personally popular, the Democratic Party held control of both houses of Congress from 1954 to the end of the Eisenhower administration and well beyond that time.
10. The political demise of Senator Joseph McCarthy was closely associated with his attacks on the Army.
11. Secretary of State John Foster Dulles believed that the U.S. military had placed too much reliance on the atomic bomb and "massive retaliation" strategy; he therefore began to shift military spending priorities toward "flexible response."
12. The Eisenhower administration maintained good relations with Castro's Cuba, and tensions did not develop until John Kennedy enlisted the CIA to try to overthrow Castro.
13. The Korean War ended very early in the Eisenhower administration with an armistice that left the Korean peninsula divided at the 38th parallel.
14. For approximately nine years after the end of World War II, the United States provided military aid to the French government in Vietnam in its struggle against the anticolonial nationalist forces led by communist Ho Chi Minh.
15. In 1948 when the Jews in Palestine proclaimed the existence of the independent nation of Israel, President Truman delayed for several months extending diplomatic recognition to the new nation because he did not want to offend the oil-rich Arab nations.

Review Questions

These questions are to be answered with essays. This will allow you to explore relationships among individuals, events, and attitudes of the period under review.

1. Analyze the causes and consequences of the economic boom of the 1950s. Explain who was left out and why.
2. Did the assumptions of containment lead the United States into unwise commitments and actions in Southeast Asia, Latin America, and the Middle East, or was the nation acting prudently in response to hostile communist expansionism?
3. What new cultural developments accompanied the prosperity and suburbanization of the 1950s? How did intellectuals regard the highly organized and homogenized new society?

Chapter Thirty-One
The Ordeal of Liberalism

Objectives

A thorough study of Chapter 31 should enable you to understand:

1. The new directions of domestic reform manifested by John Kennedy's New Frontier program.
2. The new elements added to Kennedy's program by Lyndon Johnson's Great Society proposals.
3. The reasons why the black movement became increasingly assertive in the 1960s.
4. The significance of Martin Luther King, Jr., and Malcolm X to the civil rights movement.
5. The new elements that Kennedy introduced in both the nation's defense strategy and its foreign policy.
6. The background and sequence of events leading to the Cuban missile crisis.
7. The reasons for U.S. involvement in the two Indochina Wars and why both were unsuccessful.
8. The reasons why the 1968 Tet offensive had such a critical impact on both policy toward Vietnam and American domestic politics.

Chronology of the War in Indochina

Because American involvement in Indochina stretched from the 1940s through the 1970s, the material is in several chapters. This chronology will help you see the entire span of the Vietnam War.

1945–1954	Ho Chi Minh led fight against French colonialism
1950	United States was paying for most of the French effort
1954	French defeated at Dien Bien Phu
	Geneva Conference partitioned Indochina
1956	President Diem refused to hold reunification elections

1960	National Liberation Front (NFL) (Viet Cong) organized and Second Indochina War began
1963	Diem deposed and killed
	About 15,000 American advisers in South Vietnam
1964	Gulf of Tonkin Resolution
1965	American bombing of North Vietnam began
	180,000 American troops in Vietnam by year's end
1966	Fulbright hearings began
	300,000 American troops in Vietnam
1967	Major antiwar protests under way
	500,000 American troops in Vietnam
1968	
January	Tet offense
March	Johnson announced bombing pause and his withdrawal from the presidential race
1969	American troop strength peaked at 540,000
1970	
May	Cambodia invaded
	Kent State and Jackson State incidents
December	Gulf of Tonkin Resolution repealed
1971	Pentagon Papers released
1972	
Spring	Hanoi and Haiphong bombed
Fall	American troop strength down to 60,000
December	"Christmas bombings"
1973	Cease-fire; Paris accords
1975	Vietnam unified by victory of northern forces
1978	Vietnam invaded Cambodia
	China invaded Vietnam

PERTINENT QUESTIONS

Expanding the Liberal State (pp. 829–836)

1. Describe John F. Kennedy's background and his plans for domestic legislation. How did his New Frontier fare?
2. Describe the events surrounding the Kennedy assassination. What are the varying opinions about who was responsible?

3. How did Lyndon Johnson differ from Kennedy in personality and in the ability to influence Congress?
4. What were the purposes of Medicare and Medicaid? Why were they controversial?
5. What agency was the "centerpiece" of the Great Society? What new approach tried to involve the poor themselves in shaping the programs?
6. Who opposed federal aid to education? How did Johnson's legislation manage to circumvent much of the opposition?
7. How did the effort to fund both the Great Society and a great military establishment affect the federal budget?
8. What did the Great Society accomplish?

The Battle for Racial Equality (pp. 836–843)

9. Describe the increasing civil rights activism of the early 1960s. How did this protest movement affect public policy?
10. What events prompted passage of the Civil Rights Act of 1965 (Voting Rights Act)?
11. Describe the urban violence of the mid-1960s. What did the Commission on Civil Disorders recommend in response?
12. How did the focus of racial issues and the locus of the civil rights movement change in the mid-late 1960s?
13. Describe the race riots of 1964 to 1967. What response did the Commission on Civil Disorder suggest? How did many white Americans react to the disorder?
14. What did "black power" mean? What impact did it have on the civil rights movement and on the attitudes of American blacks in general?

"Flexible Response" and the Cold War (pp. 843–846)

16. How did John F. Kennedy's approach to foreign policy contrast with Eisenhower's? What specific programs illustrated that difference?
17. What were the purpose and the result of the Bay of Pigs invasion?
18. What precipitated the Cuban Missile Crisis? How was it resolved? What was its legacy?
19. Why did Lyndon Johnson send troops to Dominican Republic? Was the action reminiscent of the interventions in the days of the Roosevelt Corollary?

Vietnam (pp. 846–854)

20. Why did the United States ignore opportunities for cooperation with Ho Chi Minh and get drawn in to supporting France's effort to reassert control over Vietnam after World War II?
21. How did the north and south parts of Vietnam differ at the time that the Geneva Conference temporarily partitioned the country?
22. Why did the United States support Ngo Dinh Diem and his refusal to hold reunification elections in 1956? What led to his downfall and assassination in 1963?
23. Recount the stages of Johnson's escalation of the Vietnam War up to 1967. Why did the conflict become a "quagmire"?
24. Why did America's twofold strategy of "attrition" and "pacification" fail?
25. Where did opposition to the war originate? How did it spread?
26. How did involvement in Vietnam affect the American economy?

The Traumas of 1968 (pp. 854–858)

27. What effect did the Tet offensive have on American public opinion concerning the war and on the course of the 1968 presidential election?
28. How did the nation respond to the assassination of Martin Luther King, Jr.?
29. What anxieties did Richard Nixon and George Wallace exploit in the 1968 presidential election?
30. How have historians differed in their explanations for the continuing involvement of the United States in Vietnam despite bleak prospects for victory?

IDENTIFICATION

Identify each of the following, and explain why it is important within the context of the chapter.

1. Lee Harvey Oswald
2. Warren Commission
3. Barry Goldwater
4. Robert Weaver
5. Immigration Act of 1965
6. sit-in
7. Student Nonviolent Coordinating Committee (SNCC)
8. Congress of Racial Equality (CORE)

10. "I have a dream"
11. "Freedom Summer"
12. "affirmative action"
13. Black Panthers
14. Malcolm X
15. Green Berets
16. Alliance for Progress
17. Berlin Wall
18. Dien Bien Phu
19. Vietminh
20. Viet Cong/National Liberation Front
21. Gulf of Tonkin Resolution
22. J. William Fulbright
23. Robert F. Kennedy
24. Hubert Humphrey

DOCUMENT

Read the section of the chapter under the heading "Urban Violence." The document below is drawn from the 1967 report of the National Commission on Civil Disorders, often called the Kerner Commission because it was headed by Governor Otto Kerner of Illinois. Consider the following questions: Why did the riots come at a time when blacks were making legal gains? How would conservative whites react to the commission's findings? What traditional American values does the report affront? What values does it affirm? More than twenty-five years later, how close is America to realizing the vision of the Kerner Commission? Does the elimination of racism remain "the major unfinished business of this nation"?

> This is our basic conclusion: Our nation is moving toward two societies, one black, one white—separate and unequal.
>
> Reaction to last summer's disorders has quickened the movement and deepened the division. Discrimination and segregation have long permeated much of American life; they now threaten the future of every American.
>
> This deepening racial division is not inevitable. The movement apart can be reversed. Choice is still possible. Our principal task is to define that choice and to press for a national resolution.
>
> To pursue our present course will involve the continuing polarization of the American community and, ultimately, the destruction of basic democratic values.
>
> The alternative is not blind repression or capitulation to lawlessness. It is the realization of common opportunities for all within a single society.

This alternative will require a commitment to national action—compassionate, massive and sustained, backed by the resources of the most powerful and the richest nation on this earth. From every American it will require new attitudes, new understanding, and, above all, new will.

The vital needs of the nation must be met; hard choices must be made, and, if necessary, new taxes enacted.

Violence cannot build a better society. Disruption and disorder nourish repression, not justice. They strike at the freedom of every citizen. The community cannot—it will not—tolerate coercion and mob rule.

Violence and destruction must be ended—in the streets of the ghetto and in the lives of people.

Segregation and poverty have created in the racial ghetto a destructive environment totally unknown to most white Americans.

What white Americans have never fully understood—but what the Negro can never forget—is that white society is deeply implicated in the ghetto. White institutions created it, white institutions maintain it, and white society condones it.

It is time now to turn with all the purpose at our command to the major unfinished business of this nation. It is time to adopt strategies for action that will produce quick and visible progress. It is time to make good the promises of American democracy to all citizens—urban and rural, white and black, Spanish-surname, American Indian, and every minority group.

National Commission on Civil Disorders, 1967.

MAP EXERCISE

Fill in or identify the following on the blank map provided. Use the map on page 848 of the text as your source.

1. All countries.
2. Mekong Delto and Gulf of Tonkin.
3. Hanoi, Saigon, Haiphong, Phnom Penh, and Bangkok.
4. DMZ.

Interpretative Questions

Based on what you have filled in, answer the following. For some of the questions you will need to consult the narrative in your text for information or explanation.

1. How did the United States get dragged into the conflict in Southeast Asia? How did Vietnam get divided?
2. From what internal and external sources did the Viet Cong receive their support? How did this make them so difficult to defeat?

The Ordeal of Liberalism ~ 345

3. What trap of competing factors kept Lyndon Johnson from either withdrawing or further escalating the war? How did the geographic position of Indochina in relation to China affect this trap?

SUMMARY

The 1960s began with John F. Kennedy squeezing out one of the narrowest presidential victories in United States history. Three years later, he was dead, and it was up to Lyndon Johnson to carry through his liberal legacy. The first three years of Johnson's presidency were legislatively one of the most productive periods ever, as Congress passed many of the civil rights, health, education, and welfare measures of the Great Society. In 1961, the nation bungled an attempt to dislodge Castro from Cuba, and a year and half later, the world came to the brink of nuclear war during the Cuban missile crisis. By the latter half of the decade, the foreign policy focus had moved halfway around the world. By the end of 1967, the United States had been involved in Vietnam for over twenty years and had 500,000 troops in the Southeast Asia war zone. The war in Vietnam had become the central issue of American politics.

CHAPTER SELF-TEST

After you have read the chapter in the text and done the exercises in the Study Guide, the following self-test can be taken to see if you understand the material you have covered. Answers appear at the end of the Study Guide.

Multiple Choice

Circle the letter of the response which best answers the question or completes the statement.

1. John F. Kennedy made an attractive presidential candidate in 1960 for all of the following reasons *except* his:
   a. family wealth and prestige.
   b. past accomplishments as a war hero and a prize-winning author.
   c. personal eloquence, wit, and charisma.
   d. promise to keep the nation on the course of the 1950s.

2. In contrast to Kennedy, President Lyndon B. Johnson:
   a. rejected the concept of dynamic governmental activism.
   b. possessed a shy and reticent personality.
   c. displayed remarkable skill in influencing Congress.
   d. sympathized with Southern conservatives.

3. A significant reason that the Medicare proposal was able to overcome opposition and win congressional approval was because it:
   a. made benefits available to all elderly Americans, regardless of need.
   b. strictly regulated the fee structure of doctors and hospitals.
   c. established annual spending ceilings by the Congress.
   d. shifted responsibility for paying a large proportion of medical fees from the government to the patient.

4. Passed partly in response to events surrounding a demonstration in Selma, Alabama, the Civil Rights Act of 1965 granted blacks:
   a. equal employment opportunities.
   b. access to higher education.
   c. federal protection of their voting rights.
   d. integration in public accommodations.

5. In response to urban racial violence, in 1968 the special Commission on Civil Disorders appointed by the President recommended:
   a. massive spending to eliminate the abysmal conditions in the ghettoes.
   b. the elimination of state government involvement in welfare programs.
   c. slowing the pace of racial change to allow the nation a "cooling off" period.
   d. a return to segregated housing patterns to lessen the emotional conflicts that sparked outbreaks in mixed neighborhoods.

6. The first major race riot of the mid-1960s occurred in the Watts section of:
   a. New York City.
   b. Los Angeles.
   c. Chicago.
   d. Detroit.
   e. Atlanta.

7. The most important and lasting impact of the "black power" movement was the:
   a. stress on the ideal of interracial cooperation.
   b. unification of black political groups.
   c. instilling of racial pride in black Americans.
   d. rejection of African ties and roots by American blacks.

8. Kennedy's "Alliance for Progress" was intended to provide:
   a. mutual reduction of missiles by the United States and the Soviet Union.
   b. additional aid to the Diem government of South Vietnam.
   c. young American volunteers to work in developing nations.
   d. better relations between the United States and Latin America.

9. In the aftermath of the Cuban missile crisis:
   a. Kennedy traveled to Vienna for his first meeting with Soviet Premier Nikita Khrushchev.
   b. the Soviets ordered construction of a Berlin Wall to stop the exodus of East Germans.
   c. a large CIA-trained army of anti-Castro Cubans unsuccessfully invaded the island.
   d. both the United States and the Soviet Union seemed ready to move toward a new accommodation.

10. Ngo Dinh Diem turned out to be an unfortunate choice as the basis of American hopes for a noncommunist South Vietnam because by the early 1960s he:
    a. resisted serious political or economic reforms.
    b. failed to attract the support of the Vietnamese upper class.
    c. was too willing to appease the Viet Cong.
    d. persecuted the nation's Roman Catholics.

11. In regard to the Vietnam Conflict, the Gulf of Tonkin Resolution:
    a. aroused strong opposition and a lengthy debate in Congress before being narrowly passed.
    b. limited President Johnson to a one-time retaliatory bombing strike on North Vietnam.
    c. was claimed by President Johnson as legal authorization for the military escalation of the U.S. role in the conflict.
    d. marked the beginning of significant international support for the American response to communist aggression in Indochina.

12. By the end of 1967, United States war efforts in Vietnam:
    a. had effectively reduced to a trickle the flow of communist soldiers and supplies into the south part of Vietnam by intensive bombings of the north.
    b. involved nearly 500,000 American military personnel in the war region.

c. had succeeded in establishing an honest and efficient, if weak, government in South Vietnam.
d. all of the above.

13. The American military in Vietnam seemed *least* capable of:
    a. winning a military victory in the major battles in which it became engaged.
    b. removing the Viet Cong and their Vietnamese allies from the North from such strongholds as Khesanh.
    c. sustaining a "favorable kill ratio."
    d. pacifying a captured region by winning the "hearts and minds" of the people.

14. The Tet Offensive by Viet Cong forces in January 1968 was most significant because it demonstrated:
    a. a display of military strength by the Viet Cong that American commanders had long insisted that the Viet Cong did not possess.
    b. that American forces had the military might to dislodge the Viet Cong from most of the positions that they had seized during the previous three years.
    c. that Saigon was a safe haven for international diplomats and businessmen despite the problems in the rest of the country.
    d. that the vast majority of the American public would increase their support for the war effort in the wake of U.S. military victories.

15. In the 1968 presidential election, George Wallace enjoyed an unusually high degree of support for a third-party candidate because he argued that:
    a. the United States should not have any military involvement in Vietnam.
    b. the movement toward racial equality should be accelerated through "affirmative action" programs.
    c. programs to alleviate poverty should be fully funded by Congress and that defense spending should be cut sharply to get the money.
    d. busing for racial integration, expanding government regulations and social programs, and soft treatment of rioters and demonstrators were destroying America.

True/False

Read each statement carefully. Mark true statements "T" and false statements "F."

1. Because it promised another round of reform like the New Deal, the nickname given to President Kennedy's agenda for social reform was the "Kennedy round."
2. The Warren Commission on the assassination of President Kennedy concluded that Lee Harvey Oswald had acted alone.
3. Barry Goldwater, the Republican nominee for President in 1964, represented the moderate-liberal wing of his party, and his defeat laid the groundwork for the conservative takeover of the Republican Party that would follow.
4. The Office of Economic Opportunity (OEO), the "centerpiece" of President Johnson's "war on poverty," tried to get members of poor communities themselves involved in planning and administering social programs.
5. The Immigration Act of 1965 gave preference to potential northern and western European migrants and sharply limited African and Asian immigration to the United States.
6. A major key to President Johnson's "Great Society" was that the programs involved reform in the approach to poverty without necessitating significant spending increases.
7. In the immediate post-World War II period, there was a major exodus of black population from the industrial cities of the northeast back to the South because of urban riots and the loss of wartime jobs.
8. By the mid-1960s the civil rights movement had begun to focus on racial discrimination that existed by custom and practice outside the South as well as on legal restrictions in the old Confederate states.
9. "Affirmative action" refers to extra efforts—for example, hiring, scholarships, etc.,—undertaken by the government and corporations to help counter the discrimination that women and minorities faced in the past.
10. Malcolm X stressed that blacks should band together and stress their racial pride through their Christian churches.
11. The Green Berets were Special Forces trained to fight guerrilla conflicts and other limited wars.

12. Despite pleas for help from anti-Castro exiles, the preparation for the Bay of Pigs invasion was undertaken by Cuban refugees without assistance from any agency of the U.S. government.
13. The Gulf of Tonkin Resolution, which authorized President Johnson to "take all necessary measures" to protect American forces and "prevent further aggression" in Southeast Asia, was inspired by an alleged attack on U.S. destroyers by North Vietnamese torpedo boats.
14. The Tet Offensive by the Viet Cong helped turn American opinion against the war in Vietnam even though the U.S. and South Vietnamese forces repelled the invasion and inflicted serious losses on the Viet Cong.
15. Despite Martin Luther King, Jr.'s philosophy of nonviolence, there were major riots in several American cities following the assassination of King.

Review Questions

These questions are to be answered with essays. This will allow you to explore relationships among individuals, events, and attitudes of the period under review.

1. What were the central elements of the New Frontier and the Great Society? Why was Johnson able to succeed where Kennedy failed? What were the long-term results of the liberal legislation of 1964 to 1966?
2. How did the reaction of many southern whites to the civil rights activities ironically serve to help the blacks' cause? How did blacks respond when it became clear that the legislative victories of 1964 and 1965 were not enough to satisfy their aspirations?
3. What was the heart of the problem in Vietnam that made military victory so difficult, if not impossible? Who seemed to understand this problem better—the Johnson administration or its critics? How was the Johnson administration trapped by the war?

CHAPTER THIRTY-TWO
The Crisis of Authority

OBJECTIVES

A thorough study of Chapter 32 should enable you to understand:

1. The reasons for the rise of the New Left and the counterculture.
2. The problems of American Indians and Hispanics, and the nature of their protest movements.
3. The meaning of the New Feminism.
4. The Nixon-Kissinger policy for terminating the Vietnam War, and the subsequent Paris peace settlement.
5. The changes in American foreign policy necessitated by the new perception of the world as multipolar.
6. The ways in which the Supreme Court in the Nixon years began a change to a more conservative posture, and the reasons for this change.
7. The reasons for the decline in the American economy in the early 1970s, and President Nixon's reaction to the decline.
8. The significance of Watergate as an indication of the abuse of executive power.

PERTINENT QUESTIONS

The Turbulent Society (pp. 861–865)

1. What led to the rise of the New Left? What were its results?
2. What were the main manifestations of the counterculture of the 1960s? What impact did the counterculture have on the larger society?

The Mobilization of Minorities (pp. 865–872)

3. How did the Indian civil rights movement manifest itself? What changes did it accomplish?

4. Describe the typical economic status of Hispanic Americans. Why did their economic development lag?
5. How did Hispanics, African Americans, Indians, and other ethnic groups challenge the "melting pot" ethic?
6. What were the accomplishments of the gay liberation movement? What resistance did it face?

The New Feminism (pp. 872–876)

7. What were the goals of the National Organization for Women?
8. How did the women's movement evolve, and how did the most radical positions taken by feminists differ from more mainstream positions?
9. What gains did women make in education, the professions, and politics in the 1970s and 1980s?
10. What happened to the Equal Rights Amendment? Why?
11. How, according to the "Debating the Past" section (page 894), did the changes in the writing of women's history reflect the evolution of the movement?

Nixon, Kissinger, and the War (pp. 876–881)

12. Explain Richard Nixon's "Vietnamization" policy. How well did it work? Why did it defuse some of the opposition to the war?
13. What direction did the antiwar movement take in reaction to the invasion of Cambodia?
14. What did the Pentagon Papers reveal about the nature of the Vietnam War?
15. What effect did the controversial and inconclusive nature of the war have on the military personnel who served in Vietnam?
16. What did the bombings and negotiations from March 1972 to January 1973 accomplish? What was the main stumbling block to final agreement?
17. What were the main provisions of the Paris accords? How did they fall apart?
18. On balance, what were the costs of the war to Vietnam and the United States?

Nixon, Kissinger, and the World (pp. 881–885)

19. Why did Nixon and Henry Kissinger decide that the time had come for rapprochement with China? What resulted from Nixon's visit and related initiatives? Why was his handshake with Chou En-lai so symbolic?

20. What was the basic thrust of the Nixon Doctrine? What were its implications in Chile?
21. What dilemma of American policy in the Middle East did the Yom Kippur War make clear? What other lessons did the war teach?

Politics and Economics in the Nixon Years (pp. 885–891)

22. What major decisions of the Warren Court most outraged conservatives?
23. What successes and rebuffs did Nixon meet in his attempts to reshape the Supreme Court? Did the Court, with four Nixon appointees, perform as he had intended?
24. What advantages did Nixon have going into the 1972 election? What were George McGovern's political liabilities?
25. What were the proximate and fundamental causes of the inflation problem of the late 1960s and 1970s?
26. Explain how the nation's manufacturing sector and, therefore, the nature of the economy was changing. How did corporate America respond?
27. Describe the general outlines of Nixon's economic policy. Was it consistent? Was it effective?

The Watergate Crisis (pp. 891–895)

28. What aspects of Richard Nixon's personality and management style led to the collection of scandals associated with the Watergate crisis?
29. Why did Spiro Agnew resign? Why did his removal and the appointment of Gerald Ford as vice president actually increase the pressure on Nixon?
30. On what charges would Nixon's probable impeachment and conviction have been based? Why did he finally resign?

IDENTIFICATION

Identify each of the following, and explain why it is important within the context of the chapter.

1. Students for a Democratic Society (SDS)
2. hippies
3. marijuana
4. "termination" Indian policy
5. American Indian Movement (AIM)

6. Cesar Chavez
7. "multiculturalism"
8. "Stonewall Riot"
9. Betty Friedan
10. Sandra Day O'Connor
11. *Roe v. Wade*
12. Henry Kissinger
13. Pentagon Papers
14. William Calley
15. "bipolar" and "multipolar"
16. SALT I
17. Leonid Brezhnev
18. "silent majority"
19. Warren Burger
20. George Wallace
21. Organization of Petroleum Exporting Countries (OPEC)
22. Gerald Ford

DOCUMENT

Read the section of the text under the heading "The Watergate Crisis." All along, President Nixon had claimed that neither he nor any of his inner staff knew any of the details of the Watergate break-in. He also denied that he had been involved in any cover-up. Through July 1974, the evidence against Nixon was circumstantial or based on contradictory testimony. Although the pressure for removal at that time was strong, the president still had many defenders. Then in August, Nixon was forced to release the tapes that are excerpted below. They cover conversations of June 23, 1972, only six days after the break-in. Read the excerpts, and consider these questions: Were these tapes necessary for Nixon's impeachment, or was there adequate evidence without them? What do the conversations reveal about the casual manner in which Nixon and White House assistant H. R. Haldeman used federal agencies for political purposes?

> HALDEMAN: Now, on the investigation, you know the Democratic break-in thing, we're back in the problem area because the FBI is not under control because Gray [Patrick Gray, acting director of the FBI] doesn't exactly know how to control it and they have—their investigation is now leading into some productive areas—because they've been able to trace the money—not through the money itself—but through the bank sources—the banker. And it goes in some directions we don't want it to go....That way to handle this now is for us to have Walters [General Vernon

Walters, deputy director of the CIA] call Pat Gray and just say, "Stay to hell out of this—this is ah, business here we don't want you to go any further on it." That's not an unusual development, and ah, that would take care of it....

NIXON: Well, what the hell, did Mitchell [John Mitchell, former attorney general and head of the president's campaign] know about this?

HALDEMAN: I think so. I don't think he knew the details, but I think he knew.

HALDEMAN (about three hours later): Well, it was kind of interesting. Walters made the point and I didn't mention Hunt [E. Howard Hunt, ex-CIA agent and White House consultant who was convicted in the Watergate conspiracy]. I just said that the thing was leading into directions that were going to create potential problems because they were exploring leads that led back into areas that would be harmful to the CIA and harmful to the government....

Recorded presidential conversation submitted to the Committee on the Judiciary of the House of Representatives by Richard Nixon, April 30, 1974.

MAP EXERCISE

Fill in or identify the following on the blank map provided. You will need to consult an atlas to complete these exercises.

1. Identify and label the following countries: China (mainland), China (Taiwan), Japan, North Korea, South Korea, Soviet Union, and Vietnam.
2. Identify and label the location of Bejing.

Interpretative Questions

Based on what you have filled in, answer the following. For some of the questions you will need to consult the narrative in your text for information or explanation.

1. How realistic was it for the United States to regard the government on Taiwan as the legitimate government of mainland China?
2. Describe the strategic geographic position of mainland China. How was this a factor in making renewed relations with China important to the United States?

SUMMARY

Opposition to the war in Vietnam became the centerpiece of a wide-ranging political and cultural challenge to traditional American society. During this turbulent era, African Americans, women, Hispanics, and Indians organized to assert their rights. Richard Nixon inherited the war in Vietnam, and he did bring it to an end. The cost of Nixon's four years of war was thousands of Americans lives and many more thousands of Asian lives, plus continued social unrest at home and an enduring strain on the economy. The end of American involvement did not mean that the goal of an independent, noncommunist South Vietnam had been secured. Nixon was more successful in his other foreign policy initiatives, opening meaningful contacts with China and somewhat easing tensions with the Soviet Union. He managed to stake out a solid constituency of conservative voters with his attacks on liberal programs and ideas. He never quite decided how to deal with a troubled and changing economy that faced the unusual dual problems of slowed growth and rapidly rising prices. Less than two years after his overwhelming reelection in 1972, Nixon resigned from office under fire from a nation horrified by his arrogant misuse of presidential power for personal political purposes in the Watergate affair.

CHAPTER SELF-TEST

After you have read the chapter in the text and done the exercises in the Study Guide, the following self-test can be taken to see if you understand the material you have covered. Answers appear at the end of the Study Guide.

Multiple Choice

Circle the letter of the response which best answers the question or completes the statement.

1. Although the philosophy of the counterculture seemed to favor all of the following, the characteristic that most defined the movement was:
   a. rejecting the inhibitions and conventions of middle-class culture and concentrating on pleasure and fulfillment.
   b. striving for racial and social justice for all peoples.
   c. breaking the power of corrupt elites who controlled American corporations and governments.
   d. demanding an end to international wars and conflicts and substituting peaceful resolution.

2. Compared to the national population, Native Americans by the 1960s had a much higher level of:
   a. family income.
   b. educational attainment.
   c. life expectancy.
   d. joblessness.

3. By the 1980s, Hispanic Americans had:
   a. become the fastest-growing minority group in the nation.
   b. yet to make any efforts to organize themselves politically or economically.
   c. strenuously opposed the concept of bilingualism in education.
   d. consistently championed the ideal of the "melting pot."

4. In *The Feminine Mystique* (1963), Betty Friedan:
   a. praised and endorsed the ideal of women living happy, fulfilled lives in purely domestic roles.
   b. discovered that many of the college-educated women in her study were deeply frustrated and unhappy, with no outlets for their intelligence, talent, and education.
   c. called for women to band together to launch an all-out assault on the male power structure.
   d. rejected the whole notion of marriage, family, and heterosexual intercourse.

5. According to most historians, a major reason that the Equal Rights Amendment (ERA) failed to gain ratification was:
   a. widespread public apathy and indifference about the issue.
   b. lack of time for proper organization of support groups to push for ratification in the states.
   c. fears by many Americans that it would create a major disruption of traditional social patterns.
   d. inadequate evidence of actual instances of political and economic discrimination toward women.

6. Nixon's policy of "Vietnamization" succeeded in:
   a. increasing the number of American military recruits.
   b. helping temporarily to quiet domestic opposition to the war.
   c. breaking the stalemate in the negotiations with the North Vietnamese.
   d. reducing the role of the White House in conduct of the war.

7. Public clamor against the Vietnam War would spread in 1971 after the Supreme Court:
   a. ordered the abolition of the Selective Service System.
   b. declared the Gulf of Tonkin Resolution unconstitutional.
   c. ruled that the press had the right to publish the so-called Pentagon Papers.
   d. overturned the war crimes conviction of Lieutenant William Calley.

8. Nixon's plan for "peace with honor" in Vietnam produced a North Vietnamese promise to:
   a. release American prisoners of war.
   b. never again invade the south part of Vietnam.

c. grant democratic rule to the government in Saigon.
d. sever its ties with the Soviet Union.
e. do *none* of the things listed above.

9. In response to a new military offensive against the south by the Vietnamese from the north in March 1975, the United States Congress:
   a. authorized President Ford to renew bombing strikes on both the northern part of Vietnam and on Cambodia.
   b. ordered an immediate withdrawal of all remaining U.S. troops.
   c. organized a rapid and orderly evacuation of American officials from Saigon and the southern part of Vietnam.
   d. refused additional funding for military support of the government in the south of Vietnam.

10. In forging a new relationship with the Chinese communists, the Nixon administration agreed to:
    a. back China in any border disputes with the Soviet Union.
    b. drop its opposition to the admission of communist China to the United Nations.
    c. immediately establish formal diplomatic relations between the United States and China.
    d. begin planning the transition of Taiwan to mainland rule by 1999.

11. Egyptian and Syrian forces launched a surprise attack against Israel which marked the start of the:
    a. 1948 War of Independence.
    b. Sinai Conflict of 1956.
    c. Six-Day War of 1967.
    d. Yom Kippur War of 1973.
    e. Suez Crisis of 1979.

12. The Family Assistance Plan, proposed by the Nixon administration, proposed to overhaul the nation's large and cumbersome welfare system by:
    a. providing a minimum guaranteed annual income for all Americans.
    b. granting greater authority for the federal government in guarding against welfare fraud.
    c. establishing a distribution of welfare funds based solely on personal need.
    d. ending cash assistance in favor of an entirely "in kind" system that would provide food, medical care, clothing, rent vouchers, etc., that the poor could not waste.

13. Conservatives were disappointed by the *Roe v. Wade* (1972) decision of the Supreme Court which:
    a. ruled in favor of the use of forced busing to achieve racial balance in schools.
    b. overturned existing statutes providing for capital punishment.
    c. clearly established the right of individuals to keep pornographic materials in the privacy of their homes.
    d. upheld the principle of affirmative action.
    e. struck down laws forbidding women to choose to have abortions.

14. All of the following factors contributed to Richard M. Nixon's overwhelming reelection in 1972 *except* the:
    a. seemingly successful negotiations moving toward an end to the war in Vietnam.
    b. acknowledged honesty and integrity of his campaign workers.
    c. disarray and confusion in the Democratic party.
    d. withdrawal of candidate George Wallace following his being seriously wounded in an assassination attempt.

15. Tapes of recorded conversations about the Watergate incident ultimately provided convincing evidence that President Nixon had:
    a. no personal connection with or knowledge of the efforts to cover up his campaign's involvement in the incident.
    b. actually planned the details of the break-in at the Democratic National Committee's office.
    c. clear knowledge that actions were being undertaken to distance his campaign staff from all appearance of involvement with Watergate.
    d. tried to blame the event on the Democrats themselves.

True/False

Read each statement carefully. Mark true statements "T" and false statements "F".

1. The New Left movement drew strength from the Civil Rights and anti-Vietnam War mood of many Americans.
2. The counterculture movement and the "hippies" of the 1960s had very little impact on the overt behavior of broader society.
3. The avowed goal of the American Indian Movement was to break down tribal allegiance and encourage Native Americans to assimilate into the mainstream of middle-class values.

4. A major result of the gay liberation movement was that homosexuals became more willing to make their sexual preference known publicly and unapologetically.
5. Betty Friedan's 1963 book the *The Feminine Mystique* helped launch the women's liberation movement by showing that many college-educated women were frustrated by their limited opportunities.
6. The Equal Rights Amendment (ERA) became part of the U.S. Constitution in 1972 when Georgia became the thirty-eighth state to ratify it.
7. The *Roe v. Wade* decision of the U.S. Supreme Court used the "right to privacy" as the basis for ruling that states could not ban all abortions.
8. President Nixon's policy of "Vietnamization" involved an effort to get the South Vietnamese military to take an increasingly large portion of the burden of combat so that the United States could reduce its ground forces involved in the war.
9. The outpouring of patriotism that accompanied the invasion of Cambodia by U.S. troops in 1970 temporarily quieted the anti-Vietnam war protest movement.
10. The Department of Defense documents released in the so-called Pentagon Papers revealed that the U.S. government had been less than fully honest in reporting to the American people about the military progress of the war.
11. According to President Nixon, the "Christmas bombings" of 1972 forced the North Vietnamese to agree to a ceasefire.
12. Henry Kissinger convinced Richard Nixon to take a bipolar vision of the world in which the United States stood essentially alone against communism everywhere it surfaced.
13. Although President Nixon began the process of opening up U.S. contact with mainland China, he was not willing to allow the mainland government to replace Taiwan in the United Nations and on the Security Council.
14. The Nixon administration faced the problem of dealing with the inflationary pressures caused by an ever-increasing proportion of the American work force being employed in high-paid, skilled jobs in manufacturing.
15. Using the justification of protecting "national security," President Nixon fostered an attitude in the members of his administration that led to efforts to stifle dissent and undermine political opposition.

Review Questions

These questions are to be answered with essays. This will allow you to explore relationships among individuals, events, and attitudes of the period under review.

1. Chronicle the several cultural and ethnic movements that arose in the 1960s and early 1970s to challenge traditional white, male-dominated society. How did more conservative forces respond? How extensive and lasting were the changes?
2. What was accomplished during the four years that the Nixon administration carried on the war in Vietnam? Could the peace have been achieved in a better manner at less human cost?
3. What were the several assumptions reflected in Nixon and Kissinger's rapprochement with the Soviet Union and China? Were the assumptions valid and the actions wise?
4. Was Watergate truly unprecedented, or was it merely a case of a president getting caught performing politics as usual? What was the lasting damage of the crisis? Did any good come from it?

CHAPTER THIRTY-THREE
The Age of Limits

OBJECTIVES

A thorough study of Chapter 33 should enable you to understand:

1. The efforts of President Gerald Ford to overcome the effects of Richard Nixon's resignation.
2. The rapid emergence of Jimmy Carter as a national figure and the reasons for his victory in 1976.
3. Carter's emphasis on human rights and its effects on international relations.
4. Carter's role in bringing about the Camp David agreement and the impact of this agreement on the Middle East.
5. Why the United States had so much difficulty in freeing the hostages held by Iran and the effect of this episode on the Carter presidency.
6. The political importance of the rise of the Sunbelt and the increasing strength of conservative, evangelical Christianity.
7. The nature of the "Reagan revolution" and the meaning of "supply-side" economics.
8. The staunchly anticommunist Reagan foreign policy.

PERTINENT QUESTIONS

Politics and Diplomacy after Watergate (pp. 896–903)

1. How did his pardon of Richard Nixon affect Gerald Ford's political standing?
2. What economic challenges did Ford face? How did he respond?
3. How did Jimmy Carter's background and personality shape the tone of his presidency and people's reaction to him?
4. What economic and energy-related problems did Carter face?
5. How did Carter manage to help bring about a peace treaty between Egypt and Israel?

6. What led to the Iranian hostage crisis? What political effects did it have on the Carter administration? How was the crisis resolved?
7. How did the Carter administration react to the Soviet invasion of Afghanistan?

The Rise of the American Right (pp. 904–909)

8. Where is the "Sunbelt?" What were the political implications of its rise?
9. Describe the basis of Christian Evangelicalism. How could it lead to both social liberalism, as in Jimmy Carter, and cultural conservatism, as in Jerry Falwell?
10. What were the elements of the New Right movement? How did it come to have such influence in the Republican Party?
11. To what extent was the tax revolt of the 1970s and 1980s as much an attack on government programs as on taxes?
12. Why did Ronald Reagan win such a decisive victory in 1980? What happened in the congressional races?

The "Reagan Revolution" (pp. 909–915)

13. What personal factors helped make Reagan politically effective? Why was he called the "Teflon president"?
14. Explain the assumptions made by "supply-side" economists ("Reaganomics") and how the Reagan administration implemented supply-side policies. How did the economy respond to the administration's policy?
15. What led to the enormous budget deficits and fiscal crisis of the mid 1980s?
16. What stance toward the Soviets and communism in general constituted the so-called Reagan Doctrine?
17. How did the Reagan administration's reaction to the 1983 barracks bombing in Beirut reveal restraint in the face of Middle Eastern terrorism?
18. Was the election of 1984 more a personal victory for Ronald Reagan or the mark of a new Republican era?

IDENTIFICATION

Identify each of the following, and explain why it is important within the context of the chapter.

1. SALT II
2. "malaise" speech
3. "human rights"
4. Panama Canal Treaty
5. Camp David Summit
6. Diplomatic relations with China
7. Ayatollah Ruhollah Khomeini
8. Sagebrush Rebellion
9. "born again"
10. Nelson Rockefeller
11. Proposition 13
12. "entitlement" programs
13. Gramm-Rudman-Hollings Act
14. Strategic Defense Initiative ("Star Wars")
15. Grenada
16. "Sandinistas"
17. Geraldine Ferraro

DOCUMENT

Read the sections of the text under the headings "The Trials of Jimmy Carter" and "The Reagan Revolution," paying attention to the differing styles and personalities of the two presidents. The excerpts below, the first from Carter's so-called "malaise" speech of July 15, 1979, and the second from Reagan's State of the Union Address on February 4, 1986, illustrate their contrasting styles. Carter's address was given at a time when he was under considerable attack for his leadership, whereas Reagan's was delivered while his popularity was at a height. Both speeches contained specific legislative agendas, but they are more memorable for their general messages than for their specific proposals. Consider the following questions: How do the two documents illustrate the differences between the leadership styles of Reagan and Carter? Each speech cited experiences or opinions of supposedly typical Americans; compare and contrast the use of these examples. The America described by Reagan in 1986 was very different from that described by Carter in 1979; had America truly changed that much? Had Reagan restored national confidence through rhetoric or through long-term solutions to difficult problems? In light of the state of the nation and the world in the early 1990s, which speech was more realistic? Which was more prophetic?

JIMMY CARTER, JULY 15, 1979.

Ten days ago I had plans to speak to you again about a very important subject—energy. For the fifth time I would have described the urgency of the problem and laid out a series of legislative recommendations to the Congress, but as I was preparing to speak I began to ask myself the same question that I know has been troubling many of you: Why have we not been able to get together as a nation to resolve our serious energy crisis?

It's clear that the true problems of our nation are much deeper—deeper than gasoline lines or energy shortages. Deeper, even, than inflation or recession. And I realize more than ever that as President I need your help, so I decided to reach out and listen to the voices of America...and I want to share with you what I heard....

Many people talked about themselves and about the conditions of our nation. This from a young woman in Pennsylvania: "I feel so far from government. I feel like ordinary people are excluded from political power." And this from a young Chicano: "Some of us have suffered from recession all our lives."...

This kind of summarized a lot of other statements: "Mr. President, we are confronted with a moral and a spiritual crisis."...

These 10 days confirmed my belief in the decency and the strength and the wisdom of the American people, but it also bore out some of my long-standing concerns about our nation's underlying problems....

So I want to speak to you tonight about a subject even more serious than energy or inflation. I want to talk to you right now about a fundamental threat to American democracy.

I do not mean our political and civil liberties. They will endure. And I do not refer to the outward strength of America—the nation that is at peace tonight everywhere in the world with unmatched economic power and military might. The threat is nearly invisible in ordinary ways. It is a crisis of confidence. It is a crisis that strikes at the very heart and soul and spirit of our national will.

We can see this crisis in the growing doubt about the meaning of our own lives and in the loss of a unity of purpose for our nation.

The erosion of our confidence in the future is threatening to destroy the social and the political fabric of America. The confidence that we have always had as a people is not simply some romantic dream or a proverb in a dusty book that we read just on the Fourth of July. It is the idea which rounded our nation and which has guided our development as a people. Confidence in the future has supported everything else—public institutions and private enterprise, our own families and the very Constitution of the United States. Confidence has defined our course and has served as a link between generations.

We've always believed in something called progress. We've always had a faith that the days of our children would be better than our own.

Our people are losing that faith....But just as we are losing our confidence in the future, we are also beginning to close the door on our past.

In a nation that was proud of hard work, strong families, close-knit communities and our faith in God, too many of us now tend to worship self-indulgence and consumption. Human identity is no longer defined by what one does but by what one owns....

Often you see paralysis and stagnation and drift. You don't like it. And neither do I.

What can we do? First of all, we must face the truth and then we can change our course. We simply must have faith in each other. Faith in our ability to govern ourselves and faith in the future of this nation. Restoring that faith and that confidence to America is now the most important task we face....

And we are the generation that will win the war on the energy problem, and in that process rebuild the unity and confidence of America....

Energy will be the immediate test of our ability to unite this nation. And it can also be the standard around which we rally. On the battlefield of energy we can win for our nation a new confidence, and we can seize control again of our common destiny....

[At this point, the speech lists six specific points emphasizing conservation and reduced energy consumption.]

I do not promise you that this struggle for freedom will be easy. I do not promise a quick way out of our nation's problems when the truth is that the only way out is an all-out effort.... There is simply no way to avoid sacrifice....

In closing, let me say this: I will do my best, but I will not do it alone. Let your voice be heard. Whenever you have a chance, say something good about our country. With God's help and for the sake of our nation, it is time for us to join hands in America.

Let us commit ourselves together to a rebirth of the American spirit. Working together with our common faith, we cannot fail.

President Jimmy Carter, television address to the nation, July 15, 1979.

RONALD REAGAN, FEBRUARY 4, 1986.

I have come to review with you the progress of our nation, to speak of unfinished work and to set our sights on the future. I am pleased to report the state of the union is stronger than a year ago, and growing stronger each day. Tonight, we look out on a rising America—firm of heart, united in spirit, powerful in pride and patriotism. America is on the move.

But it wasn't long ago that we looked out on a different land—locked factory gates, long gasoline lines, intolerable prices and interest rates turning the greatest country on Earth into a land of broken dreams. Government growing beyond our consent had become a lumbering giant, slamming shut the gates of opportunity, threatening to crush the very roots of our freedom.

What brought America back? The American people brought us back—with quiet courage and common sense; the undying faith that in this nation under God the future will be ours, for the future belongs to the free....

Family and community are the co-stars of this great American comeback. They are why we say tonight: private values must be at the heart of public policies.

What is true for families in America is true for America in the family of free nations. History is no captive of some inevitable force. History is made by men and women of vision and courage. Tonight, freedom is on the march. The United States is the economic miracle, the model to which the world once again turns. We stand for an idea whose time is now....

We speak tonight of an agenda for the future, an agenda for a safer, more secure world. And we speak about the necessity for actions to steel us for the challenges of growth, trade, and security in the next decade and the year 2,000. And we will do it—not by breaking faith with bedrock principles, but by breaking free from failed policies....

[At this point the speech went into specific proposals for a balanced budget amendment, defense spending, tax reform, and other matters.]

America is ready, America can win the race to the future—and we shall.

The American dream is a song of hope that runs through the night winter air. Vivid, tender music that warms our hearts when the least among us aspire to the greatest things....

The world's hopes rest with America's future. America's hopes rest with us. So let us go forward to create our world of tomorrow—in faith, in unity, and in love. God bless you, and God bless America.

President Ronald Reagan, State of the Union Address, February 4, 1986.

MAP EXERCISE

Fill in or identify the following on the blank map provided. For this exercise you may need to consult an atlas.

1. Circle the USSR-Afghanistan border area.
2. Locate and label the following: Iran, Lebanon, Egypt, Israel.

Interpretative Questions

Based on what you have filled in, answer the following. For some of the questions you will need to consult the narrative in your text for information or explanation.

1. Why was the Soviet Union so concerned about the revolution in Afganistan? Why did the United States support the rebel side?
2. How did the establishment of an apparently lasting peace between Egypt and Israel change the nature of Middle Eastern tension?
3. Why did the United States support the Shah of Iran? Why did his fall present so many problems for America?

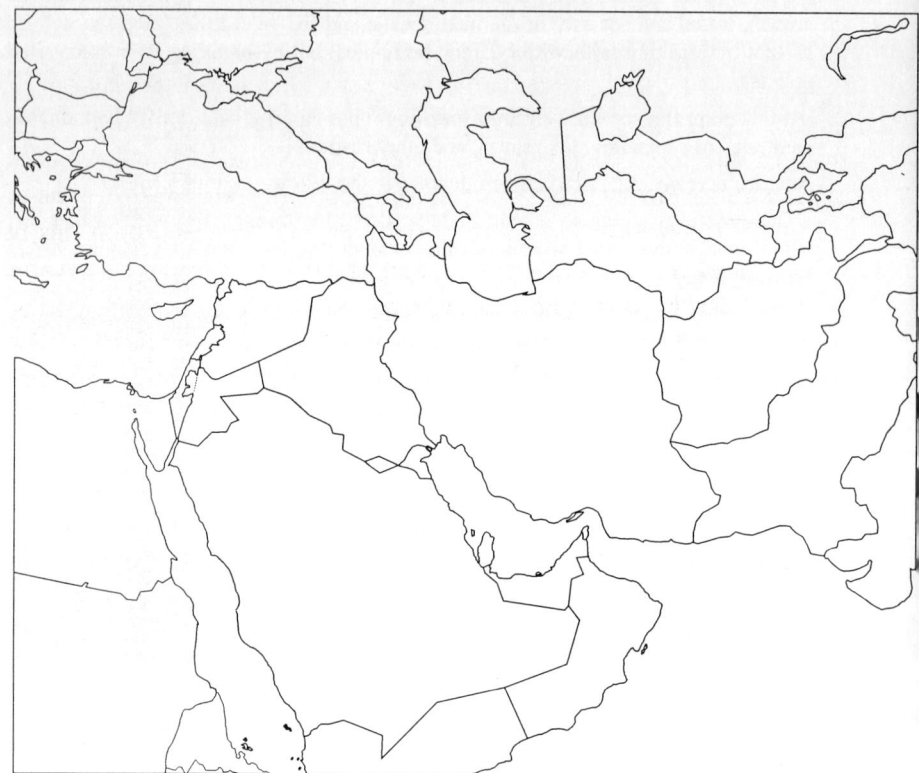

Summary

As president, Gerald Ford worked to heal the wounds of Watergate and restore respect for the presidency. His pardon of Richard Nixon was probably the most controversial act of his caretaker period in office. Jimmy Carter turned out to be a more effective campaigner than president. His administration was marked by an inability to set a tone of leadership. He made no significant strides toward solving the energy crisis and took only halting steps toward his goal of making the federal government more efficient. His last year in office was dominated by the Iranian hostage crisis, which at first boosted his popularity but later may have cost him another term. Riding the crest of a wave of his own popularity and new Republican strength from the Sunbelt and conservative Christians, Ronald Reagan won the 1980 election. He exploited deep-seated feelings of resentment over America's seeming weakness abroad and appealed to those who believed that government should play a lesser role in the economy.

Congress quickly passed his supply-side economics plan of tax reductions and spending cuts; but a year later, the nation was mired in recession. Prosperity returned and Reagan won easy reelection.

Republican control of the White House continued with the election of George Bush. The new president faced a very different world situation than had his post-World War II predecessors. The Cold War had ended along with the Soviet Union itself. Bush's popularity soared at the time of the allied victory over Iraq in the Gulf War, but economic problems at home and other factors led to his defeat in 1992 as Bill Clinton became the first "baby boomer" to be elected President.

During the 1970s, the age, racial, and regional characteristics of the American population changed. The proportion of the population classified as elderly increased; black and Hispanic figures soared; and the Sunbelt states boomed. Politically, the nation became more conservative, and much of the conservative impetus came from a New Right with strong Protestant evangelical support. Liberals, when they did not back away, shifted their emphasis to environmental issues.

CHAPTER SELF-TEST

After you have read the chapter in the text and done the exercises in the Study Guide, the following self-test can be taken to see if you understand the material you have covered. Answers appear at the end of the Study Guide.

Multiple Choice

Circle the letter of the response which best answers the question or completes the statement.

1. In his efforts to curb inflation, President Ford:
    a. initiated temporary price and wage controls.
    b. called for voluntary efforts.
    c. asked for a reduction in interest rates.
    d. urged increased federal spending.
2. Jimmy Carter's success in the election of 1976 resulted partly because:
    a. Ford refused to choose a running mate who appealed to the Republican right.
    b. Carter's considerable service in Washington assured voters of an experienced administrator.

c. Ford's personality had generated an atmosphere of bitterness and acrimony in Washington.
   d. Carter seemed to possess honesty, piety, and an outsider's skepticism of the federal government.

3. Carter hoped to base American foreign policy on:
   a. flexible military response whenever democratic governments were challenged.
   b. expansion of American economic interests.
   c. retreat from international power and responsibility.
   d. "rollback" of communist influence around the world.
   e. an active dedication to "human rights."

4. In 1979 Jimmy Carter brought two world leaders together at the Camp David presidential retreat and helped negotiate:
   a. a smooth transition of power over Laos from Vietnam to Cambodia.
   b. a peace treaty between Egypt and Israel.
   c. an end to the Arab oil boycott.
   d. the establishment of democratic governments in Nicaragua and El Salvador.

5. The 1979 Revolution in Iran resulted from:
   a. the expansion of Soviet influence in the Middle East.
   b. Iranian resentment against the repressive, authoritarian tactics of the American-backed Shah.
   c. Iranian disillusionment with the Ayatollah Ruhollah Khomeini.
   d. a desire by fundamentalist Iranian Muslims to modernize and Westernize their country.

6. The Soviet invasion of Afghanistan in late 1979 was intended by the Soviets to:
   a. overthrow the pro-Western government.
   b. support the activities of Islamic fundamentalists.
   c. settle the conflict between Afghanistan and Pakistan.
   d. keep the existing Marxist government in power.

7. The rapid population growth in the Sunbelt shifted political power to the region and tended to strengthen a political viewpoint that could be characterized as:
   a. conservative, antigovernment.
   b. liberal, government activist.
   c. moderate, middle-of-the-road.
   d. none of the above; the effect was basically neutral.

8. A common thread of evangelical Christianity is a:
   a. belief in personal conversion through direct personal relationship with Jesus.
   b. rejection of modern doctrines of racial equality.
   c. support for "secular humanism."
   d. tendency to avoid applying religious beliefs to political issues.

9. Journalists referred to the Reagan administration as the "Teflon presidency" because:
   a. of its "slick," constantly shifting and inconsistent policies.
   b. blame for problems or mistakes seldom seemed to stick to Reagan himself.
   c. Reagan's style and image failed to attract and retain public support.
   d. the President insisted upon personal planning and direction of day-to-day governmental affairs.

10. According to the theories of "supply-side" economics, the woes of the American economy had resulted from:
    a. inadequate government expenditures.
    b. excessive taxation of private investors.
    c. low interest rates.
    d. tax loopholes which favored the wealthy.

11. A factor that did *not* contribute to the large federal budget deficits of the mid-1980s was:
    a. the escalating costs of "entitlement" programs
    b. the tax cuts of 1981
    c. a large increase in military spending
    d. creation of new social programs to fight poverty

12. In its conduct of international affairs, the Reagan administration:
    a. denounced the growth of Solidarity, an independent labor organization in Poland.
    b. pursued a policy of detente with the Soviet Union, actively seeking additional arms control agreements.
    c. favored a more active and assertive role for the United States in opposing communism throughout the world.
    d. sought to pressure friendly dictatorship governments to enact internal democratic reforms.

13. President Reagan's Strategic Defense Initiative (SDI), widely known as "Star Wars":
    a. received overwhelming endorsement by the American scientific community.
    b. was proposed as a means of closing the missile gap and enhancing American first-strike capability.
    c. intimidated the Soviets into agreements for further arms reductions.
    d. was designed to intercept ICBMs.

14. Over 200 United States Marines were killed in 1983 when:
    a. Soviet forces shot down a Korean airliner that had strayed into their air space.
    b. Reagan ordered increased military support for the "contras," a Nicaraguan guerrilla movement.
    c. Marines were serving as a peacekeeping force in Beirut, Lebanon.
    d. Libyan leader Muammar al-Qaddafi ordered terrorist attacks on U.S. forces in the Mediterranean Sea.

15. Republican victory in the presidential election of 1984 seemed to indicate:
    a. a major realignment of partisan loyalties in the United States.
    b. that the Republican Party could keep control of the U.S. Senate as long as Ronald Reagan headed the ticket.
    c. a major resurgence in interest and voter turnout among American voters.
    d. that the victory was mainly a personal triumph for Ronald Reagan rather than a major across-the-board victory for Republicans.

True/False

Read each statement carefully. Mark true statements "T" and false statements "F."

1. Gerald Ford's compassionate pardon of Richard Nixon for his role in the Watergate scandal improved Ford's standing in public opinion polls.
2. President Ford faced the dual problems of inflation and recession.
3. Ronald Reagan, representing the conservative wing of the Republican Party, challenged President Ford for the Republican nomination in 1976.

4. In his campaign for president, Jimmy Carter emphasized that he was a Washington "insider" who could be more effective with Congress than President Ford had been.
5. Jimmy Carter pledged that a major focus of his foreign policy would be the defense of "human rights."
6. Jimmy Carter canceled U.S. participation in the 1980 summer Olympics in Moscow in protest of the Soviet invasion of Afghanistan.
7. Jimmy Carter's most politically damaging defeat in Congress was the Senate's refusal to ratify the controversial Panama Canal Treaty.
8. The Americans being held hostage in Iran were captured in a failed CIA attempt to overthrow the government of Ayatollah Ruhollah Khomeini.
9. The so-called "Sagebrush Rebellion" was an effort by liberal Democrats from the western states to replace Jimmy Carter as the party's nominee in 1980.
10. The term "born again" Christians was used to refer to the large number of individuals who strayed away from the church during the turbulent 1960s but who returned to regular church attendance in their thirties and forties.
11. The so-called "tax revolt" of the late 1970s emerged because there was widespread agreement on the list of government programs that needed to be cut back.
12. Although Ronald Reagan was not able to fulfill his promise to balance the federal budget, he was able to reverse the trend of the Carter years and reduce the total annual deficit.
13. The invasion of Grenada by U.S. Marines was an example of the "Reagan Doctrine" that called for U.S. intervention to support opponents of communism.
14. The Soviet Union favored Reagan's Strategic Defense Initiative ("Star Wars") because it would relieve their economy of the burden of financing a continued arms race.
15. In 1984 the Democrats nominated a female, Geraldine Ferraro, as Walter Mondale's vice presidential running mate.

Review Questions

These questions are to be answered with essays. This will allow you to explore relationships among individuals, events, and attitudes of the period under review.

1. Did Gerald Ford's pardon of Richard Nixon accomplish its purpose to "shut and seal the book" on Watergate? What else did Ford do to try to restore credibility to the presidency?
2. How effective was Jimmy Carter in applying the human-rights principle to American foreign policy? How did his approach differ from the actions taken by Ronald Reagan?
3. How did the nation's energy needs complicate both the foreign and domestic policies of presidents Ford, Carter, and Reagan?
4. How did the shift away from a bipolar world change the very foundation of American foreign policy as it had been practiced since World War II?

CHAPTER THIRTY-FOUR
Beyond the Cold War

OBJECTIVES

A thorough study of Chapter 34 should enable you to understand:

1. How the Cold War came to an end.
2. The reasons for the fall of the Soviet Union.
3. The U.S. response to the end of the Cold War and the disintegration of the Soviet Union.
4. The problems that plagued the last years of the Reagan administration.
5. The Bush administration's response to a changing world and economy.
6. The reasons that Bill Clinton won the presidency but faced great difficulties in the first three years of his administration.
7. The fundamental changes in the American economy after 1970.
8. The profound demographic changes that the nation experienced from the 1970s into the 1990s.
9. The widening gulf between economically successful African Americans and the urban black underclass.
10. The troublesome issues of drugs, AIDS, homelessness, abortion, and environmental threats.

PERTINENT QUESTIONS

America and the Waning of the Cold War (pp. 916–930)

1. Describe the process by which the Soviet Bloc and the Soviet Union itself ceased to exist. What emerged in its place?
2. How did Ronald Reagan react to Mikhail Gorbachev? What concrete agreement resulted? How did George Bush build on this relationship?
3. What caused the savings and loan crisis? How did it end?
4. Describe the Iran-Contra Scandal. What was its political impact?

5. What main campaign strategy did George Bush use to come from behind and defeat Michael Dukakis? What happened in the congressional elections?
6. What budgetary and economic problems dominated domestic concerns during the Bush presidency?
7. Why did the United States invade Panama in 1989? How did this action fit with the general direction of post-Cold War foreign policy?
8. What precipitated the Gulf War? What were the long-term outcomes after the relatively easy victory?
10. What broad issue was the key to Bill Clinton's victory in 1992? What role did Ross Perot play?
11. What obstacles to effective leadership did Clinton face upon taking office? Which of the administration's own actions compounded its problems?
12. What major domestic legislation did the Clinton administration manage to push through in its first year? In what major domestic initiative did the administration fail? Why?
13. What were the key foreign policy accomplishments of Clinton's first three years?
14. What led to the Republican sweep of congressional elections in 1994? What policy changes resulted?

Modern Times (pp. 930–949)

15. What economic transformations led to the "two-tiered" economy of the 1990s? What were the effects on lower-class, working-class, and marginal middle-class Americans?
16. Describe the "globalization" of the American economy. How was it facilitated by NAFTA and GATT? How did globalization affect industrial workers?
17. Why has the average age of Americans been increasing? What are the social, economic, and political consequences of this demographic change?
18. Describe the significant change in the nature of immigration to the United States after 1965. What two groups had the most impact?
19. Explain the reaction of many non-Hispanic Americans, particularly in areas of high Hispanic concentration, to the influx of immigrants from Mexico and other parts of Latin America. How was the situation complicated by the fact that many of these immigrants were in the country illegally?

20. Compare and contrast post-1960s accomplishments of the African-American middle class with the situation of the so-called underclass. What explains the stark disparity?
21. What were the emerging signs of heightened black-white tensions that emerged in the mid to late 1990s?
22. To what extent did the AIDS epidemic affect sexual behavior?
23. What were the key arguments on which the "right-to-life" movement rested its opposition to abortion? What gains did the movement make? How did the "pro-choice" forces respond?
24. Describe the shift of the political left to emphasis on environmental concerns. What incidents and issues attracted the most attention?
25. How did modern environmentalists differ from traditional conservationists? What new social ethic and economic approach did the ardent environmentalists propound?
26. What was at the core of the "multiculturalism" movement? What controversies illustrated the tensions surrounding multiculturalism and "political correctness"?

IDENTIFICATION

Identify each of the following and explain why it is important within the context of the chapter.

1. *glasnost* and *perestroika*
2. Berlin Wall
3. Tiananmen Square massacre
4. apartheid
5. Nelson Mandela
6. Oliver North
7. "no new taxes"
8. Saddam Hussein
9. Norman Schwartzkopf
10. Whitewater affair
11. Hillary Rodham Clinton
13. "Contract with America"
14. Newt Gingrich
15. biotechnology
16. William Gates
17. Immigration Reform Acts of 1965 and 1987
18. South Central Los Angeles riot

19. O. J. Simpson trial
20. "crack"
21. Homelessness
22. Clarence Thomas
23. Rachel Carson's *Silent Spring*
24. "Earth Day"
25. ecology

DOCUMENT

In remarks to the Summit of the Americas in Miami in December 1994, which included representatives from all Western Hemisphere nations except Cuba, President Bill Clinton addressed the issues described in the text under the headings "The Two-Tiered Economy" and "Globalization." Clinton paid homage to Franklin Roosevelt's "Good Neighbor" policy and John Kennedy's "Alliance for Progress," and he boldly declared that the United States was committed to "continuing leadership and engagement in the post-Cold War world." Read the following excerpts from Clinton's speech and consider the following questions: How does Clinton explain the linkages between the changing nature of America's domestic economy and the need for free trade? Why is the President so insistent on declaring that freer trade as promoted by NAFTA and GATT will be good for the U.S. economy? Does this speech seem to be designed as much for domestic consumption in the United States as for the representatives from the other nations?

> Our country has produced over five million new jobs during the past 22 months [since Clinton's election]. We have the lowest unemployment rate in four years, and have been voted by the Annual Panel of International Economists as the world's most productive economy for the first time in nine years. But, the thing that gives me the most hope...is that this year more high-wage jobs have come into our economy than in the previous five years combined. We hope that we are seeing the beginning of the end of a 20-year trend in stagnant wages, and the beginning of the restoration of the American Dream by reaching out to the world and into our hearts.
>
> Still, we know that millions of Americans have not felt this economic recovery. Millions of Americans are still working harder for less and feeling very uncertain, even as they read all of the good statistics in the newspaper. We have a lot of work to do. But, the truth is that the United States has never been in a stronger economic position to compete and win in the world.
>
> We are also taking bold steps to open new markets and to make the global economy work for our people. For 40 years, our markets have been more open than those of many other nations....But, now that competition is everywhere and productivity is growing, and the lessons of management, technology, and investment are readily apparent to hard working people all across the world, we cannot allow [the United

States] to continue [to be more open than other nations]. We simply must be able to export more of our goods and services if we are going to create more high-wage jobs.

Just a year ago yesterday, I signed into law NAFTA — the North American Free Trade Agreement. When Congress voted for NAFTA, that event committed the United States to continuing leadership and engagement in the post-Cold War world. It marked a new era in world trade relations for America, and it gave birth to this summit, which could not have occurred if that had not happened....

Just yesterday, I signed into law the bill implementing the General Agreement on Tariffs and Trade, the largest agreement ever for free and fair trade. GATT, like NAFTA before it, passed because we had strong bipartisan support in Congress. That is a pattern that must prevail as we continue to pursue open markets and prosperity in this hemisphere and around the world....

Finally, let me emphasize that our economic strategy seeks to prepare our own people to fill the high-wage jobs of the future....Pressures of the global economy have held wages down and increased job turnover for people who are not in a position to take advantage of the developments now occurring. We owe it to those Americans to provide the kind of lifetime education and training that will give them a chance to win in this economy as well....

More free trade is worthwhile only if its benefits actually change the lives of real people for the better.

But, as I have said over the last two years, that does not mean that we can repeal the laws of change—repeal the sweeping changes taking place in the global economy....

I am convinced that we will succeed as long as we recognize that the bonds that unite us are stronger that the forces that divide us.

Once, the United States and its neighbors were clearly divided by seemingly unbridgeable cultural and economic gulfs. But today, superhighways, satellite dishes, and enlightened self-interest draw us together as never before.

U. S. Department of State Dispatch Supplement, May 1995, vol. 6, No. 2, pp. 7–8.

MAP EXERCISE

Fill in or identify the following on the blank map provided. Use an atlas or other reference works as your source.

1. Identify and label the following eastern European nations: Russia, Poland, Hungary, Czechoslovakia, Bulgaria, Romania, Ukraine, and Belarus.
2. Identify and label Germany and Berlin.
3. Mark the old western border of the Soviet Union and shade the nations that were under Soviet dominance during the Cold War.
4. Circle the area of the former Yugoslavia which broke up into smaller republics including Bosnia.
5. Circle the area of the Gulf War and identify the nations involved.

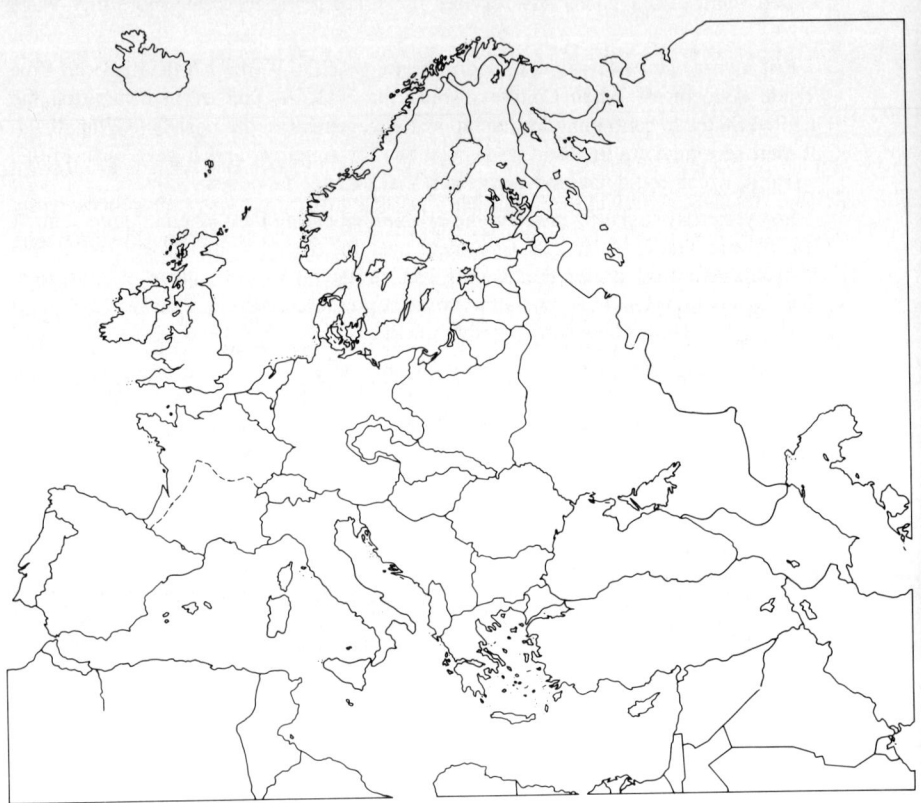

Interpretative Questions

Based on what you have filled in, answer the following. For some of the questions you will need to consult the narrative in your text for information or explanation.

1. Compare and contrast the national borders of Europe before and after the collapse of the Soviet Union and its sphere of influence.
2. Why was having a friendly government in Kuwait so important to the United States and the western European nations?
3. Why were other European nations so concerned about the civil war in Bosnia?

Summary

Although tensions had subsided somewhat, in the early 1980s Americans still thought of the world in the Cold War terms of a communist superpower confronted by the United States and our sometimes difficult allies. The incredible events of 1989–1991 saw the end of the Cold War and the demise of the Soviet Union, and the United States was not sure how to react. At home, profound, if more gradual, change was also taking place. America's manufacturing base declined in face of world competition, economic growth slowed, and poverty began to rise again. Into this mix came a new wave of immigrants dominated not by Europeans but by Asians and Hispanics. As the new century approached, the nation faced tough challenges of crime, disease, urban distress, environmental problems, and heightened ethnic and racial tensions.

Chapter Self-Test

After you have read the chapter in the text and done the exercises in the Study Guide, the following self-test can be taken to see if you understand the material you have covered. Answers appear at the end of the Study Guide.

Multiple Choice

1. The leader of the Soviet Union at the time of the fall of the Berlin Wall and the end of the Cold War was:
   a. Nikita Krushchev.
   b. Boris Yeltsin.
   c. Mikhail Gorbachev.
   d. Leonid Brezhnev.

2. The incident in Tiananmen Square signified that:
   a. communism was dead in Russia.
   b. the Eastern European nations were no longer afraid of the Soviet Union.
   c. democracy and human rights would prevail in China.
   d. none of the above.

3. "Apartheid" referred to the:
   a. system of racial separation in South Africa.
   b. land ownership patterns in Third World nations that kept peasants poor.

c. rebirth of ethnic culture and religion in the former satellite nations of the Soviet Union.
d. the revival of Germany to be the dominant economic force in Europe.

4. The so-called Iran-Contra scandal involved the Reagan administration in:
   a. a secret CIA effort to arm Iranian exiles and stage an invasion.
   b. selling weapons to the anti-American government in Iran and using the profit to aid the pro-United States Contras in Nicaragua.
   c. planting misleading intelligence information with the governments of Iran and Iraq in order to stir up a war between them.
   d. a scheme to divert frozen Iranian assets into the campaign coffers of a Republican senatorial candidate in Virginia.

5. The Bush administration responded to the alleged drug trafficking by Panamanian military leader Manuel Noriega by:
   a. invading the nation and overthrowing the Noriega government.
   b. imposing an economic boycott on all Panamanian exports.
   c. threatening to close the Panama Canal and deny the Noriega government its share of the tolls.
   d. convincing the Organization of American States to negotiate Noreiga's exile to Chile.

6. Which of the following best describes the Bush administration's approach to the problem of the growing federal budget deficit?
   a. Massive spending cuts proposed by Bush were adopted by Congress, and the deficit declined for the first time since the 1970s.
   b. Despite Bush's "no new taxes" pledge, he worked out a multi-year budget package with Congress that included a significant tax increase.
   c. Congress passed a deficit reduction plan composed of small spending cuts and large tax increases, but Bush vetoed it.
   d. Bush proposed a major tax increase, but conservative Republicans teamed with liberal democrats to defeat it.

7. A major reason that President Bush's popularity declined rapidly in the months following the end of the Gulf War was that:
   a. he quickly slashed military spending except for the "Star Wars" program.
   b. much of the public perceived that he was uninterested in domestic issues even though the economy was in a recession.

c. a majority of voters apparently opposed his "pro-choice" position on abortion.
   d. the economy experienced rapid inflation despite slow economic growth.

8. The official United Nations-authorized objective in the Gulf War was to:
   a. remove Saddam Hussein from power in Iraq.
   b. occupy Iraq's oil fields.
   c. reunify Kuwait and Iraq.
   d. expel Iraq's military forces from Kuwait.

9. The general theme stressed most consistently by Bill Clinton in his 1992 presidential campaign was:
   a. the economy.
   b. equal rights for all minorities.
   c. an immediate freeze of military spending.
   d. health care reform.

10. Which of the following was *not* an episode that tarnished President Clinton's early popularity?
    a. his effort to end the military ban on homosexuals serving in the U.S. armed forces.
    b. his controversial appointments to major government positions in the Justice Department and elsewhere.
    c. his decision to send U.S. troops into Bosnia for humanitarian relief.
    d. his clumsy handling of the investigation into his banking and real estate ventures.

11. President Clinton's first budget involved:
    a. a substantial tax increase on upper-income Americans.
    b. a substantial tax decrease designed to stimulate the economy.
    c. no changes in taxation, but did cut spending significantly.
    d. minor tax adjustments and a major increase in spending.

12. Hillary Rodham Clinton emerged as an extremely influential First Lady whose principal focus in the first year or so of the Clinton administration was on:
    a. mental health.
    b. child welfare.
    c. educational improvements.
    d. health care reform.

13. The American economy in the period from the late 1980s to the mid-1990s was characterized by all of the following *except:*
    a. a decrease in the rate of poverty.
    b. a decline in the relative importance of heavy manufacturing.
    c. an increase in the number of families that needed more than one income to maintain their desired standard of living.
    d. unequal distribution of wealth and income, with the middle 40 percent experiencing a decline in wealth.

14. From 1965 to the early 1990s there was significant relative and actual increase in immigration by all of the following groups *except:*
    a. Asians.
    b. Mexicans.
    c. Puerto Ricans.
    d. Europeans.

15. Which of the following best represents the economic status of African Americans by the 1980s?
    a. Despite the efforts of the 1960s all classes of blacks were falling further behind whites.
    b. The black middle class had made significant gains but the gap between the black middle class and underclass had widened.
    c. Working-class blacks made significant strides, but white-collar options remained closed, so middle-class blacks made little gains.
    d. Except in the South, average family income for blacks matched that of whites by the 1990 census.

True/False

Read each statement carefully. Mark true statements "T" and false statements "F."

1. In the reforming Soviet Union *glasnost* referred to the dismantling of repression and *perestroika* referred to economic restructuring.
2. The white South African leader who worked with President Carter to end apartheid was Nelson Mandela.
3. Although cautiously optimistic about changes in the Soviet Union, Ronald Reagan refused to meet face-to-face with Mikhail Gorbachev as long as the Communist Party continued to exist.
4. Unlike the Reagan-Mondale campaign of 1984, the George Bush-Michael Dukakis presidential campaign tended to focus on straightforward discussion of the issues rather than personal attacks.

5. The effectiveness of George Bush's presidency was limited by his rigid ideology that prevented pragmatic compromise.
6. The Gulf War was initially popular with the American public, but support waned sharply as casualty figures rose.
7. Because Ross Perot split the Democratic vote in 1992, the Republicans gained control of the U.S. Senate despite Clinton's presidential victory.
8. The "Whitewater affair" concerned allegations that President Clinton had been sexually involved with a woman that he met while on a rafting trip in the Grand Canyon.
9. The annual rate of Gross National Product (GNP) increase was higher in the 1950s and 1960s than it was in the 1970s and 1980s.
10. The U.S. birthrate began to slow in the 1970s and at the same time life expectancy increased so the average age of Americans was noticeably higher by 1990 than it had been in 1970.
11. Asians constituted the largest group of illegal immigrants to the United States in the 1970s and 1980s.
12. Although Asian immigrants often faced discrimination from Americans of Anglo-European heritage, they were generally able to settle in African-American neighborhoods without arousing any tensions.
13. In the early to mid-1990s, a majority of black children were born into single-parent families.
14. The major riot in South Central Los Angeles in 1992 was sparked by turf conflict between black and Hispanic gangs.
15. The advocates of making abortion legal chose to call themselves "pro-choice" rather than "pro-abortion" in order to stress that they were defending the woman's right to make her own decision.

Review Questions

These questions are to be answered with essays. This will allow you to explore relationships among individuals, events, and attitudes of the period under review.

1. How did the United States respond to the end of the Cold War and the disintegration of the Soviet Union? To what extent were the approaches of reduced military spending and increased world responsibility contradictory? Give examples.

2. Explain the fundamental changes in the nature of the American economy that were evident by the end of the 1980s. What caused such transformation? How did middle America cope?
3. Describe the remarkable demographic shifts that occurred after 1965. What were the immediate economic and social impacts of these shifts? What implications do these shifts have for twenty-first-century America?

Writing a Historical Book Review

Writing a book review as an assignment in a history course is designed to promote at least four important objectives: (1) effective writing, (2) substantive knowledge about a particular historical topic, (3) the development of a historical perspective and an understanding of the nature and use of historical research, and (4) an ability to think critically about the work of others. A typical summary "book report" can at best teach only the first two objectives. A critical book review goes beyond mere summary to inquire into the overall worth of the work. There are six steps to preparing a review of a historical work. With some modifications, these steps also apply to writing reviews of other nonfiction works.

1. *Select a book.*

Your instructor may provide a reading list, but if he or she does not, you will find that locating an appropriate work can be a very important part of the learning process. Start, of course, with the Suggested Readings at the end of your text and with the book catalogue (computer-based or cards) in your college library. Check standard bibliographies such as *Harvard Guide to American History,* and try consulting the footnotes or bibliographies of other works. When you locate a likely book, give it a quick once-over. Glance at the table of contents and the bibliography, and read the prefatory material to make sure that the book is appropriate to your assignment. Ask yourself if the topic seems interesting, for you will probably write a better review if you have some affinity for the subject. Most important, talk to your instructor; he or she has read many books and has probably graded hundreds of reviews, so seek your instructor out for advice.

2. *Determine the purpose of the book and the intended audience.*

The best place to determine both purpose and audience is usually in the preface, foreword, or introduction. What demand did the author intend to fulfill with the book? Did the author write because there was no satisfactory work available on the subject? Did the writer feel that he or she had a new point of view on a well-worn topic? Perhaps the author wrote a popular account of a subject about which previous works had been dull and dry. Ascertaining the author's purpose is important, for, assuming that the purpose is worthwhile, the writer should be judged by whether he or she achieved what he or she set out to accomplish. Also determine the audience for which the work was intended. Was the work directed mainly at professional historians, at college students, or at the general public?

3. *Learn the author's qualifications and viewpoint.*

Find out the author's academic background. Is the author a journalist, a professor, or a professional writer? Has this writer published other books on related topics? Consult your library catalogue; check *Who's Who in America, Contemporary Authors, Directory of American Scholars,* or other directories. Viewpoint, however, is generally more important than credentials, since an author must be judged mainly by the quality of the particular work you are examining. A Pulitzer Prize-winner may later write an undistinguished book. But many first books, often derived from the authors' doctoral dissertations, are outstanding. Knowing the author's point of view, however, may put a reader on guard for certain biases. A Marxist historian will often write from a predictable perspective, as will an extreme rightist. Biographers are often biased for or against their subjects. For example, after the assassination of John F. Kennedy, many of his intimates, most notably Arthur Schlesinger, Jr., wrote biographical works. A reviewer could not adequately analyze Schlesinger's *Thousand Days* without knowing something about his close relationship with the slain president. Look for information on point of view in prefatory materials, in the body of the book, and in reference works with entries about the author.

4. *Read the book.*

Read critically and analytically. Be sure to identify the author's thesis—the main argument of the book. Look for secondary theses and other important points. See how the author uses evidence and examples to support arguments. Are his or her sources adequate and convincing? Does the author rely mainly on primary—firsthand, documentary—sources or on secondary sources? Consider the author's style and presentation. Is the book well organized? Is the prose lively, direct, and clear? Take notes as you read so that you can return to particularly important passages or especially revealing quotations. Remember that being critical means being rational and thoughtful, not necessarily negative.

5. *Outline the review.*

The following outline is only a suggestion; it is not a model that you should necessarily follow for all reviews. You may find it appropriate to add, combine, separate, eliminate, or rearrange some points.

I. Introduction

   A. Purpose of the book

   B. Author's qualifications and viewpoint

II. Critical summary

   A. Thesis of the book

   B. Summary of contents, indicating how the thesis is developed (Use examples. While this will generally be the longest part of the review, you should make sure that your paper does not become a mere summary without critical analysis.)

   C. Author's use of evidence to support the thesis and secondary points

III. Style and presentation

   A. Organization of the book

   B. Writing style (word choice, paragraph structure, wit, readability, length, etc.)

   C. Use of aids (photographs, charts, tables, figures, etc.)

V. Conclusion

   A. Historical contribution of the book (How does the book fit into the prevailing interpretation of the topic? Does it break new ground? Does it answer a troublesome question? Does it revise older interpretations? Does it merely clarify and simplify the standard point of view? You may need to consult other sources when considering this point. See, for example, the "Debating the Past" sections in your text.)

   B. Overall worth of the book (Would you recommend it? For what type of audience would it be set suited? Did the author accomplish the intended purpose?)

6. *Write the review.*

Follow your outline. Use standard written English. When in doubt, consult *The McGraw-Hill College Handbook* or a similar reference. If your instructor does not assign a standard format, the following style is accepted.

I. At the top of the first page, give the standard bibliographic citation of the work under review. (Reviews seldom have titles of their own.)
II. The review should be printed double-spaced on good-quality paper. The typical review is from 450 to 1,200 words long.
III. If you quote from the book under review, simply follow the quotation with the page number(s) in parentheses. For example: "The author makes the incredible assertion, 'Jefferson turned out to be America's worst president' (p. 345)."
IV. If you need to cite other sources for quotations, points of view, or facts, use a standard citation style.

You may find it helpful to read published book reviews as a guide to the preparation of your own. Most historical journals, including the *American Historical Review* and the *Journal of American History*, publish many short reviews at the end of each issue. *Reviews in American History*, which prints longer reviews, is especially useful. To determine where reviews of the particular book you have chosen have been published, consult the *Book Review Digest* or the *Book Review Index*. Assume that your audience is college educated and well read, but do not assume that your hypothetical reader has in-depth knowledge about the subject of the book under review.

Preparing a Historical Research Paper

A research paper helps students develop competencies very much like those that are enhanced by doing a book review. One of the best ways to develop a historical perspective is to actually write some history, even a short research essay. In addition, preparing a paper gives students the opportunity to become more competent in research skills and in the organization of diverse materials into a meaningful essay. The suggestions that follow are of a general nature, designed to enable an instructor to adapt them to the kind of project that best suits the class. These suggestions are directed to students taking the introductory course who may be writing their first historical research papers at the college level.

1. *Select a topic.*

This should be done with the advice of the instructor. Many instructors have a list of suitable topics to offer their students. If no such list exists, you should consider the following questions: (a) Will the topic help you understand the course? (b) Can a paper on the topic be finished during the term? (Students often bite off more than they can chew. It is better to select a manageable topic, such as "Lincoln's Veto of the Wade-Davis Bill," than one such as "Abraham Lincoln: President.") (c) Is sufficient material available to do an adequate job of research? (d) Does the topic interest you? There are, of course, other factors to consider, but if the answer to any of the above is "no," then the value of the project is lessened considerably.

2. *Locate sources.*

Sources for a research paper fall into two general categories: (a) *primary material*—sources produced by people who took part in or witnessed the events being researched (letters, diaries, pictures, newspaper accounts, and so forth); and (b) *secondary material*—sources produced after the fact and generally written relying on the primary sources. To locate these sources, you should first consult a bibliographic guide, such as the *Harvard Guide to American History* or *American History and Life*. This will enable you to identify a number of secondary sources whose bibliographies whose give you more material (primary and secondary) to look into.

You should also examine historical journals, particularly those that concentrate on the field into which your topic falls. You should read related articles, paying attention to the sources they cite, and book reviews, which will tell you of new works on the subject. Once a source is located, you should write its full bibliographic citation on an index card or in a form appropriate to your software. This will make it easier to organize your bibliography during the hectic days just before the paper is due. Consult *The McGraw-Hill College Handbook* for examples of bibliographic and footnote form. Most colleges have collections of primary material—on microfilm or printed—to aid students in this kind of research. Be sure to remember that you must give citations for material located via the Internet or World Wide Web just as you would those found in a traditional library. If the source is one generally available in printed version, such as a historical journal, provide normal citation followed by a notation that it was cited from the on-line version. If the source is only available on-line, cite the sponsoring entity and give the Internet or Web address.

3. *Do the research.*

The research process has as many approaches as there are researchers, but until you develop the method best suited to you, here are some helpful hints. Begin by reading general accounts of the circumstances surrounding the topic you have chosen. For example, if your topic is "Witch Trials at Salem," read a general study of late-seventeenth-century Massachusetts. Then turn to the more specific secondary sources. (Consult the Suggested Readings in the back of the text for background sources.) Take notes on index cards, one citation to each card (or the software equivalent). In this way, you will have notes that can be arranged in the order you desire when the time comes to write. Do not worry about having too many notes. It is better to have too many than too few, which would mean additional research at the last minute. Also, when taking notes, be sure to record the location (title, volume, page) so that you will not have to backtrack to find a citation. If you do the work the first time, you will not have to waste time retracing your steps at the end.

4. *Organize the paper.*

If your research is done systematically, the organization of the paper will all but take care of itself. There are, however, a few hints that might be helpful. First, do not leave this to be done last. Even while you are pulling material together, you should be organizing it into a loose outline. This will show you where gaps exist and reveal which areas need work, and will often cause you to redirect your efforts in a more productive way. In this way, the process of organizing is ongoing, and so when the research is done, the paper is organized. Still, you should prepare a final outline just before you begin to write. This forces you to go over all the material once again, makes it fresh in your mind, and gives you the opportunity to make any last-minute adjustments.

5. *Write the paper.*

Again, if the previous steps have been carefully taken, writing the paper is easy. The notes you have accumulated should be organized to correspond with your outline. However, be sure to pay attention to your thesis so that the paper will not be just a string of notes. Write a rough draft of the paper, with documentation on a separate page. At this stage, citations may be in an abbreviated form, but they should be complete enough for later reference. Beware of the tendency to overuse quotations. As a general rule, you should quote only when the actual wording is as important as the idea being transmitted or when "colorful language" spices up the narrative. In most cases, however, it is best simply to put the information in your own words and cite the source.

For general information on the use of the language, consult *The McGraw-Hill College Handbook* or another handbook used in freshman English classes.

6. *Prepare the final draft.*

After the rough draft is finished and at least one revision has taken place, the clean copy should be prepared. Notes may be placed at the bottom of each page, at the back, or in the narrative depending on the instructor's preference. The bibliography should be placed at the end of the paper. Other additions—title page, table of contents, an outline—may be included or omitted as the instructor desires.

By paying careful attention to the directions given by your instructor and by following the portions of this guide that apply to the project you undertake, you should develop basic research and writing competencies that will help you in many other classes.

Answers to Self-Test Questions

Chapter 1

Multiple-choice

1. c	5. a	9. b	13. c
2. d	6. b	10. b	14. b
3. a	7. a	11. a	15. b
4. c	8. c	12. d	

True-False

1. False	5. True	9. True	13. False
2. True	6. False	10. False	14. True
3. False	7. True	11. False	15. False
4. True	8. False	12. True	16. True
		17. True	

Chapter 2

Multiple-choice

1. b	5. d	9. b	13. b
2. c	6. e	10. a	14. a
3. a	7. b	11. a	15. a
4. c	8. c	12. c	16. b

True-False

1. False	5. False	9. True	13. False
2. True	6. False	10. False	14. True
3. True	7. True	11. False	15. False
4. False	8. False	12. False	16. False

Chapter 3

Multiple-choice

1. c	5. d	9. b	13. b
2. a	6. a	10. a	14. d
3. a	7. d	11. c	15. a
4. d	8. a	12. d	

True-False

1. True	5. True	9. False	13. False
2. False	6. False	10. True	14. True
3. False	7. True	11. False	15. True
4. False	8. False	12. True	

Chapter 4

Multiple-choice

1. a	5. c	9. c	13. a
2. b	6. d	10. c	14. b
3. c	7. a	11. a	15. a
4. d	8. a	12. b	

True-False

1. False	5. False	9. False	13. False
2. True	6. False	10. False	14. False
3. False	7. False	11. True	15. True
4. True	8. True	12. True	

Chapter 5

Multiple-choice

1. b	5. b	9. b	13. a
2. d	6. d	10. a	14. c
3. a	7. c	11. c	15. b
4. c	8. a	12. d	

True-False

1. False	5. False	9. False	13. False
2. False	6. False	10. True	14. True
3. False	7. False	11. True	15. False
4. True	8. True	12. False	

Chapter 6

Multiple-choice

1. a	5. a	9. d	13. d
2. c	6. d	10. b	14. b
3. b	7. a	11. a	15. d
4. c	8. e	12. a	

True-False

1. True	5. False	9. True	13. False
2. True	6. True	10. True	14. False
3. True	7. True	11. True	15. True
4. False	8. False	12. True	

Chapter 7

Multiple-choice

1. b	7. a	13. d	19. d
2. d	8. d	14. a	20. b
3. a	9. b	15. b	21. a
4. b	10. a	16. b	22. a
5. b	11. b	17. a	23. a
6. c	12. c	18. c	24. c
			25. a

True-False

1. True	7. True	13. False	19. False
2. True	8. False	14. False	20. False
3. False	9. False	15. False	21. False
4. False	10. False	16. False	22. True
5. True	11. True	17. False	23. False
6. False	12. False	18. False	24. False
			25. False

Chapter 8

Multiple-choice

1. c	5. a	9. c	13. a
2. d	6. a	10. b	14. a
3. c	7. a	11. d	15. d
4. b	8. c	12. e	

True-False

1. True	5. False	9. True	13. True
2. True	6. True	10. False	14. False
3. True	7. False	11. False	
4. True	8. False	12. False	

Chapter 9

Multiple-choice

1. c	5. a	9. a	13. b
2. a	6. c	10. b	14. c
3. b	7. d	11. b	15. d
4. c	8. d	12. d	

True-False

1. False	5. False	9. False	13. True
2. True	6. False	10. True	14. True
3. False	7. True	11. False	15. False
4. False	8. True	12. True	16. True
			17. False

Chapter 10

Multiple-choice

1. c	6. b	11. a	15. c
2. a	7. a	12. b	16. a
3. a	8. b	13. d	17. d
4. b	9. c	14. b	18. e
5. d	10. c		

True-False

1. True	5. False	9. False	13. False
2. False	6. True	10. False	14. True
3. True	7. True	11. False	15. True
4. True	8. True	12. False	

Chapter 11

Multiple-choice

1. c	5. b	9. b	13. a
2. b	6. d	10. a	14. d
3. d	7. c	11. c	15. d
4. c	8. c	12. d	

True-False

1. False	5. False	9. False	13. True
2. True	6. False	10. True	14. False
3. True	7. False	11. False	15. True
4. True	8. False	12. False	16. True

Chapter 12

Multiple-choice

1. d	5. d	9. b	13. a
2. b	6. a	10. a	14. c
3. c	7. a	11. c	15. b
4. c	8. d	12. d	

True-False

1. False	5. True	9. False	13. False
2. True	6. True	10. False	14. False
3. False	7. True	11. True	15. True
4. True	8. False	12. False	

Chapter 13

Multiple-choice

1. a	5. b	9. a	13. e
2. b	6. b	10. a	14. c
3. c	7. c	11. a	
4. d	8. b	12. a	

True-False

1. True	5. False	9. False	13. True
2. False	6. False	10. False	14. False
3. False	7. True	11. True	15. True
4. True	8. True	12. True	16. False

Chapter 14

Multiple-choice

1. d	5. d	9. c	13. c
2. e	6. c	10. a	14. a
3. a	7. b	11. b	15. d
4. d	8. b	12. b	

True-False

1. True	5. False	9. False	13. False
2. True	6. True	10. True	14. True
3. False	7. False	11. False	15. True
4. False	8. False	12. True	

Chapter 15

Multiple-choice

1. b	6. d	11. a	16. a
2. c	7. d	12. b	17. b
3. a	8. c	13. e	18. a
4. e	9. a	14. a	19. c
5. c	10. d	15. d	20. b

True-False

1. False	6. False	11. True	16. True
2. False	7. False	12. False	17. False
3. False	8. False	13. True	18. False
4. True	9. False	14. False	19. True
5. False	10. True	15. False	20. False
			21. True

Chapter 16

Multiple-choice

1. d	5. d	9. c	13. bc
2. c	6. a	10. d	14. a
3. d	7. d	11. b, d	15. c
4. a, c	8. a	12. d	

True-False

1. False	5. False	9. True	13. False
2. False	6. True	10. True	14. False
3. False	7. False	11. True	15. False
4. True	8. True	12. False	

Chapter 17

Multiple-choice

1. b	5. a	9. a	13. d
2. d	6. b	10. c	14. b
3. c	7. a	11. c	15. ad
4. c	8. e	12. b	

True-False

1. True	5. False	9. False	13. False
2. False	6. True	10. False	14. False
3. True	7. False	11. False	15. True
4. True	8. False	12. False	

Chapter 18

Multiple-choice

1. b	5. a	9. a	13. d
2. d	6. b	10. d	14. b
3. a	7. b	11. b	15. c
4. d	8. b	12. d	

True-False

1. False	5. False	9. False	13. True
2. False	6. True	10. True	14. True
3. True	7. False	11. False	15. False
4. False	8. False	12. False	

Chapter 19

Multiple-choice

1. b	5. a	9. a	13. b
2. d	6. a	10. d	14. d
3. d	7. d	11. b	15. b
4. a	8. b	12. a	

True-False

1. False	5. False	9. True	13. False
2. False	6. True	10. True	14. False
3. False	7. True	11. True	15. False
4. True	8. True	12. True	

Chapter 20

Multiple-choice

1. b	5. d	9. a	13. c
2. b	6. b	10. d	14. a
3. d	7. d	11. a	15. a
4. a	8. b	12. b	

True-False

1. False	5. False	9. False	13. False
2. False	6. False	10. False	14. True
3. True	7. False	11. False	15. False
4. True	8. False	12. False	

Chapter 21

Multiple-choice

1. d	5. d	9. b	13. c
2. a	6. d	10. b	14. d
3. d	7. a	11. e	15. c
4. b	8. c	12. d	

True-False

1. False	5. False	9. True	13. False
2. False	6. True	10. False	14. False
3. True	7. True	11. False	15. True
4. True	8. True	12. True	

Chapter 22

Multiple-choice

1. c	5. d	9. b	13. d
2. b	6. c	10. b	14. a
3. b	7. c	11. d	15. d
4. c	8. b	12. b	

True-False

1. True	5. True	9. True	13. False
2. False	6. False	10. True	14. True
3. True	7. False	11. True	15. True
4. False	8. False	12. False	

Chapter 23

Multiple-choice

1. c	5. a	9. c	13. d
2. d	6. d	10. b	14. b
3. d	7. d	11. b	15. c
4. c	8. c	12. b	

True-False

1. True	5. False	9. False	13. False
2. True	6. False	10. True	14. False
3. False	7. False	11. False	15. True
4. True	8. False	12. True	

Chapter 24

Multiple-choice

1. d	5. d	9. c	13. b
2. c	6. d	10. c	14. a
3. c	7. d	11. b	15. c
4. a	8. d	12. c	

True-False

1. True	5. True	9. True	13. True
2. True	6. True	10. False	14. True
3. False	7. True	12. False	15. True
4. False	8. False		

Chapter 25

Multiple-choice

1. c	5. d	9. d	13. b
2. b	6. c	10. b	14. c
3. d	7. b	11. b	15. d
4. a	8. a	12. a	

True-False

1. False	5. True	9. True	13. False
2. True	6. False	10. True	14. False
3. False	7. True	11. True	15. False
4. False	8. True	12. False	

Chapter 26

Multiple-choice

1. d	5. d	9. c	13. b
2. b	6. b	10. c	14. b
3. a	7. a	11. d	15. a
4. c	8. c	12. a	

True-False

1. True	5. True	9. True	13. True
2. True	6. True	10. False	14. True
3. False	7. True	11. False	15. True
4. False	8. False	12. False	

Chapter 27

Multiple-choice

1. d	5. d	9. b	13. b
2. a	6. c	10. a	14. d
3. c	7. d	11. d.	15. a
4. b	8. c	12. b	

True-False

1. True	5. False	9. False	13. True
2. False	6. True	10. False	14. False
3. False	7. True	11. True	15. False
4. True	8. True	12. False	

Chapter 28

Multiple-choice

1. b	5. b	9. c	13. d
2. b	6. a	10. b	14. d
3. a	7. d	11. d	15. a
4. d	8. a	12. a	

True-False

1. False	5. False	9. False	13. False
2. True	6. False	10. False	14. False
3. False	7. False	11. True	15. False
4. True	8. True	12. True	

Chapter 29

Multiple-choice

1. d	5. c	9. c	13. d
2. a	6. a	10. a	14. b
3. b	7. b	11. b	15. c
4. e	8. bd	12. a	

True-False

1. False	5. False	9. False	13. True
2. True	6. True	10. False	14. False
3. False	7. False	11. False	15. False
4. False	8. True	12. False	

Chapter 30

Multiple-choice

1. d	5. d	9. d	13. d
2. b	6. d	10. c	14. c
3. c	7. b	11. a	15. d
4. c	8. c	12. b	

True-False

1. False	5. True	9. True	13. True
2. False	6. False	10. True	14. True
3. True	7. True	11. False	15. False
4. True	8. True	12. False	

Chapter 31

Multiple-choice

1. d	5. a	9. d	13. d
2. c	6. b	10. a	14. a
3. a	7. c	11. c	15. d
4. c	8. d	12. b	

True-False

1. False	5. False	9. True	13. True
2. True	6. False	10. False	14. True
3. False	7. False	11. True	15. True
4. True	8. True	12. False	

Chapter 32

Multiple-choice

1. a	5. c	9. d	13. e
2. d	6. b	10. b	14. b
3. a	7. c	11. d	15. c
4. b	8. a	12. a	

True-False

1. True	5. True	9. False	13. False
2. False	6. False	10. True	14. False
3. False	7. True	11. True	15. True
4. True	8. True	12. False	

Chapter 33

Multiple-choice

1. b	5. b	9. b	13. d
2. d	6. d	10. b	14. c
3. e	7. a	11. d	15. d
4. b	8. a	12. c	

True-False

1. False	5. True	9. False	13. True
2. True	6. True	10. False	14. False
3. True	7. False	11. False	15. True
4. False	8. False	12. False	

Chapter 34

Multiple-choice

1. c	5. a	9. a	13. a
2. d	6. b	10. c	14. d
3. a	7. b	11. a	15. b
4. b	8. d	12. d	

True-False

1. True	5. False	9. True	13. True
2. False	6. False	10. True	14. False
3. False	7. False	11. False	15. True
4. False	8. False	12. False	